SHORT

COLLECTIVE
RESPONSIBILITY

DAVID HILL

The right of David Hill to be identified as author of this work has been asserted by him under the Copyright, Designs and Patents Act 1988.

The views expressed are those of the author alone and should not be taken to represent those of His Majesty's government, the Ministry of Defence, HM Armed Forces or any government agency, unless quoted. The events outlined are real.

<u>Books by David Hill, in paperback and Kindle</u>
Breaking the Military Covenant
Citadel of Waste
Shoreham - Collective Responsibility

The Mull of Kintyre Trilogy:
Their Greatest Disgrace - The campaign to clear the Chinook ZD576 pilots
The Inconvenient Truth - Chinook ZD576: Cause & Culpability
Chinook ZD576 - The Concealed Evidence

The Red Arrows:
Red 5 - An investigation into the death of Flight Lieutenant Sean Cunningham
A Noble Anger - The manslaughter of Corporal Jonathan Bayliss

All titles published by Nemesis Books.
nemesisbooks@aol.com

The issues related in these books are ongoing, and they will be regularly updated. If you have purchased a previous edition, please contact the publisher for a free Kindle or pdf version.

https://sites.google.com/site/militaryairworthiness/home

All proceeds to St Richard's Hospice, Worcester
https://www.strichards.org.uk/raise-funds/

Contents

Author's declaration and note 1

IN SEARCH OF THE TRUTH

Introduction 3
Shoreham Airshow 6
The accident aircraft 10
The pilot, Andrew Grenville Hill 14
Airworthiness and maintenance of ex-military aircraft 19

PERCEIVED TRUTH

The accident manoeuvre 28
Accident causation 37
The AAIB Investigation (2015-17 and 2019) 44
Who was the Hunter Aircraft Design Authority? 54
Serviceability 61

NO TRUTH

AAIB test flights (2015) 82

JUDICIAL TRUTH

A legal quirk, and High Court rulings 98
Sussex Police Investigation 112
The decision to charge 115

TWISTED TRUTH

The Trial (16 January - 6 March 2019) 121
Request to reopen AAIB investigation 176
Other voices (2019 - 2022) 178
The torturous route to the Inquest (2015 - 2022) 183

The Inquest finally opens: 30 November 2022 197

ACTUAL TRUTH

Collective responsibility 205
Folland Gnat T.1 G-TIMM (XP504), 1 August 2015 214
Where do matters stand? 217
An alternative explanation? 219
Final conclusions 220

ANNEX - Links to the death of Sean Cunningham 222
Terms and abbreviations 224
The Author 225

Figures

1. Details of accident manoeuvre
2. The Reason 'Swiss Cheese' Model of accident causation
3. Mk14 Fatigue Meter
4. G-BXFI's relocated *g*-meter
5. Mk2 Accelerometer
6. Gravitational axes with respect to pilot
7. Pilot Andrew Hill's head tilt, just before Point X

Dedication

Maurice Abrahams, 76, from Brighton
Dylan Archer, 42, from Brighton
Anthony Brightwell, 53, from Hove
Matthew Grimstone, 23, from Brighton
Matthew Jones, 24, from Littlehampton
James Mallinson, 72, from Newick
Daniele Polito, 23, from Goring-by-Sea
Mark Reeves, 53, from Seaford
Jacob Schilt, 23, from Brighton
Richard Smith, 26, from Hove
Mark Trussler, 54, from Worthing
and
Those who survived but with injuries, some life-changing.
The emergency first responders, many of them volunteers.

Author's declaration and note

I am not related to, nor do I know, Shoreham accident pilot Andrew Hill.

The aim of this book is to explain why Mr Hill was cleared of Gross Negligence Manslaughter. It is not an 'Andrew Hill is innocent' campaign. The undisputed fact of the matter is he completely messed up his intended manoeuvre, resulting in 11 deaths and many injuries. But it is little understood that the Crown's case was that he acted deliberately - the 'gross' element of the charge. The jury chose to disagree, and returned a verdict of not guilty.

To aid a broader appreciation of the issues, it is necessary to explore *other* facts that were not in dispute; which, by High Court order, the jury was not allowed to hear and Hill still isn't permitted to mention. These reveal why it was not he who was severely criticised by the Air Accidents Investigation Branch (AAIB) and Health and Safety Executive. A key question is this:

Having previously made safety recommendations that, if implemented, would have prevented the accident, and complained loudly about being ignored, why did the AAIB not want its reasoning, and its 452-page Shoreham report, revealed in court?

The answer is thought-provoking, deeply disturbing, and what prompted me to write this book. This insight will allow you to better understand the case. To ignore it is to ignore the wider truth.

Meanwhile, justice remains to be served.

David Hill, January 2025

IN SEARCH OF THE TRUTH

Introduction

Shoreham, 22 August 2015. On a fine summer's day, the huge crowd awaited the display of a vintage ex-RAF Hawker Hunter jet, flown by Andrew Hill. A bringer of pleasure to all with his skill as a display pilot, and trusted by those he flew as an experienced British Airways captain.

At 1322 BST the aircraft crashed onto the busy A27 dual carriageway. Five vehicle occupants were killed, and six passers-by. A further 12 were injured. These 11 men played no part in their own deaths. They were going about their lawful business, but unluckily at a time which placed them in the path of this crash.

Incredibly, miraculously, Hill survived the impact and fireball. But he could not tell the tale as the accident had wiped his memory. He was now a pariah.

Later, shown video of the accident, he admitted he screwed up. Big time. Anyone familiar with display aerobatics could see what went wrong. But he couldn't explain it. A living hell. But not as bad as that experienced by survivors and bereaved, their lives inexorably changed. And the psychological effects remain with the injured, and the courageous first responders who braved heat, flames and noxious fumes to tend them.

But admitting an error is not the same as being solely responsible for it. The axiom of any aircraft accident is they rarely have a single cause. One should never simply look at the final, proximate act. Accident investigations are *required* to also look at organisational influences, unsafe supervision, pre-conditions and unsafe acts. Not to apportion blame, but to prevent recurrence.

However, regulatory and legal authorities like to present the notion of a perfectly serviceable aircraft behaving normally - until the pilot errs. In fact, errors are frequent, the pilot usually recovering the situation; but sometimes he is unable to and a crash occurs.

Moreover, if the investigation uncovers evidence of failings that did not contribute directly, these *must* still be assessed and dealt with. This is made difficult by the regulatory authority having huge influence over the direction the legal authorities take; primarily because the latter do not have the necessary investigative, technical or airmanship expertise. And in aviation, a close-knit and highly specialised community, it is difficult to find expert investigators who will be truly independent.

And so, to a related principle; justice as an abstract concept. There is judicial truth, and actual truth. Even if the investigation is independent, transparent and efficient, those with most to lose play a major part, expending inordinate resources seeking to have the adverse either removed, or excluded from evidence led in court. In this case, if the whole truth had been permitted it is unlikely Hill would have been in the dock alone; if at all. Therefore, as we proceed one of the questions I would like you to ask is this. *If he was so obviously disadvantaged, yet still found not guilty, was the decision to prosecute fundamentally flawed?*

Conversely, how often does such a scenario result in wrongful conviction? More than you might believe. In July 2017, four months after the Shoreham accident report was issued, HM Inspectorate of Constabulary and the Crown Prosecution Service Inspectorate accused the police and Crown Prosecution Service of routinely failing to disclose crucial information about cases, undermining the right to a fair trial. The Criminal Law Solicitors' Association said clients could be put in the *'dreadful position'* of being advised to plead guilty to receive maximum credit without all the evidence having been presented to the court.[1] Andrew Hill didn't plead guilty, but he was in the 'dreadful position' of not being permitted to defend himself with the evidence gathered by the Air Accidents Investigation Branch. Justice must not only be done, it must be seen to be done.

With Hill in a coma, and then advised not to speak, the media indulged in uninformed speculation. Their 'experts' presented hypotheses as proven facts, as they sought to outdo their contemporaries. These opinions took hold. At best, they were a small part of the complete picture; at worst, deceit. The simpleton's investigation. *He blundered, so only he can be to blame.*

Internet forums heaved with bile. *Shouldn't have had a pilot's licence. An accident waiting to happen. He flew a perfectly serviceable aircraft into the ground. What proper pilot would make such a mistake? Take your punishment like a man.* What most meant was, *there but for the Grace of God.* If they thought they really knew something, or had any evidence that would have prevented the accident, their duty was to report their concerns to their superiors; be that when Hill was in the RAF, or with Virgin Atlantic or British Airways. Or to the Civil Aviation Authority who granted him his display licence, or the owner/operator of the accident aircraft. There is no evidence of

---

1 https://www.independent.co.uk/news/uk/home-news/Police-crown-prosecution-service-disclosure-lawyers-trial-a7846021.html

any such notifications.

Hill chose to plead not guilty to the charges laid, and was cleared by a unanimous verdict. Legal authorities thought from Day 1 the case was going to be a slam dunk, a maker of reputations. And therein lies the most likely explanation for the rush to prosecute. The person who 'got' the Shoreham killer would be fêted. The tried and tested methods they deployed, concealing the truth while lying to and deceiving the courts and bereaved, revealed behaviour so exceptionally bad you will wonder why *they* remain free. The truth will shock you to the chasm of your soul.

So, please proceed with an open mind, or at least knowing Hill admitted he got it terribly wrong. Did the contributory and aggravating factors revealed by the investigation increase the risk factor to an intolerable level? Were these existing failures known, by whom, for how long, and why was nothing done? Did the same people contribute to or influence the decision to do nothing? Did *they* bear any responsibility? Were they judging their own case? Had they done it before? Were they in the process of doing so again in parallel cases? I will answer all these questions, and demonstrate the truth to you.

Shoreham Airshow

Shoreham-by-Sea (usually just Shoreham) is a coastal town of around 25,000 in the county of West Sussex. It lies equidistant between Brighton and Hove to the east, and Worthing to the west, 80 miles south of the centre of London.

The airfield, properly Brighton City Airport, dates to the early 20th century, when it was proposed that an *'international ground for aviation purposes be established at Shoreham'*.[2] Brighton and Shoreham Aerodrome was inaugurated on 20 June 1911. The following January, flying schools were established.

The airshow began in 1989, starting as a fete. Coincidentally, the Battle of Britain Memorial Flight was displaying its Lancaster, Spitfire and Hurricane nearby. The control tower at the airport called these aircraft up and asked if they would do a fly through at Shoreham, which they did, and this was the start of a successful airshow that continued on an almost annual basis.

The show was organised by the Royal Air Forces Association (RAFA) in aid of the RAFA Wings Appeal, the largest single service charity in the UK, providing welfare support to any member of the Royal Air Force, past or present. Shoreham was the showcase event, raising around 75% of its income, and usually held over two days. Annual planning began immediately after the end of the previous show, offering static and flying displays by various aircraft types, such as fast jets, helicopters, aerobatic aircraft and historic aircraft. Also, ground displays by local organisations such as flying clubs, the Armed Forces, and of classic cars. The aim was to present a garden party atmosphere.

Occasionally, the show coincided with the 4-day Bournemouth Air Festival, 90 miles along the coast to the west. This had benefits, as the shows could share costs with aircraft able to display at both during the same sortie. Crowd numbers weren't affected as Shoreham and Bournemouth didn't share catchment areas - indeed, record crowds have attended Shoreham when shows overlapped.

Unfortunately, Shoreham suffered two accidents before 2015. In 2007 a Second World War Hawker Hurricane crashed near Lancing College, adjacent to the airfield. The pilot was killed. In 2010 a Swift S-1 aerobatic glider stalled during its final low-level turn and crashed onto the runway. The pilot

---

2 Bexhill-On-Sea Observer, 16 October 1909.

survived, but with serious back injuries. The Hurricane crash assumes import later.

Display procedures and approvals

The Civil Aviation Authority (CAA) provides regulatory oversight of air displays in the UK, the main relevant publications in this case being:

- CAP403: Flying Displays and Special Events: Safety and Administrative Requirements and Guidance (including Flying Display Pilot Authorisation and Evaluation).
- CAP632: Operation of Permit to Fly ex-military aircraft.
- CAP733: Guidance for those seeking to obtain a Permit to Fly Aircraft.
- CAP553: British Civil Airworthiness Requirements (BCAR) Section A - Airworthiness Procedures where the CAA has Primary Responsibility for Type Approval of the Product.

The CAA's position is that ex-military aircraft on the UK civil register are not normally acceptable for the issue of a Certificate of Airworthiness. Instead, it will grant a Permit to Fly if satisfied the individual aircraft satisfies BCAR, chapters A3-7, and A8-23/24/25. These aircraft may only operate in UK airspace unless granted a specific exemption.

As one might expect, these and other publications are regularly updated to take account of experience gained, and changes in legalisation. For example, CAP403 has been amended and re-issued 14 times since the accident, the 21st Edition being published in February 2024. As far as possible I will refer to the regulations of the day, and to this end I have relied primarily on the AAIB report, which is excellent in this respect.

There exists the British Air Display Association (BADA), but it has no regulatory role.[3] Its aim is *'to encourage, promote and advance Safety and Standards in British Air Displays'*; but encouraging and promoting is a long way from being responsible and accountable. Indeed, the only mention of BADA is that it co-hosts pre- and post-season seminars with the CAA and Military Aviation Authority (MAA).

At this point you may be wondering why I'm mentioning the Ministry of Defence (MoD). It was largely concealed that it played a crucial part as an integral part of the AAIB investigation; and assisted the police and prosecution, providing the latter's lead witness at trial. The impact this had

---

3 https://www.bada-uk.com/2011/01/about-us/

will become evident, especially the key part it played in Hill's acquittal. Yes, you read that correctly. It is likely he would have been acquitted anyway, but the Crown, AAIB and MoD made sure. Unintentionally, but with unerring efficiency.

I have limited experience of such matters, having only been on the committee of a military tattoo for two years, in 1975/76. Thankfully, this did not include flying. These were the first two years it was held, and with hindsight we were making it up as we went along, relying almost entirely on the Army sending experienced operators along with the vehicles being displayed and driven by the public. There was certainly no oversight, except from the Army barracks whose Commanding Officer was mostly concerned with the damage we'd cause to his really quite smart sports fields.

...Driven by the public. I still twitch a little that anyone who rolled up and had the patience to stand in the queue, was allowed to drive the new Fox armoured vehicle with its semi-automatic gearbox and half a steering wheel sticking out from under the dash. At least we had the sense to cordon off a large area, because ordinary car drivers (and many teenagers without a licence) took some time to work it out and drive in a straight line.

The potential for chaos was huge. We were enthusiastic, but complete amateurs. My point being, such things evolve over a long time. When the Wright Brothers first took to the air, they didn't simultaneously publish guidelines on how to display their aircraft to thousands. And the most difficult aspect is that, when run by enthusiasts, if a key member leaves there is no real structured succession plan, or handover for the replacement, who essentially must start again.

Similarly, most airshows, including Shoreham, are organised and run mainly by volunteers. They, too, are enthusiastic; although far less amateurish, with most having prior experience in aviation. Even so, my guess is most who read the accident report had no idea there was so much to consider. Some will have set out to learn and do better; others will have realised they'd bitten off more than they could chew and quietly stood down. And it's not just about competence, but the ability to devote time.

CAP403 *'strongly recommends'* there is a Flying Control Committee for displays of seven or more items. That is, it isn't mandatory. Frankly, implementing these CAP documents to the letter requires a full-time committee of professionals. And even then, on matters of airworthiness and serviceability of the display aircraft they are entirely at the mercy of the CAA and those who own and maintain the aircraft. The CAA is the 'glue' that is meant to bind all this together but, as the AAIB made very clear, for various reasons - lack of resources being prominent - it could only offer a light touch, the impression being display organisers were left to get on with it. Heavily criticised, the part-timers were let down by the full-time professionals. Regulations are no use whatsoever if there is no regulatory oversight, and are allowed to be treated as optional.

The Flying Display Director (FDD)

The FDD is the individual responsible to the CAA for the safe conduct of a flying display. The Shoreham FDD had been responsible for previous displays, was a display pilot and Display Authorisation Evaluator, and formerly Head of the CAA General Aviation Department. Shoreham had selected him for his *'significant experience in running air displays and his wide recognition within the air display community'*.

The Flying Control Committee (FCC)

The FCC's role is to assist the Display Director in monitoring display standards, provide specialist knowledge for specific display items, and offer in-depth opinion in the case of infringement of the regulations.

The CAA requires the Committee to have the:

> *'Authority of the Event Organiser to curtail or stop, on the grounds of safety, any display item or, in extreme cases, the whole flying display'.*

The FCC at Shoreham consisted four experienced pilots located on or near the appropriate display lines. They had the written authority of the event organiser (RAFA) to override the FDD on any flight safety related matter, and to stop any or all of the flying display on public safety grounds.

The accident aircraft

Aircraft history

The Hawker Hunter T.7 is a single-engine, swept-wing, military jet trainer capable of speeds close to the speed of sound. It entered service in August 1958, initially with 229 Operational Conversion Unit at RAF Chivenor, and served until the disbandment of 208 Squadron on 31 March 1994.

G-BXFI was delivered to 222 Squadron (RAF) in July 1955 as a single-seat F.4, and allocated military tail number WV372. Shortly, it suffered an engine fire and its rear fuselage was badly damaged. It was repaired, returning to service in May 1959 after conversion to a T.7 trainer, with two side-by-side ejection seats, by the Sir Armstrong Whitworth Aircraft Ltd. In 1997, three years after leaving RAF service, it was transferred to the civil register.

The aircraft was owned by petroleum magnate Graham Peacock, operated by Canfield Hunter Ltd, and maintained by Weald Aviation Services Ltd at North Weald airfield in Essex. On 22 August 2015 the total airframe hours were 5,976. (For any Hunter, the US Federal Aviation Administration regard anything over 2,500 hours as 'high time').

Aircraft approval

Ex-military aircraft on the UK civil register must operate in accordance with CAP632, necessary for aircraft lacking a Certificate of Airworthiness.

The AAIB report reproduced several relevant G-BXFI documents, including at Appendices C and L:

- Permit to Fly, Certificate number PR 048467/006, issued on 17 October 2003.
- Airworthiness Approval Note No: 26172, Issue 2, 3 July 2008. (The document reproduced is the internal CAA version. The actual Approval Note was issued on 14 September 2008, and differs in that the 'applicant' is listed as Jet Heritage, not 'CAA Internal Purposes', and was signed by a different CAA official).

The Civil Aviation Authority (CAA), as the regulatory body, issues the Approval Note after reviewing an aircraft and its documentation, based on a technical report submitted, usually, by the owner/operator. The Note is unique to the aircraft and forms the basis of its airworthiness approval, and defines the Build Standard for acceptance (although in very general terms). It is a snapshot of the aircraft's status at the time it was placed on the civil register, but may be revised by the CAA to reflect changes in an aircraft's modification standard or a change of a limitation or requirement.

The CAA will then issue a Permit to Fly, making a statement that it is:

'...satisfied that the aircraft is fit to fly having regard to the airworthiness of the aircraft and the conditions to be attached to the Permit'.

The Permit includes conditions and limitations under which the aircraft may be flown, and any relevant airworthiness, operation or maintenance requirements that are to be met. It ceases to be in force:

1. If any condition (other than a condition of the Permit requiring an inspection, modification or maintenance) is not complied with, or;
2. If the aircraft, engines or propellers, or such of its equipment as is necessary for the airworthiness of the aircraft, are modified or repaired, unless the repair or modification has been approved by the CAA or by a person approved by the CAA for that purpose.

The CAA defines 'airworthy' as:

'The status of an aircraft, engine, propeller or part when it conforms to its approved design and is in a condition for safe operation'.

MoD defines 'airworthiness' as:

'The ability of an aircraft or other airborne equipment or system to operate without significant hazard to aircrew, ground crew, passengers (where relevant) <u>or to the general public over which the airborne systems are flown</u>'.

In general, Permits to Fly are issued at greater risk than aircraft having a Certificate of Airworthiness, as they recognise there are 'unknowns' in the audit trail. For example, G-BXFI was originally an RAF aircraft, and it is not RAF policy to retain an audit trail. Indeed, since 1992 it has not been routine practice to maintain airworthiness of a type; hence airworthiness of individual aircraft can seldom be demonstrated. But the Permit assumes it has been - the first major deficiency. I need not argue this point. The full background was provided to the Nimrod Review, accepted, and the Review's report accepted by the government and MoD.

For fixed wing aircraft with a mass greater than 2,730 kg (including Hunters) the initial application for a Permit must be submitted by an organisation approved for that purpose. When issued, the Permit is considered to be 'non-expiring'. In order to revalidate it an annual submission must be made to the CAA confirming that the aircraft continues to satisfy the requirements of its Permit. This must include confirmation that the aircraft is compliant with the requirements of the Approval Note and all applicable Mandatory Permit Directives. When verified, a Certificate of Validity is issued.

A major question emerges - *When transferred from the military to civil register, was a seamless transition achieved?* The Air Accidents Investigation Branch answered it, setting out a number of reasons why G-BXFI was non-complaint - and I will reveal and explain others. In other words, by the CAA's own regulations the Permit to Fly should have ceased to be in force. It was invalid on the day it was issued, and remained so in 2015. In fact, there seems to have been no transition to speak of, the Approval Note and Permit predicated on the RAF (not MoD) providing most of the services they (allegedly) did pre-1994; which they were not funded to, was never their job, and in any case had rid themselves of the expertise to carry out the small part they played. The audit trail was non-existent.

So, how was G-BXFI (or indeed any Hunter) maintained in an airworthy state, and how could the CAA be satisfied it was? Put another way, did the 'unknowns' constitute too great a risk?

Organisational

The Canfield Hunter Chief Pilot produced an Organisational Control Manual. Effectively, this was a contract between the regulator (the CAA) and Canfield, setting out the terms under which the aircraft would be operated. The CAA approved it, and it became the formal basis for the operation of G-BXFI.

Pilot approval

Pilots seeking to display aircraft must be granted a display authorisation. The Hunter is a Category G aircraft (single engine jet) and authorisations are type specific. They do not differentiate between Marks, so Hill was permitted to fly both single and twin seat Hunters, and variants with more powerful engines.

Pilots are approved by Display Authorisation Evaluators appointed by the CAA; the approvals are by Category only, not type. At the time the CAA regulations gave details of the Categories and Groups. However, some Categories were also annotated by type, leading to confusion. Following the accident, Category G was further subdivided into G1 and G2 for straight wing and swept wing single engine jets. This makes no practical difference to the award of a Display Approval, but it does with respect to pilot currency.

After evaluation, pilots are free to design and perform any display sequence within the limitations imposed in their authorisation, along with those of the aircraft. They are not restricted to the sequence flown in front of the Evaluator. All pilots are mentored by their peers as they gain experience, and if they infringe the rules during a display it can be terminated and their Display Authorisation suspended or revoked by the CAA.

Here, the Air Accidents Investigation Branch confirmed:

- Hill was licensed and authorised to operate the Hunter at flying displays in accordance with the requirements existing at the time of the accident.
- It was his fifth aerobatic display in a Hunter during the 2015 season, and he met the recency requirements.

Likewise, before his trial in 2019 the prosecution stated:

'Hill held an Aircraft Type Rating Exemption for the Hawker Hunter from June 2011. This covered him to fly the Hunter, Jet Provost Mk1-5, and Strikemaster aircraft. [Essentially an armed version of the Jet Provost T.5]. The required certification had been renewed as required and was valid at the time of the Shoreham display. Hill also held a European Union Class 1 Medical Certificate with no limitations, issued on 20 January 2015. It is clear that Hill had all the necessary permits and authorisations to perform the planned aerobatic display and that he was medically fit to fly the Hawker Hunter at the Shoreham Air Show'.

Regarding the training required for Hunters, the Chief Pilot at Canfield Hunter said in court:

'If it were a very low experience pilot, (it would take) ~30 sorties before he went solo. For an ex-military pilot I would expect to complete the training within one long sortie, if they had the appropriate background. The difference in this case was that Hill was going to become part of the team, so he had a much more in-depth training, because he needed to have a greater skillset than just to operate the aircraft on its own'.

The pilot, Andrew Grenville Hill

Andrew Hill was born on 22 March 1964, making him 51 at the time of the accident. That is not old for a pilot, but it is getting on a bit for a fast jet pilot. He has two siblings, a brother and sister, both younger. He married Ellie, herself an airline pilot, in 1999.

He attended Sheldwich Primary School, then went to a boarding preparatory school, Betteshanger, and then to Tonbridge School; all in Kent. While at Tonbridge he was an RN Combined Cadet Force cadet, and awarded a flying scholarship in 1981.

Upon finishing secondary education, he took a gap year and then went to Christ's College, Cambridge, studying engineering and computer science. While there, he joined the University Air Squadron on a Flying Scholarship, gained his Private Pilot's Licence, and set his sights on a career in the RAF. In his final year he was commissioned into the RAF as an Acting Pilot Officer in July 1984, becoming a career pilot when he graduated with Honours in July 1985.

He served in the RAF from July 1985 to October 1994. Initially, he attended RAF Cranwell for six months officer training, progressing through basic and advanced pilot training on Jet Provosts and then Hawks; at which point he gained his wings and was considered a qualified pilot. But qualifying in a training aeroplane is a long way from being a qualified front-line pilot. Further training took place on Hawk, being exposed to events occurring at a much higher speed, and being tested to see if he had the initiative and dynamics to be a true fast jet pilot.

A natural hiatus ensues before being allocated a slot at a front-line squadron or, in Hill's case, being selected for Flying Instructor training on Jet Provosts - in which a degree of preference was allowed, he preferring Yorkshire to Wales. Normally, the top ~20% in any course will be selected for this. His appetite for displaying was whetted at RAF Linton-on-Ouse, winning the annual station competition held between Instructors, going on to represent the Station at the Command competition; the winner becoming the RAF's Jet Provost display pilot.

Part of his advanced Hawk work was at RAF Chivenor in Devon and RAF Brawdy in south-west Wales; where he was part of the Tactical Weapons Unit, learning to fight the aircraft. At the end of the tactical weapons course he was streamed on to Harrier. There, pilot training was different in that the first part of the course was undertaken on helicopters. Only upon passing that could he progress to advanced training. This took nine months, while conventional fast jets (Buccaneer, Jaguars, etc.) took six.

Posted to RAF Gütersloh in Germany he flew Harriers, and by 1992 was deemed combat-ready. He carried out active service in Northern Iraq in 1993, enforcing no-fly zones. By now he had decided not to extend his commission, planning to leave towards the end of 1994. Upon his return from the squadron's base in Turkey, he became a flight simulator liaison officer, still flying Harrier.

In 1992 he was presented with the L G Groves Memorial Prize for Air Safety, awarded for:

'The most important contribution made during the year towards the safety of aircraft and flying personnel, either by practical work or by the writing of constructive papers'.

The citation read:

'For writing for the Harrier GR7 a PC-based electronic Operating Data Manual which is accurate, versatile and quick, and has contributed considerably to the overall safety of Harrier operations'.

Essentially, the software program took over the burden of calculating the various parameters necessary to ensure the correct speed at take-off. He left the RAF before the program was formally adopted, so with some colleagues formed a company, AGH Software Solutions Ltd, to mature it, sustain it to the required safety standard, and update it as the aircraft was modified to operate off the RN's Invincible Class carriers. He also developed a Weapon Planning Aid for Harrier GR7 and Hawk T.1.

He joined Virgin Atlantic Airways in 1995, and a year later British Airways, being promoted to captain in 2002 and flying Boeing B757 and 767, and Airbus A319, A320 and A321.

To continue his interest in fast jets he attained his display authorisations, in 2003 once again flying the Jet Provost, and soon began instructing civilian pilots. Airshow aerobatic techniques (rapid manoeuvring or manoeuvring that is outside the norm for the aircraft) are not taught during military flying training, or if one is doing competition aerobatics. They are specific to the safe execution of display flying - where one is looking to show off the aircraft in an attractive manner, not show off one's skill. Later, in an unfortunate turn of phrase, one pilot-turned-journalist described such displays as *'gladiatorial'*.

In late 2005, with his wife, he embarked on a self-build project, assembling a

Van RV8 tandem 2-seat single engine aircraft in the garage of their home. Upon completion in October 2007 he regularly flew from his Hertfordshire farmhouse, using it to commute to North Weald Airfield. In 2008 he obtained permission from the CAA to perform aerobatic displays in it. With experienced display pilot Alister Kay he launched a two-man formation flying team, known as the RV8Tors. The pair flew their matching aircraft at air shows and weddings, and by 2012 it was estimated they had displayed to nearly three million people. In 2011 he began to display the Hawker Hunter with a group called Team Viper.

At the High Court in 2019, Hill fully admitted that he got the accident manoeuvre totally wrong - he just couldn't recall what happened to cause this. In fact, when video of the accident was played in court, and errors were pointed out, he identified some that the prosecution had missed. He was found not guilty, the prosecution unable to prove its allegations.

Cognitive Impairment

The basis of his defence, advanced not by himself but by medical experts, was he had suffered a form of Cognitive Impairment, possibly caused by cerebral hypoxia (lack of oxygen to the brain). The National Health Service in the UK defines Mild Cognitive Impairment (MCI) as:

'A term used to describe minor memory and thinking problems, such as:

- *memory loss (amnesia).*
- *difficulty concentrating.*
- *problems with planning and reasoning.*

These symptoms are not severe enough to cause problems in everyday life. MCI can be caused by an underlying illness, such as depression, anxiety or thyroid problems. If the underlying illness is treated or managed, symptoms of MCI often disappear and cause no further problems. But in some cases, people with MCI are at increased risk of going on to develop dementia, which is usually caused by Alzheimer's disease'.[4]

For comparison, here is what the US government says:

'Problems with a person's ability to think, learn, remember, use judgment, and make decisions. Signs of cognitive impairment include memory loss and trouble concentrating, completing tasks, understanding,

---

4 https://www.nhs.uk/conditions/dementia/about-dementia/causes/

remembering, following instructions, and solving problems'.[5]

By necessity this is somewhat broad-brush, as the precise diagnosis and degree of impairment will differ from person to person. It can be the sign (not cause) of a disease; for example dementia, which is progressive. Other forms of Cognitive Impairment can occur suddenly and quickly disappear when the cause is removed, such as trauma, sleep deprivation, and the side-effects of medication. Other factors include heat, fumes, dehydration, illness, hyperventilation, blood sugar, and fatigue. In aviation, these might exhibit as disorientation, distraction or incapacitation. Alcohol is a well-known factor, but was confirmed not to be in this case. A typical manifestation is that well-learned automatic tasks can still be carried out, but executive decisions such as reaction time to unexpected events can suffer.

The prosecution alleged that, because Hill was seen in cockpit video, viewed over his right shoulder, to be moving, then he was fully aware and in control. This does not follow. To someone sitting next to him he might have appeared completely normal, but to him the world around him would be making little sense. Such an event can occur without any apparent immediate cause or stimulus, and can last anywhere from a few seconds to 15-20 minutes.

As expert witness Dr Henry Lupa said: *'The lights are on, but there's nobody at home'*. Which is probably the best summation offered during the case, and readily understood by the lay-person.

Hill has no recall of events after the evening of Wednesday 19 August, three days before the accident, until brought out of an induced coma in hospital. This amnesia is also a common result of trauma, and of being administered exceptionally strong painkillers. After assessing what drugs he was given at the scene, and then in hospital, one expert opined it would be more surprising if he *didn't* have amnesia.

Being the cornerstone of his defence, it might be thought this 'argument' about Cognitive Impairment would form a major part of this book. Indeed, three expert witnesses took the stand, but their evidence was more a friendly exchange of views about a subject that is very poorly understood by the medical profession. No evidence was supported by hard facts, and claims made by the prosecution were refuted. With the legal test being *beyond reasonable doubt*, and the prosecution introducing considerable doubt, the

---

5 https://www.cancer.gov/publications/dictionaries/cancer-terms/def/cognitive-impairment

defence merely having to reiterate it to the jury, the jurors had a simple task. It was not for the defence to prove Hill was cognitively impaired. It was for the prosecution to prove he wasn't. They couldn't.

That is not to criticise these eminent physicians in any way. And I am certainly in no position to debate the medical evidence. Rather, I simply convey to you the case that was accepted by the court. The problem the prosecution expert (an RAF officer) faced was there were very few 'facts' to offer opinion on. Instead, he offered opinion based on what he could not demonstrate were facts.

Airworthiness and maintenance of ex-military aircraft

The book proceeds on the basis that G-BXFI's Airworthiness Approval Note (3 July 2008) was based upon the RAF being the Aircraft Design Authority, and therefore the management and control of all associated activities being carried out in accordance with MoD's regulations and procedures. The Note offered the aircraft owner no other option.

Airworthiness

Airworthiness is concerned solely with safety, and there are three distinct aspects: attaining and maintaining type airworthiness, and continuing airworthiness of individual aircraft.

Attaining (Aircraft type)

Hawker Aircraft Ltd were contracted by the forerunner of MoD to produce an airworthy design, prove this, and certify it so. They would produce a Safety Argument (today, Safety Case), which is tied to a specific Build Standard and a Concept of Use (today, Statement of Operating Intent and Usage). This must be up-issued when the form, fit, function or use changes.

Maintaining (Aircraft type)

Upon delivery, the responsibility for Design Control was passed to MoD (brought *Under Ministry Control* - a formal process), meaning Hawker no longer had the autonomy to make design changes. They remained the Aircraft Design Authority, and Maintained the Build Standard through the innumerable changes demanded by MoD and required by (e.g.) legislation. Likewise, subsidiary Design Authorities for aircraft equipment, such as avionics.

The Aircraft Design Authority underwrites the safety and performance of the Design Authority Build Standard for the whole aircraft, so long as it is used within the limits of the Master Airworthiness Reference. (The MoD document applying to Type Airworthiness which, when issued, provides authority for Service regulated flying). Part of Maintaining the Build Standard is upkeep of the technical information necessary for...

Continuing (Individual aircraft)

As 'attaining' delivers the data necessary to maintain the aircraft, and 'maintaining' ensures this remains valid, it can be seen that the continuing airworthiness of an individual aircraft cannot be assured or certified if airworthiness is not maintained. There will be no valid audit trail, no maintained Build Standard, and hence no valid Safety Case based on it. One may use engineering judgment up to a point, but there comes a time when that will tell you the uncertainty (risk) is too great. If asked to show an individual aircraft is airworthy, the first thing one demonstrates is that it is at the Build Standard called up in the Safety Case, upon which all aircraft and aircrew publications are based; or that deviations are acceptable, correctly recorded and justified.

To a degree one can play tunes here, but the principles remain sound.

Applicability to G-BXFI

The CAA classifies Hunter as having an 'Intermediate' level of design complexity, meaning there is no requirement for maintaining airworthiness of the type (as above) by the manufacturer or an equivalent organisation. (CAP553, 2.1.2). But someone must do it, and it must be stated in the Approval Note. The CAA said it was the RAF.

At the time of the accident, the CAA required that ex-military jets on the UK civil register were maintained by organisations holding approvals under British Civil Airworthiness Requirement (BCAR) A8-20, 23 or 25. Moreover, 'M5 maintenance' and 'E4 design' approvals are required to allow the maintenance organisation to restore and maintain former military aircraft for operation on the civil register. The privileges granted to a BCAR A8-20 approved organisation allow it (as above) to self-certify that an aircraft continues to meet the requirements of its Permit to Fly and to issue a Certificate of Validity. The CAA has no requirement to check that such self-certifications are valid, but it does perform general compliance audits as part of its oversight of approved organisations. This of course requires adequate resources. The Air Accidents Investigation Branch (AAIB) reported these were lacking, and routine but crucial regulatory oversight functions were not implemented.

Weald Aviation Services Ltd, holding BCAR A8-20, were contracted at the time of the accident to provide all aircraft maintenance and continuing airworthiness functions for G-BXFI. But that is not the same as being able to maintain airworthiness, the AAIB correctly reporting that core activities were simply not happening. (Indeed, BCAR A8-20 doesn't refer to the subject, or even Safety Cases, and offers no guidance). And because they *are* core, that meant all Hunters were potentially affected. The further danger being that if the regulator cannot ensure this is done on Hunters, what confidence is there for other types?

This is precisely the scenario MoD found itself in post-Nimrod Review (2009-on), its 'solution' being to scrap entire aircraft fleets. For example, Nimrod MR2, MRA4 and R1, and Air Cadet gliders. Of even greater concern, It continued to operate fleets it could not demonstrate the airworthiness of, such as Hawk T Mk1 used by the Red Arrows; a situation that persists. Self-evidently, the entire process upon which the G-BXFI Permit to Fly was predicated was fatally compromised, and remains so - witness subsequent deaths in unairworthy aircraft. Both MoD and CAA purport to follow 'best practice'. But the current 'best' is not good enough; the solution being to implement mandated regulations.

Note: The AAIB report does not actually say who the 'maintenance organisation' was, only that it was contracted by Canfield Hunter. This became academic at the criminal trial in 2019 when two Weald Aviation employees appeared as witnesses.

A maintenance organisation does not necessarily have the approvals or skills to be a Design Authority. And I have known many 'Continuing Airworthiness Managers' with not the slightest idea what maintaining airworthiness involves, who does it, or under what process and procedures. That is not a personal failing - one usually learns and manages 'continuing' first; graduating to managing 'attaining'; and being allowed to 'maintain' only when deemed competent in the others. Today, *'I manage airworthiness'* is a common claim (especially post-Nimrod Review), but very few can explain each component of maintaining a Build Standard, who does the work, or what the primary output is. (MoD regulations now barely mention the subject, and the CAA's are no better). So, if you decide to read the AAIB report, or any MoD accident report, often when it says 'airworthiness' it means 'serviceability'; not realising the aircraft type is not airworthy in the first place. Case in point, and I will return to this later.

Aircraft and Aircrew Publications

The G-BXFI Airworthiness Approval Note states:

'This aircraft is approved for issue of a Permit to Fly provided that it is operated in accordance with the limitations and procedures contained in

the Aircrew Manual and the Flight Reference Cards referred to in Section 6, and those identified in section B, plus the conditions of the Permit to Fly. [It] must be maintained...in accordance with the Air Publication Manuals and schedules referred to in Section 6'.

Section 6 lists MoD's AP101B-1303-series, saying Jet Heritage Ltd has a complete set (for the T.7A).[6] It also lists four of the T.7's AP113B-1302-series, and those applicable to the engine and ejection seats. There is no mention of Issue status, whereas in MoD the latest Issue of the Operating Data Manual must be listed in the Master Airworthiness Reference.

Plainly, this requires the publications to be up-to-date. Prior to 1994 this was the responsibility of MoD's Aircraft and Equipment project offices, with authority for aircraft and aircrew publications delegated to specialist departments, and contracts let on the Design Authorities. On Hunter, this work ceased completely upon it leaving service in 1994; yet G-BXFI's Approval Note includes an unequivocal statement that, in 2008, responsibility rested with the RAF. For the AAIB to have reproduced the Note without further comment, it must have been satisfied that it was the latest one, current at the time of the accident.

(In 2019 the AAIB claimed to the Coroner the Note had been superseded at some point between 2008 and 2015; but could offer no evidence of this and declined to explain why it had accepted the 2008 Note as current. The CAA, who would have issued any replacement, were not invited to comment. The AAIB report has not been updated to reflect this fundamental point, so it remains the official position that the 2008 Note was current in 2015).

When sold into private hands all Hunters needed upgrades, so by definition these publications were immediately out-of-date. And due to the MoD policy of funding reducing by 20% per year in the last five years of life, there is no guarantee they were up-to-date any time after 1990. Consequently, both the Approval Note and Permit to Fly were based on a false premise, and invalid.

The Flight Reference Cards for an aircraft Mark are crucial to safety. They comprise detailed checklists for essential operations during various phases of flight, including emergencies. A summary of the Aircrew Manual, they are provided as flip cards to be kept on the pilot's person, so the two must <u>always</u> be aligned. They were issued as a supplement to the Pilot's Notes (today, the

---

[6] Six Hunter T.7s were modified to Hunter T.7A to serve with No 237 Operational Conversion Unit at RAF Lossiemouth, with Buccaneer instrumentation.

Aircrew Manual), with Canfield's pilots expecting Weald Aviation to provide updates; but they received nothing. Hill's, dated March 1971, had been handed down to him, with no means of updating them.

Moreover, Hunter publications are a mix of the pre-1970 6-Volume system, and the newer 16-Topic system. The old system made clear the difference between on-aircraft and off-aircraft servicing, but the new system mixed them. This required a higher level of maintainer training; a key factor being they had to know how the equipment worked, not just how to remove and install it; which was fine in 1969, but not by 1995 due to MoD contracting-out maintenance and running down engineering training. For example, it ceased ejection seat training for armourers. This was a root cause in the killing of Red Arrows pilot Sean Cunningham in 2011, when off-aircraft servicing of his seat was attempted on-aircraft to save money, and botched. (A root cause is one which, if removed from the accident sequence, would have prevented it).

In MoD this work (and much more besides) is carried out under Post Design Services (PDS), defined as Maintaining the Build Standard. If it is not, both the Safety Case (the primary output) and Master Airworthiness Reference become progressively invalid, meaning a decision must be taken on grounding. In fact, MoD's rules say that if the Service does not ask for funding to Maintain the Build Standard, and state the level of PDS required, its bid for funding for the operation of the entire aircraft fleet is rejected out of hand; the aim being to *force* it to consider the subject.

There are 17 core components, and the key is to understand which must be carried out as a centralised management function. In other words, they shouldn't be stove-piped (each aircraft or equipment project team doing their own small element of what should be a consolidated task). Yet in the early-90's this became the norm. Instead of a single contract to conduct PDS, a company might receive multiple contracts from each MoD user, each costing more to administer than they were worth. The result was at least two extra layers of red tape, huge waste, and significant risk of critical disconnects. Then followed the biggest single violation; the administrative decision in 1993 that all this was a complete waste of money. And hence, and the Nimrod Review...

Because this *is* so crucial, it is largely invisible to front line, who tend to take for granted that the publications (to them, the most tangible output) are valid. On G-BXFI there was an audit trail gap of at least 21 years (1994-2015). The AAIB correctly recommended all publications be at the latest amendment state, but did not go so far as to cite a CAA Letter to Owners issued on 10 March 2005:

> *'Owners of aircraft operating under a Permit to Fly are reminded that in order for an aircraft to be properly maintained it is essential that the latest service information is taken into account'.*

Later, the CAA seemingly disagreed with itself, saying to use the versions in force when the aircraft was decommissioned; meaning it accepted that the Build Standard had not been maintained. Confusion reigned.

Modification state

When Hunter left service, MoD's regulations governing modifications (one of the 17 core components) comprised some 26 pages and nine Annexes in a Defence Standard mandated in all aviation contracts. At Section 4 the G-BXFI Approval Note states:

> *'The applicant* [Jet Heritage Ltd] *confirms that all modifications classified as B/2 or above (with exception of armament and related modifications) have been embodied on the aircraft'.*

'B' refers to what the contractor must do, '2' the Service. That is, Class AA, A and B had been embodied, C and D not necessarily. (There are other Classes which the Approval Note doesn't mention, and I won't go into).

A Class C modification must be:

> *'Embodied on reconditioning or repair. In the case of repair only, embodiment is to be limited to those modifications which can be embodied without further stripping'.*[7]

Moreover, Section 4 of the Note states:

> *'All relevant Special Technical Instructions (STI) have been complied with and Servicing Instructions (SI) satisfied'.*

Both are termed Special Instructions (Technical), defined as covering:

> *'Short-term repair procedures, examinations of equipment, restrictions on use, preventative measures to avert or contain a fault, or hazard warnings or cautions. They are intended to permit rapid action on the part of users who are, or might be, affected by the fault, while a design solution is being sought and applied'.*

Both apply to work packages to be carried out within a specified time or other limit, to seek and repair, or prevent, a potential fault. An STI is a single application (non-recurring), an SI details repetitive (recurring) work.

MoD's regulations (from 1993-on) were confusing, brought about by constant

---

7 Defence Standard 05-125/2, Section 7.4.4.4.

upheaval. The mandated ones stated the MoD project offices were responsible for issuing STI/SIs.[8] However, following the RAF's decision to run down airworthiness management, disband the specialist project offices, and rid themselves of the expertise, they decided that the work now defaulted to ATP3(RAF) (Aircraft Technical Publications) - formerly part of MoD Procurement Executive but recently transferred to the RAF's Air Member Supply and Organisation. Hitherto, the MoD(PE) project offices delegated some of the work to ATP, but upon their demise ATP were unable to pick up the tasks they'd never carried out (as they were being run down as well). The audit trail was further compromised, and remained so through further reorganisations.

In short, *after 1994 there was no MoD Hunter project office or section in ATP3*. It was incumbent upon the CAA to ensure the formal 'design solution' had been found; or the STI/SIs made permanent and publications updated. And that this process was sustained through-life. But by whom, and under whose regulatory oversight? Once again, the CAA stated this was the RAF; MoD correctly denying this.

Once again, for these and other reasons the Airworthiness Approval Note and Permit to Fly were invalid.

The above is but a brief summary of one small element of Maintaining the Build Standard. The essential point is that before 1993 a named individual was responsible and accountable for the airworthiness of each equipment and aircraft type. (An individual might be responsible for scores of equipments; for example, all Navigation or all Comms equipment). Thereafter it was dangerously fragmented, with no single person in charge, encouraging gaps in audit trails. All I can say is that until the early-1990's this was basic trade training for any engineer. Then, suddenly, it wasn't. Many aircrew have been killed due to the resultant dumbing-down, including Chinook ZD576 (29 killed in 1994), Hercules XV179 (10 killed in 2005), and Nimrod XV230 (14 killed in 2006).

An important principle

It is often said the pilot signs to say the aircraft is airworthy; and the AAIB report repeated this. A common fallacy. This is the responsibility of the chief engineer of the maintenance organisation, or an engineer to whom he has

---

8 Defence Standard 05-125/2, Chapter 7.13.3.

delegated the authority. The pilot is responsible for the safe operation of an aircraft he has been told is airworthy and serviceable. If it is not, but he has been told it is, then he can bear no responsibility in this respect. If he errs (as in this case) one must study the effect of the anomaly (unairworthiness and unserviceability) on the accident sequence as a whole, not just the proximate (final) act.

Here, the AAIB opined that G-BXFI being neither airworthy nor serviceable was not directly related to the proximate cause; yet also presented evidence casting significant doubt on this. But at the most fundamental level, if an aircraft is not airworthy it should not be flying. Exceptions are permitted, for example under 'military risk' during conflict. That can never apply to display flying, be it military or civilian.

If an aircraft is deemed airworthy, but carrying 'acceptable' faults, the pilot may accept them. If he does not, he should not fly. Plainly, if there are faults or defects which are not revealed to him, he cannot make an informed decision and, again, cannot be held responsible.

A major cultural issue here is that if the pilot is ex-military, he will have been taught and expected to routinely accept far greater risk, and placed under intolerable pressure to fly manifestly unfit aircraft operationally. Seldom, if ever, will the true status of the aircraft be revealed to him. The aforementioned Chinook, Nimrod and Hercules cases in a nutshell. (And many others). The transition to display flying can be difficult, especially knowing many thousands are waiting in anticipation. It is a different kind of pressure, but nonetheless real. This does not excuse any poor airmanship (if it could be proven), but it is a major mitigating factor when considering liability.

(Having left the RAF in 1994, Hill would have escaped the worst of its financial decision to no longer maintain airworthiness; the *savings at the expense of safety* policy reiterated by the Nimrod Review in 2009).

PERCEIVED TRUTH

The accident manoeuvre

Prior to the airshow, the Display Director sent out a written briefing to all pilots taking part. This set out local restrictions, the minimum distance from the display axis, and a reminder of the meaning and expectations following a *'stop stop stop'* call. (Whereby the pilot can be directed to stop his display).

On the morning of 22 August 2015, Hill flew his own light aircraft from his home in Hertfordshire to North Weald Airfield. Between 1000 and 1100 he received a telephone briefing from the Director. It was short, as he regarded Hill as a competent display pilot who was familiar with the Shoreham site. It covered all the required items and he had no concerns about his preparation.

Pre-flight checks had been carried out on G-BXFI the previous day by a Weald Aviation engineer, later a witness at trial. At Hill's request, the aircraft had been fully fuelled. Two cameras were mounted within the cockpit. A Go-Pro secured to the bulkhead between the two seats, facing forward and providing a partial view of the instruments, pilot movements, and through the canopy and windscreen. The other, a Dog-Cam, was positioned against the base of the windscreen, facing out over the nose of the aircraft. The former continued recording for ~23 minutes after impact, but the latter's video was poor due to distortion caused by the windscreen. These cameras are not designed to capture aircrew audio, the dominant noise being from the engine. From this, investigators can often determine changes in power, or in extreme cases engine breakup.

Hill set off on the 75-mile flight to Shoreham at 1304, his display scheduled for 1321. He initially flew to a designated holding location just off the coast at Brighton, before he was called in by the Air Show Controller. He flew west, just off and parallel with the south coast, for about eight miles; inverting the aircraft briefly to check for loose articles.

On reaching Shoreham, he turned right to fly inland towards the airshow site and straight along the display line. The airfield is situated approximately ¾ mile north of the coast. He was #9 in the flying aircraft displays, coming immediately after a display of model aircraft.

He began by performing a low-level flypast from south to north, following the display line which was parallel to the tarmac runway, just over 230m from the front of the on-site crowd, which was on his right hand side.

He pulled up while turning right and performed a Derry Turn (a manoeuvre whereby the aircraft completes ¾ of a roll) and came out in a banking left turn. This turn continued until the aircraft was facing back towards the display side of the crowd, flying in a southerly direction at an angle of approximately 30° to the display line. (Figure 1, bottom white arrow). About ½ a mile north of the airfield the aircraft commenced the beginning of the 'Bent Loop' which was to end in disaster.

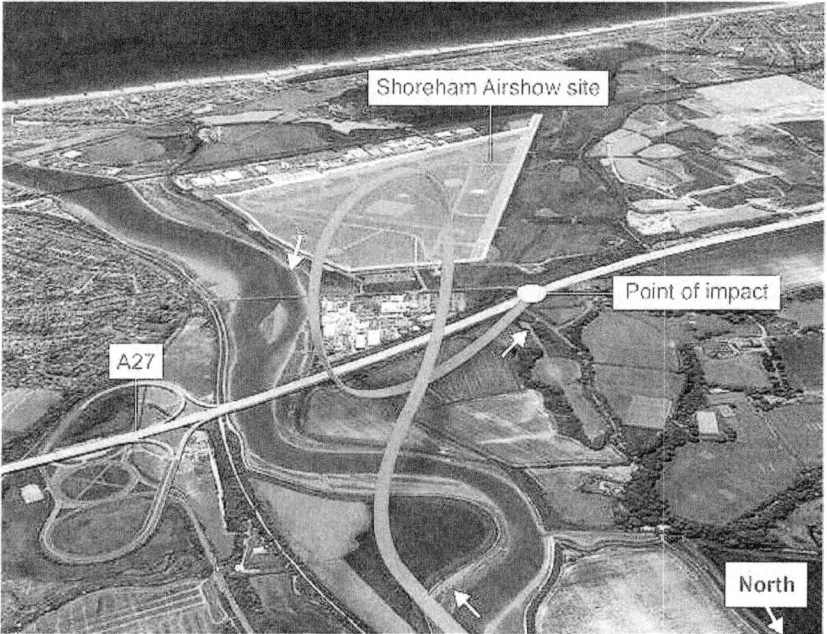

Figure 1: Details of accident manoeuvre *(AAIB)*

It pulled-up at 310 ±15 knots Groundspeed, at a height of 225 ±25 feet above mean sea level (185 ±35 feet above ground level), and with an engine speed of ~7,500 rpm. (The maximum permitted was 8,100 ±50 rpm). As he approached the vertical he initiated a roll to the left. During the climb the engine speed first reduced, then increased to about 7,200 rpm, then reduced again nearing the apex. The aircraft was almost inverted with its wings level at the apex, at a height of 2,700 ±200 feet and Indicated Airspeed of 105 ±2.5 knots. During the subsequent descent the aircraft accelerated, its ground track aligned to the west along the A27 Shoreham Bypass. The nose was raised but insufficient height was available to recover to level flight before it impacted the westbound carriageway at 225 ±25 knots Groundspeed, with a nose-up attitude of 14 ±3°.

A 'normal' loop is entered from straight and level flight. The nose of the aircraft is then pitched up continuously, passing through the inverted attitude at the apex and continuing through the downward vertical until the aircraft returns to the required height in a straight and level attitude. The entry and exit ground tracks are the same.

A typical Bent Loop is performed by entering a loop and, towards the end of the first quarter, just before vertical, rolling the aircraft while continuing to pitch the nose up. The aircraft continues pitching nose-up, pulling through the second half of the loop, which results in the exit track being different from the entry track, determined by the amount of roll applied. Hill stated his normal technique was to adjust most of the track in the upward vertical, and then refine the track in the downward portion of the loop by blending roll and pitch in the last quarter to position and align with the desired exit track. This was approximately 60° right of the entry track.

There are two variants of Bent Loops:

(a) Those with gently rolling pull on the way up, like the first half of a Barrel Roll. While graceful, they inherit the dangers of a Barrel Roll, where the blend of roll and pitch is difficult to accurately reproduce. All other factors (e.g. power) being equal, the energy at the apex (highest height, and ideally wings level inverted in roll) will be the same...*but* the kinetic energy v potential energy balance is different. This is crucial, because a reduced height not only makes recovery more difficult (or impossible), but the speed will be higher, recovery requiring yet more height.

(b) Experienced display pilots tend to perform the roll briefly and crisply when the aircraft is in the upward vertical. This is safer, since the pitch rate ('pull') is stopped, or reduced, for the short roll period - the aircraft still ascending. Therefore, the aircraft should arrive at the apex with more height, and less speed, than a conventional loop.

The accident manoeuvre was intended to be type (b), as flown in his other displays. But the error meant it was 'in between'. Hill later used ground video taken at Shoreham in 2014 to illustrate the differences.

Performance gates

All pilots work to gate parameters, such as the height necessary to achieve a particular manoeuvre, or speed to be at a particular point of the manoeuvre. To be outwith gate parameters is potentially catastrophic.

Note: It is important not to confuse Airspeed and Groundspeed. Airspeed is the vector difference between Groundspeed and wind speed. On a still day, at sea level, Airspeed is equal to Groundspeed. But if the wind is blowing in the same direction the aircraft is moving, Airspeed will be less than Groundspeed. The effect here was to confuse; for example, the prosecution said speed at entering the manoeuvre was 291 knots Groundspeed, and most (if they even thought about it or noticed) would infer this was even lower than the AAIB's 310 knots Indicated Airspeed (IAS). In court, the two were conflated. It is easy to do when considering a flight with the wind direction relative to the aircraft's heading constantly changing.

Height at pull-up

It was widely reported that Hill breached a 500 feet minima when pulling-up from 185 ±35 feet. The AAIB:

'The aircraft was carrying out a manoeuvre involving both a pitching and rolling component, which <u>commenced from a height lower than the pilot's authorised minimum for aerobatics</u>, at an airspeed below his stated minimum, and proceeded with less than minimum thrust. This resulted in the aircraft achieving a height at the top of the manoeuvre less than required to complete it safely, at a speed that was lower than normal.

The underlined phrase was misleading, and clearly intended to be taken as criticism; with the reader expected to believe Hill should have been at 500 feet. At trial, the prosecution adopted the same tactic. In fact, his Display Authorisation permitted a minimum flypast height for Category G aircraft of 100 feet, with 500 feet being the minimum for aerobatics. He was permitted to <u>commence a climb</u> into a vertical manoeuvre from <u>100 feet</u>. Therefore, the smooth pull into a loop from 185 ±35 feet was not a violation of his Display Authorisation.

The AAIB did add, however:

'Guidance concerning the minimum height at which aerobatic manoeuvres may be commenced is not applied consistently and may be unclear. Recorded information from other aircraft, and other flying displays' Radar data and video recordings, indicated that instances of aerobatic manoeuvres occurring below 500 feet above ground level more than 1 km from the airfield, or flight below the heights specified in a display plan, were not limited to one aircraft, pilot or venue. There was evidence that other pilots do not always check or perceive correctly that the required height has been achieved at the apex of manoeuvres'.

While important this be said, once again it conflated these two phases of the manoeuvre; the casual reader thinking Hill breached his height at entry, and the AAIB was blithely saying *'so did others'*. Rather, the point is Hill did <u>not</u> breach his entry height, and (apparently) nothing had been done about those who did.

I think it essential to emphasise this. Even today, almost every commentary claims Hill was 'too low' at entry; despite the facts being accepted by the prosecution, Judge and jury.

Speed at loop entry

It was alleged that before the aircraft pitched up, Hill failed to select full power on the throttle. He was at 310 ±15 knots IAS at entry instead of his normal 350; although expert witnesses later stated 300 was adequate.

I will discuss later a specific problem with engine system unserviceability that <u>may</u> have affected power, but it is worth noting now that Hunter variants are fitted with different models of the Avon engine. The T.7 has the 100-Series engine, and is of lower power than others using the 200-Series. Experienced pilots opined this makes no practical difference to the way a display is flown, although they know the larger engine allows them to enter a loop at around 20 knots slower or, for example, if the cloud base is marginal and an absolute minimum apex height is necessary.

Rather, the main consideration in the T.7 is the reduced view due to the dual cockpit/canopy shape. This assumes import later when discussing precisely *when* Hill's Cognitive Impairment was said to commence, it being associated with him tilting his head sharply to get a better view.

Speed through the climb

The important question is why the speed through the climb was lower than planned. All other things being equal, this is determined by the throttle setting and hence engine power, and the engine's efficiency; noting that power in the climb is less important than achieving the gate numbers. Expert witnesses later confirmed that applying full power was unnecessary; the real issue the two <u>reductions</u> in power. The prosecution claimed these were deliberate acts by Hill; which would indeed be negligence. However, the AAIB noted that the fuel pump which the engine performance relied upon was unserviceable and unairworthy. I return to this later.

Speed and height at apex of loop

Due in part to the power reductions, Hill did not achieve the apex gates.

The ideal gate height was 4,000 feet, the sum of: 3,000 feet (needed to carry out the downward half of the loop), the minimum authorised height of 500 feet for conducting aerobatics in a Hunter, and an additional 500 feet safety margin. At the apex, while inverted, achieved height was around 2,700 ±200 feet, and Airspeed 105 ±2.5 knots instead of 150.

The apex height came from a radar signal detected by the National Air Traffic Services (NATS); whereby a Height Encoding Altimeter provides the data to an onboard Transponder, which is interrogated by NATS. The NATS radar does not detect height itself. The Encoding Altimeter works by using outside (static) air pressure. Such instruments can be remarkably accurate if calibrated correctly.

However, instruments such as Airspeed Indicators, which rely on both Pitot ('ram air' if you like) and Static pressure, are susceptible to large inaccuracies during manoeuvring, which can result in ram air briefly entering the Static ports. They are particularly vulnerable during sharp turns. This well-known phenomenon, which aircraft designers always seek to mitigate, was not mentioned, the AAIB confining itself to:

'It was not possible to test or check the integrity of the aircraft's Pitot and Static systems due to the extensive structural disruption resulting from the accident'.

A separate issue is that of friction, and the effect on the instrument's movement (e.g. the hand staff, quadrant, pinion). This is usually termed 'stiction', mitigated so long as the instrument and its internal vibrator are serviceable. The accident damage meant this was impossible to determine. (In instruments lacking a vibrator 'light tapping' is permitted to free any stickiness. The manuals don't say what with).

The AAIB reported the Main Altimeter was under-reading by ~100 feet. In general this is not a huge error; a good rule of thumb is that the allowable error in a Pitot Static instrument is the width of the pointer. So, no criticism can be implied of the instrument or maintenance organisation. However, the report omitted that the presence of drop tanks causes the Airspeed Indicator and Mach Meter to under read; although the issue is worse when nearing the speed of sound.

The AAIB also noted GPS height data was 50-200 feet higher than the pressure altitude transmitted via the transponder. While GPS is very accurate in latitude/longitude, the inherent errors in height are relatively large, and those stated are very good for the UK.⁹ One is not permitted to rely solely on GPS height (primarily due to these errors and Air Traffic Control expecting you to use the local pressure setting to avoid conflict with other aircraft). And during manoeuvring the system can lose sight of the satellites, needing time to reacquire them. I feel mention of this was a bit of a red herring.

Reading the plethora of papers on this speed/height aspect, one becomes utterly bewildered by the sheer variation in figures presented. I've quoted just one set, but none can be proven 100% accurate. The best thing to say is that in general terms they were not contested. That is, height at entry was fine, speed perhaps a little slow, power dropped twice during ascent, and he was too low and too slow at apex.

Escape manoeuvre

At this stage Hill would have been expected to conduct an escape manoeuvre, by rolling the aircraft upright. The AAIB:

'Although it was possible to abort the manoeuvre safely at this point, it appeared the pilot did not recognise that the aircraft was too low to complete the downward half of the manoeuvre. An analysis of human performance identified several credible explanations for this, including: not reading the altimeter due to workload, distraction or visual limitations such as contrast or glare; misreading the altimeter due to its presentation of height information; or incorrectly recalling the minimum height required at the apex. Although it was possible to abort the manoeuvre safely at this point, it appeared the pilot did not recognise the aircraft was too low to complete the downward half'.

(The AAIB's consideration of 'glare' is both correct and intriguing, in a report signed by its Chief Inspector, a recently retired Military Aviation Authority officer. It would be interesting to know if he realised MoD's formal position, following the loss of two RN Sea Kings in a mid-air in 2003, was that glare need not be considered, in design, risk assessment, or accident investigations. If he did, allowing this one word to remain is to his immense credit).¹⁰

At the time, CAP403 referred to training for escape manoeuvres only as a ground training 'emergency' item. There was no requirement for a pilot to

---

9 GPS height errors vary depending on where you are. In south India/Sri Lanka it may show you 330 feet lower than you are; in Iceland 230 feet higher. In the UK it is around 165 feet higher; plus system errors of ±150 feet.
10 RN Board of Inquiry report, Sea Kings ASaC Mk7 XV650 & XV704, 23 March 2003.

demonstrate proficiency before obtaining Display Approval. However, it is common ground among pilots that specific training is required regarding rolling a swept wing jet at low airspeed; and then the manoeuvre must be regularly practised. Under AAIB interview Hill confirmed he had been taught and was aware of the escape manoeuvre for the Jet Provost, but had no specific recall of heights and speeds used when he flew the Harrier.

The AAIB reported:

> 'He had not practised this escape manoeuvre in the Hunter and commented that he would not be sure of the outcome of attempting it at the speed achieved at the apex of the accident manoeuvre'.

Instead, he committed to the loop and a vertical descent. *Why?*

The errors

Immediately after the crash there was general agreement among experienced aviation witnesses that the manoeuvre was flown so badly there must have been something wrong, either with the aircraft or pilot.

On 4 September 2015, nine days later, the AAIB issued a statement saying there were no technical faults with the aircraft. It is unclear if it based this on examination of the mostly destroyed aircraft, or examination of the aircraft's records - which said it was serviceable and airworthy. Thus, the entire focus quickly shifted to pilot error.

But when its formal report was issued 18 months later (March 2017), the AAIB confirmed the aircraft was neither serviceable nor airworthy, listing a number of technical faults. (I need to stress this. I am not claiming the aircraft was unairworthy or unserviceable. The AAIB confirmed it wasn't, and I merely seek to explain to the reader some additional reasons which were not spelt out in its report).

There was no attempt to reconcile this contradiction, or assess the effect it had on the direction the investigation had taken. The AAIB claimed this had no direct relationship with the proximate cause. But they were clearly root causes, as the aircraft should not have been flying. Yes, it was clear errors had been made in the cockpit, but at this early stage it was not known why; and to disassociate them with the condition of the aircraft was wrong.

The effect was to prematurely eliminate all other components of the investigation (e.g. Technical, Legal) to concentrate on Airmanship. The correct approach is to give equal weight to each, establish the known facts, and from them derive the lead anomaly, any follow-on anomalies, and the lead event that led to them. Only then can *theories* be offered, which *must* match *all* these facts.

The AAIB Inspectors understood this. Regarding the lead anomaly - lack of airworthiness - they got very close indeed. However, it is equally plain that, as soon as the implications were appreciated (i.e. there was shared liability, and so there should be a sense of collective responsibility) they stopped. Or, more likely, were stopped. The final report is utterly scathing of other parties, but then suddenly that part of the investigation ceased. The points at which their words are cut-off are obvious.

Thus the investigation was **incomplete, flawed and deficient**. I emphasise these words because they constitute a formal legal test, and assume huge importance later when discussing High Court rulings. Hill made errors. But they were not the only ones - and it was these that were to be hidden.

Immediate action

On 25 August 2015 the CAA issued Safety Directive SD-2015/003 grounding all UK civil-registered Hunters, pending the AAIB investigation.

Additionally, flying displays over land by vintage jet aircraft were significantly restricted; limited to flypasts, which means 'high energy' aerobatics were prohibited. The CAA announced it would begin *'additional risk assessments on all forthcoming civil air displays to establish if additional measures should be introduced'*, and that it had commenced a full review of air display safety.

The only principle which governs the grounding of aircraft is that of airworthiness. In other words, the CAA at least strongly suspected this was the case, and a major factor.

No mention was made of military-registered Hunters, the implication being the problem was <u>known</u> to be confined to aircraft on the civil register. What systemic problem applied to civil, but not military? The Permit to Fly and Airworthiness Approval Note process. Thus, the grounding criteria was met.

These actions were prudent; but lacking a proactive Safety Management System they were reactive.

Accident causation

The root causes of most accidents are usually deficiencies in systems, whether these are for management, design, certification, maintenance, and/or operation. Most accidents can be traced to one or more of four levels of failure. The normal method of describing this is the Reason Model of accident causation, after the late Professor James Reason; more commonly the Swiss Cheese Model:

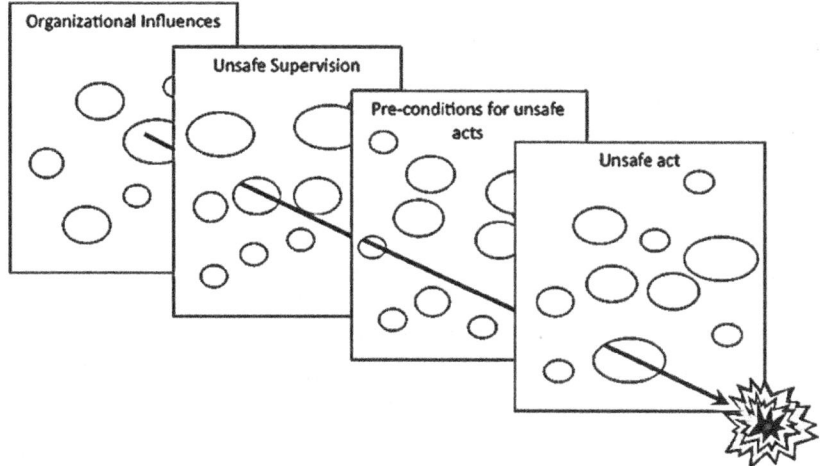

Figure 2 - The Reason 'Swiss Cheese' Model of accident causation.

Defences against failure are modelled as layered barriers, represented as slices of Swiss cheese:

Organisational Influences - Resource management (e.g. equipment, information, facilities), organisational climate (e.g. culture, structure, policies) and processes (e.g. instructions, procedures, regulations).

Unsafe Supervision - Inadequate supervision (leadership, oversight), failure to correct known problems (e.g. ignoring safety hazards) and supervisory violations (e.g. bullying, illegal orders).

Preconditions for Unsafe Acts - Environmental factors (e.g. technological, physical), condition of operators (e.g. mental, physiological, and physical) and personnel (e.g. readiness).

Unsafe Acts (Errors and violations) - Errors are unintentional behaviours and may be skill-based, decision-making or perceptual. Violations are wilful disregard of rules and regulations; they may be routine (habitual and tolerated by the governing authority), or exceptional (isolated and neither typical of the operator nor condoned by management).

The holes denote individual weaknesses in individual parts of the system, and are continually varying in size. The system as a whole produces failures when a hole in each slice momentarily align, permitting the 'accident trajectory'; so a hazard passes through the holes in the defences, leading to a failure.

The hazards/failures may exist all the time, but not every aircraft will crash because the holes are seen to be constantly moving and only rarely, if ever, align. The model includes active and latent failures. The latter is useful in accident investigation, encouraging the study of factors that may have lain dormant, often for years, until they finally contribute to the accident.

Inadequate defences may make errors more dangerous, but some errors will overcome even the most robust defences. In practice, defences should be strengthened in recognition errors will occur. There must be regulatory oversight to ensure they remain strong. Therefore, to truly analyse (any) accident one must assess why defences failed. The normal approach is to map the failings - in this case those noted by the AAIB, and importantly those not noted - to the Model. Doing so is the best way of illustrating why one cannot simply blame the final act - in this case the pilot errors - when multiple examples of unsafe violations, preconditions, unsafe supervision and organisational failures exist. Natural justice, not to mention investigative protocols, demands it be fully understood why these pre-existing holes were allowed to persist after being identified. Put another way, a root cause in most aircraft accidents is recurring systemic failings. The AAIB fully understands this. Legal authorities seem not to, although most police officers will intuitively understand that (e.g.) if someone cuts a car brake line, then one should not blame the driver if he cannot stop in time to avoid an accident; and if it can be proven he was going too fast, there must still be collective responsibility. However, the police understanding this, and the Crown Prosecution Service (CPS) applying it, are two very different sides of the same coin. Again, case in point.

But what if these assumed random events are aligned by conscious violations? That is no longer an example of the Reason Model since it is not random - it is gambling. Here, the layered defences were systematically dismantled. This error/violation aspect is crucial to any assessment of the case, primarily because it is the difference in law between negligence (inadvertent) and gross negligence (deliberate). The AAIB noted multiple breaches of the defences in each of the four slices. Plainly, and regardless of the reason(s), the most obvious unsafe acts were the <u>errors</u> made by Hill. But more serious were the <u>habitual, intentional violations</u> prior to the accident, and the serious offences committed afterwards by other parties. I summarise these in the following chapters.

An error can be negligence; for example, <u>if</u> Hill made a poor decision and the resultant cascade of problems overwhelmed him to the extent he failed to recover. But by charging him with Gross Negligence Manslaughter, the CPS accused him of deliberately violating the rules and regulations he was bound by. Not to be facetious, but some might call that attempted suicide when applied to flying a fast jet. However, I think most reasonable people would agree he did not set out that day to crash his aeroplane. He committed errors, but he did not violate. In effect, the CPS were also gambling, deciding to prosecute without first establishing the facts, assessing contributory and aggravating factors, or determining the lead anomaly. Some might think that malfeasance, but it is probably better I describe it as pandering to public opinion for political reasons.

The investigation, and implementing recommendations, are part of the overall Safety Management System, the aim being to prevent recurrence. The prosecution of Hill did nothing to advance this aim. By ignoring the Reason Model, and concentrating on the final act, the CPS attacked the System head-on, compromising future safety. One solution for consideration is the government declaring an amnesty for past transgressions, and giving fair warning that future violations, at any stage, will be prosecuted. I accept this would be unsatisfactory to the Shoreham families (and countless others) but it must be recognised that legal authorities will not take retrospective action against Departments of State such as MoD and Transport - or themselves. And make no mistake, *their* violations are among the worst.

Risk Management and Safety

A hazard is a potential source of harm. There are many types of impact, but here we are concerned with those that cause Risk to Life. Risk Analysis is the identification and evaluation of the probability of occurrence and impact. Risk Assessment determines the significance and value of the identified hazards, and estimated risks to those affected. Risk Management is the control of risk through development and implementation of mitigation plans. Continual assessment of mitigation action is necessary, along with contingency planning to cater for its failure, and the resources to manage this. When known in advance a risk will occur, or pre-exists, it is a Certainty and must be dealt with before proceeding.

Regarding Safety Management Systems (SMS) the AAIB reported:

> 'An SMS enables an organisation to determine its approach to safety and to identify the hazards to which it is subject. There was no mention of SMS in CAP403 in force at the time, and no evidence that the available guidance had led to the adoption of SMS or equivalent practices among the operators [plural] of displaying aircraft. The operator of G-BXFI was <u>not required</u> to have an SMS and <u>did not have one</u>. <u>Likewise, neither the display organiser nor the CAA General Aviation Unit had, or were required to have, an SMS</u>'.

The law does not actually require an organisation to have an SMS. Health and Safety Executive guidance is that if the business is *'small or low risk then you'll probably be able to demonstrate risk management'* without an SMS. But 'small' can be high risk. Like very many of the issues I raise, MoD actually gets it right. You <u>must</u> have a Safety Management Plan for every activity (e.g. a project, operating an aircraft), but you can tailor it to your needs. Where MoD falls down is it does not fund implementation - again, the core failing raised in the Nimrod Review.

The resultant shoulder-sloping was described very well by the AAIB:

> <u>'Ownership of risk</u>
>
> The investigation heard conflicting views about who held the ownership of flying display risk. The Flying Display Director (FDD) and the organisers of the Airshow believed that the CAA held the risk, and the CAA considered that the risk was held by the organisers and the FDD. The FDD stated his belief that the CAA issued an Article 162 permission for a flying display only when it was "satisfied that the situation is safe" and that it would intervene if it believed that "everything is not satisfactory". The organiser expressed the view that the CAA remains "the gatekeeper" of all safety and risk management relating to air displays'.[11]

In other words, there wasn't a Risk Management Plan setting out boundaries of responsibility or a conflict resolution process. A properly constructed, independently approved and applied Safety Management Plan would have seen to this.

---

11 AAIB report, 1.17.4.2.

Oddly, perhaps, the CAA's CAP1059 (Safety Management Systems: Guidance for small, non-complex organisations) is actually quite good. But it doesn't explain why it's not mandatory.

The spectators, and especially the deceased who were simply driving by and had no interest in the display, had no say in this. They placed their trust in the Committee getting it right, and the CAA applying strict regulatory oversight. It was misplaced.

Nevertheless, the Flying Display Committee had produced a log containing 10 hazards *'subject to risk assessment'* :

1. Airside unauthorised access
2. Mid-air collision - Display and non-Display aircraft
3. Mid-air collision - Display formation
4. Ejector seat impacts crowd
5. Loss of control due to pilot disorientation
6. Location road and of local built up areas
7. Public assembly on A27 and local roads
8. Aircraft crash outside the airfield boundary
9. Fast jet aircraft collision into crowd area
10. Fatigue amongst key safety staff

Here is the 'risk assessment' relating to #8:

Mitigation

Display regulations require pilots to observe the normal Rules of the Air when outside the display area. There are the major restrictions on displaying aircraft that require them to be at specific minimum heights when over specific areas around the display site. Pilots will be specifically briefed on this restriction at the display briefing.

Action required

All crews to be briefed on safety requirements and mandatory operating regulations prior to each display flight. All flights to be monitored by the FDD and FCC to ensure compliance with the regulations, observance of agreed display programme and consistency of presentation. FDD and FCC to have direct radio contact with the display pilot and can intervene to stop the display at any time'.

That is not a risk assessment. There is no indication of contingency planning or confirmation of resource availability and sustainment. It is no more than initial jottings repeating a few key phrases from CAA recommendations; which, the AAIB confirmed, was sufficient to see it waived through without independent scrutiny. The 'actions required' bear little relationship to the hazard/risk. *Who was responsible for delivering a valid risk mitigation?*

Human Factors in aviation: The Dirty Dozen

All accidents have an element of human error at their root, and it doesn't just apply to the final act. Aviation safety, in its entirety, is based on the inevitability that humans <u>will</u> make errors. And if you fail to correct an error, it becomes a mistake. Safety Management Systems have evolved to minimise errors, through better training, assessment, monitoring and supervision. How these errors are dealt with can either support or sabotage aviation safety.

Understanding this is critical to preventing mistakes, but is seldom addressed in accident reports which (certainly in MoD) are issued by those who invariably made, or represent those who made, those mistakes.

The Dirty Dozen represents 12 common causes of human error in aviation safety, or conditions that can act as precursors, to accidents or incidents. The concept was developed by Gordon Dupont, in 1993, whilst he was working for Transport Canada, and has since become a cornerstone of Human Factors in Maintenance training courses worldwide, as exemplified in the CAA's CAP715. There is no order of priority, although lack of communication is often presented as #1:

1. Lack of Communication
2. Distraction
3. Lack of Resources
4. Stress
5. Complacency
6. Lack of Teamwork
7. Pressure
8. Lack of Awareness
9. Lack of Knowledge
10. Fatigue
11. Lack of Assertiveness
12. Norms

How many had already occurred, been set in motion, reported as a result of previous accidents, or condoned by the regulator - and most importantly, not of the pilot's making - before the accident flight? If the answer is even one, then there must be collective responsibility. (The conservative answer is nine). Mistakes not only developed, but ambivalence and failure to act allowed them to become violations.

I will return later to Human Factors, as the subject assumed huge import during Hill's trial.

The AAIB Investigation (2015-17 and 2019)

The AAIB is an independent unit within the Department for Transport, based in Farnborough, Hampshire. It investigates civil aircraft accidents and serious incidents within the UK, its overseas territories and Crown dependencies. It also provides assistance and expertise to international air accident investigations and organisations. Its purpose is to improve aviation safety by determining the circumstances and causes, and promoting action to prevent recurrence. It has a duty to investigate thoroughly, and submit recommendations that will enhance safety and prevent recurrence. It does not have executive authority to ensure its recommendations are implemented, it cannot bring prosecutions, nor may it attribute blame. The decision to investigate accidents rests solely with the Chief Inspector. Perhaps more importantly, he decides which are *not* to be investigated.

The Branch is occasionally asked by MoD to assist in its investigations, where its input is restricted to reporting on the evidence from the scene. It is not permitted unfettered access to that evidence, which (e.g. MoD or the police) may remove and conceal before the AAIB's arrival. Nor is it permitted to comment on legal, airmanship, or matters of certification; in civil accidents it does all of these.

The organisation consists six Groups, each headed by a Principal Inspector, plus a Business Support Unit. Above them sit the Chief Inspector and his Deputy. It produces four types of investigation reports; Field Investigation, Formal, Annual Safety, and Special Bulletins. Additionally, a Monthly Bulletin summarises these and, as in this case, it may issue Supplements which update, amend or correct previous reports. (A Supplement does not mean the investigation has been reopened).

There is a 3-level investigation status:

1. Under investigation - the investigation is underway and includes the drafting of the report prior to consultation.
2. Consultation stage - when an investigation is largely complete and a confidential draft report has been sent out for formal consultation. This includes the time taken to consider representations and amend the draft report prior to publication.
3. Publication scheduled - the report has been approved for publication by the Chief Inspector.

In this case the time taken to complete (2) explains why it announced its report would be published in Autumn 2016, but was delayed until March 2017. The unknown it faced was what interested parties, such as the CAA, airshow organisers, and owner/operator/maintainer, would say in response to their advance notifications. The pilot would have to be given the opportunity to respond. The families would have to be briefed, along with legal representatives. The police investigation had been in abeyance awaiting the report, and they would have to prepare an initial briefing to the Crown Prosecution Service. There were many fingers in the pie, and a lot of politics to negotiate, before the public were allowed to read the official, sanitised version. In turn, this delayed the initial legal proceedings. Similarly, after the court case a Supplement was issued, delaying the Coroner's Inquest. The AAIB is under no obligation to assist the Coroner in this respect; it is the Coroner who must assist the investigation. If the Coroner fails in this duty, the AAIB must put its interests second, risking recurrence.

The nature of the task means the AAIB's workload is variable and unpredictable. At time of writing 31 civilian aircraft accidents are under investigation, 11 of them fatal. The problem it faces is that there <u>must</u> be sufficient trained staff to cover infrequent major accidents - it cannot simply recruit when something pops up. In this, it is similar to the emergency services. As such, there will be occasions when staff are looking for something to do, others when there aren't enough hours in the day for months on end. Being an investigator is a vocation. My guess is few Inspectors aspire to the Chief Inspector's job, and having to deal with beancounters continually looking to cut funding; who never realise they are making 'savings' at the expense of safety - including their own, whether they fly or not. Once again, a problem familiar to MoD, and the main thrust of the Nimrod Review.

My approach

To understand why Hill was found not guilty, first one must appreciate a legal aspect of the case. By High Court order the content of the AAIB report could not be led in court, and none of its staff appeared as witnesses. I will discuss these rulings in more detail later when assessing the effect. But immediately a serious question arises:

If the prosecution is permitted to base its entire case on selected extracts from an AAIB report which is incomplete, flawed and deficient, the jury is able to read it before trial, and the defence is not permitted to even mention it, is there is any real prospect of a fair trial?

In effect, the prosecution was hoping the jurors had not read it, the defence hoping they had.

How to tackle the report? I could take you through it line by line, but you would lose the will to live. The other extreme is to ignore it, as it wasn't allowed in court. That would be ridiculous, because you need to know why the prosecution case failed.

I will use the AAIB's own summary, which is mostly excellent. However, there are two major caveats. First, some of it is not entirely factual, or is open to misinterpretation. Second, there are important facts which have been ignored, omitted, or removed during review.

Some subjects must be taken in chronological order; on others that is less important. The best way, I hope, is to provide a brief feel for the content, and then discuss each component of the accident sequence separately as they naturally arise in the narrative. To meet my aim of explaining the acquittal, and to avoid over-complication, I will concentrate on what became important, namely:

- The effect of g-forces.
- Test flights conducted to further knowledge of the accident manoeuvre.
- Allegations of poor airmanship.

It is no coincidence that these were poorly addressed in the report, but explored in detail at the criminal trial.

I will also discuss matters of certification (airworthiness and serviceability) that were not developed, and explain why G-BXFI should not have been flying at all. *Who benefitted from this being obscured?* Put another way, what the report omitted was in many ways more important than what it included.

Summary of report [12]

Some 452 pages long, it is in a standard AAIB format, making repetition unavoidable and interpretation difficult. Correctly, there is no comment on potential liability or culpability. But it unavoidably offers signposts; and the CAA and the Airshow organisers are heavily criticised, whereas Hill is not.

In places, absence of evidence is confused with evidence of absence. Often, unverified or unexplained 'facts' are discussed in an authoritative manner, while offering little balance. Uninformed readers (primarily the police and

---

12 https://www.gov.uk/aaib-reports/aircraft-accident-report-aar-1-2017-g-bxfi-22-august-2015

Crown Prosecution Service) drew incorrect inference. This is particularly disappointing because in the past it has been the AAIB who pointed out the same tendencies in MoD reports. It would seem it is the AAIB who has regressed. One must ask what, or who, has changed to bring this about.

A relatively minor point is the persistent use of 'defect' when it really means 'fault'. The former has legal connotations relating to product liability. That is, an item may be declared faulty, and the fault investigation will determine liability. If it is deemed a design failure, then it becomes a defect. MoD was required to heed this from 1991, resulting in updates to all airworthiness regulations. To avoid confusion I have taken the liberty of correcting this where necessary. I am not being pedantic. If it were case of simply replacing 'defect' with 'fault', then perhaps so. But here there was a real design defect, which the AAIB did not report as such, leading to an untrustworthy Fatigue Index of the aircraft. That is, not only was it a defect, but it affected the basic structural integrity and safety of the aircraft.

Notwithstanding, the report revealed a root cause of the accident:

'The aircraft had been issued with a Permit to Fly and its Certificate of Validity was in date, but <u>the issues identified in this investigation indicated that the aircraft was no longer in compliance with the requirements of its Permit to Fly</u>. CAA oversight of the maintenance organisation and the operator did not identify the deficiencies with the aircraft's airworthiness'.

Readers were left in no doubt as to where the most serious failings lay. It is one of many passages that, if read out in court, would lead a jury to ask: *Why is the pilot on trial?* Coupled with the CAA not requiring a Safety Management System, all this pointed to a high degree of liability and lack of fitness for purpose as a regulator. Then it emerged the CAA did not require *itself* to have one…

The investigation identified the following causal factors:

- The aircraft did not achieve sufficient height at the apex of the accident manoeuvre to complete it before impacting the ground, because the combination of low entry speed and low engine thrust in the upward half of the manoeuvre was insufficient. (While mentioned in the body of the report, this summary item omitted the power reductions).
- An escape manoeuvre was not carried out, despite the aircraft not achieving the required minimum apex height.

The following contributory factors were identified:
- The pilot either did not perceive that an escape manoeuvre was necessary, or did not realise that one was possible at the speed achieved at the apex of the manoeuvre.
- The pilot had not received formal training to escape from the accident manoeuvre in a Hunter and had not had his competence to do so assessed.
- The pilot had not practised the technique for escaping from the accident manoeuvre in a Hunter, and did not know the minimum speed from which an escape manoeuvre could be carried out successfully.
- A change of ground track during the manoeuvre positioned the aircraft further east than planned, producing an exit track along the A27 dual carriageway.
- The manoeuvre took place above an area occupied by the public over which the organisers of the flying display had no control.
- The severity of the outcome was due to the absence of provisions to mitigate the effects of an aircraft crashing in an area outside the control of the organisers of the flying display.

I will discuss some of these in more detail later as they require context, but note the last three conflate cause of accident and cause of death. The AAIB was correct to note these, but it is always wise to separate them by identifying the point of divergence, otherwise it can be prejudicial.

Regarding the final acts, the AAIB investigators were severely constrained by Hill's physical condition and amnesia. Interviewed on seven separate occasions, in accordance with restrictions advised by his doctors, he was able to describe his normal practice but not the actual event. His lack of recall was not disputed at any time, by any party. More pertinently, he was entirely consistent across seven high-pressure interviews during which his questioners would be looking for any signs of recall.

I believe the format of the report, and the placing of 'factual' but inaccurate evidence up front, tended to colour judgments - especially anyone who was, perhaps, just seeking to write a short paragraph or two in a newspaper. I doubt if many actually waded through all 452 pages, far less understood them. It transpired the prosecution barristers and many of their 'expert' witnesses certainly hadn't. Nor the Crown Prosecution Service. Otherwise, they would have realised that, as the report proceeded and developed, it sometimes picked apart its own 'facts'.

Special Bulletins and Supplement

Bulletin S3/2015

Published on 4 September 2015, this provided preliminary information gathered from ground inspection, radar data and imagery. The content was a simple statement of what little had emerged at the time.

Bulletin S4/2015

Published on 21 December 2015, this included seven recommendations, under these general headings:
- Safety of first responders when the aircraft is fitted with ejection seats.
- Non-compliance with ejection seat regulations.
- Lack of knowledge of military aircraft within civilian maintenance organisations, and establishment of minimum standards for publications.
- Review of effectiveness of Mandatory Permit Directive relating to the engine.
- Review of procedures that allowed an invalid Permit to Fly Certificate of Validity to be issued.

Bulletin S1/2016

Published on 10 March 2016, this dwelt on risk management associated with air displays, issuing a further 14 recommendations, encompassing:
- Poor guidance to display organisers.
- Competence of display organisers.
- Risk Assessments.
- Information exchange between pilot and organiser.
- Displays rules regarding minimum heights and distances from spectators.
- Lack of independence of Display Authorisation Evaluators, and rules governing Authorisations.
- Reporting of safety occurrences at displays, and suspension of pilots who breach rules.

The intent was to inform the air display community prior to the 2016 display season.

In total, 44 pages focussing on safety concerns, all aimed at the CAA; most pointing to systemic failings. A further 11 safety recommendations were made in the report itself. The AAIB later summarised this:

'The regulator (CAA) believed the organisers of flying displays owned the risk. Conversely, the organiser believed that the regulator would not have issued a Permission for the display if it had not been satisfied with the safety of the event. The aircraft operator's pilots believed the organiser had gained approval for overflight of congested areas, which was otherwise prohibited for that aircraft, and the display organiser believed that it was the responsibility of the operator or the pilot to fly the aircraft's display in a manner appropriate to the constraints of the display site.

No organisation or individual considered all the hazards associated with the aircraft's display, what could go wrong, who might be affected and what could be done to mitigate the risks to a level that was both tolerable and As Low As Reasonably Practicable. Controls intended to protect the public from the hazards of displaying aircraft were ineffective'.

Supplement, 19 December 2019

Issued after the trial, many characterised this as the AAIB having a second bite. It concentrated on Cognitive Impairment, referring to prosecution 'evidence' that had already been discredited in court, as if it were fact. In particular, it discussed evidence and reproduced stills from the cockpit video which was prohibited by High Court order. In doing so the AAIB sailed close to the wind, risking contempt.

The AAIB engaged yet more 'expert witnesses' to analyse Hill's actions to determine if they contained new or significant material, or new insight. If they offered opinion that differed from the previous 'experts', then that would be new and/or significant. But it would seem the AAIB was only looking for supporting opinion, and would only consider adverse opinion if it referred to new video. Put another way, whatever the trial experts said (who were held by law to a higher standard), this would never override the AAIB. This general concept was upheld by the High Court - the AAIB could never be wrong by virtue of its position. Unsurprisingly, the investigation was not reopened. It might be asked, then, why the Supplement was issued. Certainly, the content provoked some barbed comment by military pilots on aviation forums, including:

'The AAIB supplementary report reads rather like a publication of the Flat Earth Society'.

'The AAIB are excellent at engineering and technical analysis, but

incredibly poor at understanding the fleshy bit holding the stick. Good grief, the supplement reads as if written by a GCSE student who skimmed through a human factors book while waiting for the bus'.

At first I thought this harsh. Hitherto, my experience of the AAIB was nothing but positive. But as it admitted, it was suffering from a lack of resources, and at the time had just experienced a mass exodus of Inspectors. My mind was changed when I began to appreciate just how many errors and, especially, omissions there were across the entire report - most of which served to assist the prosecution.

By issuing the Supplement, the AAIB made its position clear. Hill was guilty. It didn't matter that others had committed violations and given him an unairworthy aircraft. It didn't matter how many experts said he suffered from Cognitive Impairment, or that the jury had believed this (in fact, was directed to), and the prosecution accepted it.

Appendices

The report contains 15 appendices, all written by other parties. For the most part the AAIB simply accepted all 15 without comment. For current purposes the two most important are: Appendix C - Permit to Fly, and Appendix L - Airworthiness Approval Note. As I said, they are predicated, incorrectly, on the RAF being the Aircraft Design Authority. The most obvious omission is a lack of discussion of this, meaning it was omitted that this was directly related to the lead anomaly. Without establishing that, an investigation is incomplete.

Was this a lack of understanding, or deliberate? At first I thought the former, but when asked later by the Coroner, the AAIB misled her. In short, while the AAIB correctly said the Approval Note and Permit were not adhered to (a criticism of the operator and maintenance organisation), it omitted they weren't valid in the first place (serving to protect the CAA). At first glance this seems a little strange, as elsewhere it left the CAA without a name. This emphasises that the dynamics of the investigation changed significantly at one or more points, the AAIB transitioning from being neutral to, effectively, part of the prosecution.

Assessment

It is only logical that the three stages of airworthiness - attaining, maintaining and continuing - are addressed in sequence during an investigation, as each is a prerequisite for the next. But the AAIB's report completely omits the section on maintaining airworthiness. There is simply no discussion, yet without this there can be no stable, known baseline for assessing serviceability before flight. Even so, the AAAIB confirmed a number of unserviceabilities.

The apparent dearth of expertise meant there was no fast jet, display, or aerobatic experience available in the AAIB. Importantly, the cockpit video, owned by Hill, was not shown to him during the investigation. It was only when disclosed as part of the criminal process that it was shown to reveal many aspects which had been missed, not addressed, or misrepresented. This was a matter of common ground between prosecution and defence at the trial, rendering the AAIB report deeply deficient. (Noting that the AAIB were not represented in court so had no opportunity to comment).

Nor does the report reflect the Human Factors issues identified by the defence, which again were not disputed. Also, the accident timeline is vague and imprecise, failing to identify the point at which Hill's errors began. When allowed to view the evidence, other pilots identified it immediately; and at trial it was (again) common ground that no errors occurred before this point.

The AAIB relied upon a report written by an RAF medical officer, who appeared as the prosecution's expert medical witness - but refused to release the source data. Inadvertently, this strategy worked against the prosecution. Had it been disclosed and debated between parties prior to the trial, the prosecution would have been spared the embarrassment of it being sliced and diced by defence expert witnesses.

On a more positive note, perhaps the strongest aspect of the report is it offers comparison with similar accidents, highlighting that many of its most important recommendations had been made before, but ignored by the CAA.

It also references the death of Red Arrows pilot Jon Egging at Bournemouth in 2011, where Cognitive Impairment was deemed a root cause. Yet while accepting MoD's assessment, it spends an extraordinary time trying to disprove essentially the same arguments on Shoreham. Suffice to say, MoD did not revisit the Egging case (as it was required to do if it believed the AAIB argument plausible).

AAIB reports must be seen to be as accurate as humanly possible, because there is no independent mechanism for challenging their accuracy, save requesting a review by the Chief Inspector - who is judging his own case. There is no obligation on the AAIB to correct its errors. It is deemed correct by virtue of its position, even when proven wrong. The AAIB claim this is justified by the *Rogers v Hoyle* case (discussed later), whereby the AAIB's (undoubted) experience and (alleged) independence in assessing *competing evidence* was deemed of paramount importance.

The problem here is - after the criminal trial it was the AAIB who introduced competing evidence that was contrary to what had been accepted by both defence and prosecution. An independent assessment was required of what, after all, could only be opinion, because on its own admission it had no expertise on Cognitive Impairment. But as the final arbiter it could disregard evidence which did not fit the official CPS/AAIB/MoD line, the 2019 Supplement suffering from confirmation bias and, in effect, re-running the prosecution with a predetermined verdict.

Root causes

I have mentioned these, but deliberately not gone into Root Cause Analysis. (A collective term that describes a wide range of approaches, tools and techniques used to identify causes of non-conformity). This, because the concept cannot be applied equally to every accident. More often than not a hybrid approach is needed.

The main problem is proximity - how far does one regress to identify an event that, if it didn't happen, would have prevented the accident? A rather extreme and crude example: if Andrew Hill's parents hadn't..., then he wouldn't... Such analysis soon gets bogged down, as no two people will agree the criteria. A huge amount of common sense and (mainly engineering and airmanship) judgment is required - both of which are notable by their absence in this investigation. However, to its credit the AAIB did identify lack of airworthiness and serviceability, which were undoubtedly proximate.

Prevention is a complex matter of implementing regulations, learning from experience, and implementation again. This is called 'continual review and assessment', and it is mandated in airworthiness regulations. But like most such mandates it is rendered optional by not being resourced, both in financial and manpower terms. Perhaps above all else, one has to have the right kind of people in charge of this, and providing oversight.

Shoreham, in a nutshell.

Who was the Hunter Aircraft Design Authority?

The role of a Design Authority or Design Custodian

A contractor must be appointed as Design Authority or Custodian, to be responsible for the design and certification of the materiel. Once the equipment is in service, his primary task is to Maintain the Build Standard, and with it the Safety Case.

By reference to MoD procedures...

By default, the appointment supposes the contractor is original designer, and has maintained appropriate resources to support the work. MoD policy is to require a guarantee of 15 years support from first delivery, with extensions negotiated thereafter. This will be less only if the intended life of the equipment is less. The ability of a given contractor to sustain the obligation must be continuously monitored. It is over 30 years since this was resourced.

If this contractor no longer exists, then another with similar resources and skills is appointed. If the original designer exists, but has no wish to continue as Design Authority, then a Custodian must be appointed. The essential difference is the Authority holds the Master Drawing Set, the Custodian a set of Secondary Masters. If there is a Custodian, the original designer must agree to remain under directed sub-contract to provide (e.g.) technical bulletins, so that the Drawing Set and Safety Case may be updated. If he is unwilling or unable to do this, then arrangements must be made to transfer the Master drawings - for example, buying-out the design. Thus, ownership of Intellectual Property Rights is an important consideration, and is *always* stated in the contract.

While the CAA's procedures do not use the same terms (which is actually a major problem given it mandates use of MoD procedures and regulations for legacy aircraft), it only requires the above to be satisfied for 'complex' designs; whereas MoD mandates it for all designs. (The fundamental issue being it facilitates systems integration, and the functional safety of the system in which the aircraft operates).

Managing these scenarios is familiar and routine to anyone versed in maintaining airworthiness; but alien to those who have 'only' done attaining or continuing. In MoD, the procedures at the time of G-BXFI's transfer to the civil register were set out in a mandated Defence Standard; and the role of the Technical Agency, the named individual responsible for Maintaining the

Build Standard and Safety Case. He assessed and appointed Design Authorities/Custodians, having the power to take away the appointment if the work was not carried out satisfactorily. For this reason, and the fact he could delegate Financial Approval to a senior company engineer to commit MoD funding to safety-related tasks without prior approval, this is the only time MoD must name someone in a contract.

However, in 1993 the RAF decided it was no longer necessary to maintain airworthiness or have valid Safety Cases (hence, the Nimrod Review, after XV230 crashed as a result of this work not being done), and stopped updating the Defence Standard. It has since been cancelled without replacement, which is all you need to know about why airworthiness is so poorly managed in MoD.

The crucial issue here is this. When G-BXFI left service in 1994 the CAA assumed the airworthiness regulatory role. *But who actually did the work expected of the Design Authorities and MoD?*

G-BXFI

The G-BXFI Airworthiness Approval Note, issued on 14 September 2008, states:

'The Design Authority now rests with the RAF'.

Note : Not MoD - there is a huge difference.

This would require, for example, the RAF to have arrangements in place to maintain technical data, and resolve technical and design issues. Also, crucially, Safety Cases/Reports. And, because G-BXFI underwent an avionics and instrument upgrade after it was sold by MoD, the RAF would have to acquire and retain (or engage) expertise on equipment they do not use. An unlikely scenario, given they don't on equipment they do have.[13]

A company can be accredited as a design organisation, but Design Authority is a higher appointment. One attains accreditation in the hope of being awarded contracts. At this point, being considered good enough to be a Design Authority is a distant aspiration. In recent years MoD has sought to combine these terms, but in the process over-simplified it to the point of creating a safety hazard. Weald Aviation having 'design approval' for G-BXFI did not in any way imply they could be, or were, the Design Authority. As I said, there are 17 core components of Maintaining the Build Standard. Having 'design approval' facilitates at most four of them. It was the CAA's job to ensure this

---

13 The aircraft was newly fitted with 2 x VHF radios, an IFF Transponder, GPS, and Height Encoding Altimeter.

work could be sustained. But, a maintenance organisation, with design approval, was allowed to make decisions on G-BXFI's airworthiness without (presumably) realising that the aircraft type was not airworthy. The AAIB omitted (perhaps because it was so obvious) that airworthiness facilitates serviceability, meaning Weald's decision to declare G-BXFI serviceable could have no audit trail.

Once again, I deliberately use MoD's terminology because of the Approval Note's premise. Yes, MoD establishments may attain design approvals (although very few post-1994, with the privatisation of most that had them), but they can only be appointed Design Authority if they have proven they can maintain the Build Standard. In MoD this can only apply to minor modifications (e.g. taking under 50 man-hours to embody), and even then must be subject to Aircraft Design Authority oversight (as they must be 'Design Incorporated' into the Drawing Set).

If MoD or the RAF were the Design Authority, the Hunter project team would be one of the largest in MoD. But regulations and procedures simply do not cater for the concept. It is therefore highly unlikely the CAA sought the RAF's opinion on its assertion, because they would immediately be told *No we're not, and never have been.*

To confirm this, I submitted a Freedom of Information request on 13 September 2019, asking if any part of MoD was Hunter Design Authority when the Approval Note was issued. Initially it refused to reply, saying many teams would have to be consulted and many archives searched, as the Hunter left service in 1994. It claimed this would take 37 hours and cost £925, which exceeds the £600 (24 hour) limit. This of course was a lie. If it didn't know, how could it say it would take 37 hours? Upon appeal, on 5 November 2019 it confirmed no part of MoD was Hunter T.7 Design Authority in 2008.[14] Why the initial refusal? The request made it aware of the CAA's claim, forcing an assessment of the implications and possible liability. Often, MoD will (correctly) seek guidance as to where the information might reside. If it really doesn't know, the correct thing to do is issue a holding reply. Flat refusal reveals much. The eventual answer probably came as a relief - *Thank goodness we're not at fault*. Ah, but did you then engage with the CAA and legal authorities to report this vital evidence?

For MoD Hunters, British Aerospace were contracted by MoD until the Out-of-Service date. (In 1999 they became BAe Systems). For the Hunter T.7 this

---

14 MoD letter FOI2019/11951, 5 November 2019.

was 1994, coinciding with the demise of the Blackburn Buccaneer on 31 March 1994, for which it acted as a trainer. As a natural consequence, the airworthiness audit trail for the T.7 ceased on that date; and needed to be resurrected when the aircraft were sold to be operated privately.

The G-BXFI Approval Note demonstrates the CAA at least thought of the subject. But it did not verify what was only an assumption, and presumably no-one involved had ever worked in MoD. The result was a huge gap in the audit trail, which just got worse as the error persisted. This has not been explained, nor the consequences examined. And the exit date of 1994 is significant, because for the previous three years the RAF had been implementing its policy to run down airworthiness management, cutting direct funding by ~28% each year. As a matter of RAF policy, the audit trail was virtually non-existent after 1991.

Airframe life

The key parameter is the Fatigue Index. Every aircraft suffers fatigue damage caused by fluctuating loads applied to the airframe. To prevent catastrophic structural failure, each type of aircraft and some of its major components are given a safe fatigue life, at which they must be retired from service or modified (re-lifed) to permit further flying.

Fatigue life is measured in units of Fatigue Index, which is a non-dimensional number. In order to initially calculate this, the designer needs to know how the aircraft is going to be used. For military aircraft this is set out in the Statement of Operating Intent and Usage (SOIU), forming part of the Aircraft Document Set. The Safety Case <u>must</u> reflect the SOIU and Build Standard. If that Use or Intent changes at any point, then it must be updated. It follows there must be an appointed Aircraft Design Authority who is contracted to Maintain the Build Standard. There wasn't.

G-BXFI's Permit to Fly requires, at Section 8:

> 'Fatigue is to be accounted for in accordance with section 4 of Airworthiness Approval Note 26172 <u>after each days flight</u>'.

The Approval Note quotes the Aircraft Servicing Manual:

> 'A Mk14 Fatigue Meter has been fitted...and the operational life has been accounted for in accordance with AP101B-1302-1, Section 2, Chapter 3'.

...and states MoD Form 725 shall be used for this purpose.

The manual sets out the procedures in detail:

> 'Fatigue Meter readings are recorded to MoD Forms 725 (Hunter), which

are sent to HQ Strike Command (RAF) [who no longer existed when the Approval Note was issued] *on a monthly basis, where consumed Fatigue Index is calculated. The replacement of unserviceable fatigue meters is a high priority task. Flying with an unserviceable fatigue meter, or taking an incorrect reading, carries a penalty in terms of fatigue. Careless or incomplete recordings could result in the premature retirement of an aircraft because of doubt over its true fatigue life'.*

When no Fatigue Meter readings are available, the fatigue life is to be calculated by using 1.5 times the aircraft's historical average per sortie. (One 'penalty'). (This varied between operators).

Who would Weald Aviation send its MF725s to (if indeed raised at all)?

Figure 3 - Mk14 Fatigue Meter

The Approval Note lists the Fatigue Index and limitations for key components. The Centre Fuselage is limited to 100FI by the Frame 25 tie bars (or tie rod, a structural strengthening component capable of carrying tensile loads only), and hence governs the total life of the aircraft. There is no recovery scheme. The Fatigue Meter is mounted on the main spar, running through the wings, and accessible via the lower fuel vent access door.

To put it bluntly, meticulous monitoring, recording and management of airframe fatigue is how you avoid the aircraft falling apart in flight.

The AAIB reported that Weald Aviation only recorded the meter readings once a year. Between these, fatigue monitoring relied on the pilot reporting any high loads seen on the g-meter (accelerometer) in the cockpit. The g-meter in G-BXFI was unserviceable. But the AAIB did not mention:

1. The requirement to apply the *1.5 times average* method (or an alternative); and if, in the circumstances, this was now a universal requirement, regardless of g-meter serviceability.

2. The anomaly, whereby the Fatigue Index was unverifiable, is an example of an 'other factor' which, while (apparently) unrelated to the proximate cause of the accident, nevertheless had to be addressed because it was directly related to the lead anomaly. The AAIB did not record what action was taken, or why the CAA permitted this. (I discuss the g-meter in the next chapter).

Airworthiness Approval Note and Permit to Fly

The G-BXFI Approval Note was not a verified statement, it was an illogical and incorrect assumption, meaning there was no valid basis for the Permit to Fly. I conclude, therefore, that the CAA must accept a major part of the blame. Had it acted properly the problem-fault sequence would have been broken. That does not exonerate the pilot, but demolishes the Crown's claim that he alone was responsible.

The CAA confirmed to the owner/operator/maintainers/pilot - and by extension the display organisers and public - that all the above was in place and valid. They pinned everything on the historical safety of the Hunter, which would require, at a minimum, a Safety Case that was valid on 31 March 1994; and maintained thereafter. Even if MoD could produce it (and the likelihood of that lies between infinitesimally small and zero), *someone* had to be responsible for subsequent versions. The CAA say it was the RAF. MoD confirm is wasn't. Whose fault is that? Not anyone at Canfield Hunter or Weald Aviation.

But... Surely the penny dropped when Weald first tried to invoke the conditions of the Approval Note, only to be told by the RAF *We don't know what you're talking about*. And I note the same questions must be asked of Hawker Hunter Aviation, who operate Hunters on the military register. And of their regulator, the Military Aviation Authority.

The CAA's 'approval process' does not address sustainment, or if contractual cover exists to maintain the various 'civilian' Hunter Build Standards; which are all different to when MoD last flew the aircraft. A valid Hunter Aircraft Design Authority Safety Case, and Configuration Control upon which it is dependant, will now be convoluted. *Who controls this, and pays for it?*

The AAIB report made no comment on any of this. And the implication is that MoD, who contributed so much to the report, didn't actually read it; or if it did, didn't understand the ramifications. (Both are equally likely). It follows that the audit trail for transfer to the civil register was incomplete.

Bottom line. No valid Permit to Fly or Airworthiness Approval Note, no fly. Non-negotiable.

What part did Andrew Hill play is this?

None. In this sense he was 'only' the pilot, with no delegated authority. The owner would perhaps listen to him, along with the Weald Aviation Chief Engineer, on matters affecting serviceability. He would be asked if he was prepared to fly with certain 'acceptable' faults. But did they appreciate what was involved in maintaining airworthiness, and what was <u>not</u> being done? I doubt it very much. The Chief Engineer did not appear in court, and his witness statement has not been released. There is very little in his subordinates' history that would lead *them* to understand. That is not a criticism, far from it. But it is of the CAA system that allows them to think they're all 'doing airworthiness', when actually they're only involved in the final act before the aircraft flies.

Serviceability

G-BXFI was accepted onto the civil register in 1997 on the basis that maintenance activity would follow the aircraft's military programme, and be recorded on documents based on military documentation; which is predicated on airworthiness having been maintained.

In 2011 the aircraft changed ownership and the nominated maintenance organisation elected to change the programme to a bespoke one based around an annual 'minor check', and a 'major check' every two years, each incorporating tasks from the MoD programme. When the aircraft was purchased by Canfield Hunter in July 2012, Weald Aviation completed an inspection of the maintenance records. Due to a lack of clarity regarding the aircraft's maintenance status, and after discussion with the CAA, they decided to transfer the aircraft back onto a military-based programme.

In order to ensure the aircraft met regulatory requirements it underwent a 'Minor Star' inspection, completed in December 2012. The subsequent application recommending the issue of a Certificate of Validity for its Permit to Fly was accepted by the CAA. During this period Weald's approvals were subject to CAA audit, the report of which the CAA would not provide to the AAIB. *Why?* At this point, the AAIB should have escalated to the Department for Transport, pointing out the Department was now impeding its own investigation.

On 3 January 2013 the CAA conducted an Aircraft Continuing Airworthiness Monitoring audit of the aircraft. A specific item on the checklist referred to compliance with Mandatory Permit Directive (MPD) 2001-001, imposing a calendar life on the engine, with an option to extend it using an Alternative Means of Compliance (AMOC) approved by the CAA; but there was no reference to an AMOC in the CAA report. In November 2013 Weald issued a new Certificate of Validity for G-BXFI's Permit to Fly, valid from 28 November 2013 until 4 December 2014. Between November 2013 and the end of March 2014 the aircraft underwent a 'Primary' inspection. Between December 2014 and March 2015 it underwent another period of scheduled maintenance which included a 'Primary Star' inspection.

The CAA conducted an audit of Weald's British Civil Airworthiness Requirement (BCAR) A8-20 approval in November 2014, including a review of G-BXFI's Certificate of Validity. There were no findings. In March 2015

Weald issued another Certificate of Validity, valid to 10 March 2016.

Master Altimeter

The aircraft was subject to a post-maintenance 'shake-down' flight on 20 March 2015, after which the pilot reported the aircraft had a number of faults, including a problem with the Mk30B right altimeter. However, there were no corresponding entries in the aircraft's technical log.

The instrument is a combined 'digital' (numeric) and analog (pointer) display. A Maintenance Work Order (MWO) stated *'Master altimeter servo encoder 30B not working in flight'*, and indicated it had been replaced on 23 March 2015. Also, that it would not power-up during subsequent maintenance. Weald determined the fault was linked to an inconsistent electrical power supply, due to the compass unit drawing excessive current. The AAIB did not say what action had been taken regarding the compass unit and power supply. The MWO stated:

'Unserviceable altimeter #993 replaced with serviceable altimeter #874. Pitot static checks carried out from pitot probe to unit (satisfactory)'.

The MWO indicated that the pitot-static system had been leak-tested after replacement of the altimeter. Weald informed the AAIB that the replacement altimeter was taken from another Hunter, G-BZSE, which was undergoing refurbishment. They were unable to confirm when G-BZSE had last flown, but its most recent Certificate of Validity expired in 2011. The AAIB determined that the altimeter fitted to G-BXFI at the time of the accident was in fact Serial Number 786, not 874 as the maintenance records indicated. Weald informed the AAIB that the altimeter taken from G-BZSE was the only spare available to them, claiming the serial number had been transcribed in error.

No functional test of the altimeter system, to confirm electrical synchronisation between the two instruments, was carried out after replacement. (Whereby one instrument is slaved to the other via a Desynn transmitter, the test including the transmitter itself). There were no pilot reports following this work, Weald saying they had no other means of knowing if there was problem with the altimeters. There were no further entries in the technical records.

It was also noted that a number of other instruments were unserviceable, including the *g*-meter and Master Airspeed Indicator. Also, the manual aileron trim gauge, which had been entered in the Technical Log as an

'Acceptable Defect'. Of most concern, a fuel pump diaphragm was rotted, having not been inspected for many years.

All rather important, when the accusation was the aircraft was too low and too slow, and there had been two unexplained power reductions. Pilots I have spoken to deemed these deficiencies, individually and collectively, unacceptable. Perhaps above all else, the inability to ascertain when G-BZSE last flew is the biggest red flag. To not know when an aircraft last flew is so fundamental, one would expect the regulator to jump.

Ejection seat issues

The AAIB engaged Survival Equipment Services (Ltd) of Tetbury to attend the scene, make the seats safe, and prepare a report, the scope being:

- To determine if the pilot of aircraft G-BXFI had made any attempt to egress from the aircraft via the escape system.
- To ascertain if the ejection seat and its associated systems had functioned and, if so, by means of what initiation.

SES were not the maintenance organisation for G-BXFI's seats. They attended the following day, and their report was comprehensive and excellent. The AAIB used it as the basis for their much abbreviated Appendix B ('Ejection Seats'), but did not credit SES.

G-BXFI was equipped with two Martin-Baker Mk4HA ejection seats. (The single-seat variants used Mk2 seats). The design is capable of safe ejection at ground level if the aircraft's flight path is parallel to the ground and it has a forward speed of at least 90 knots. While Hill did not try to eject, the impact disrupted the fuselage under the cockpit to the extent it initiated the ejection sequence. Only a partial ejection took place, as the damage prevented correct pressurisation of the ejection gun and firing of secondary cartridges. There was insufficient thrust to allow the seat to clear the aircraft in the normal manner. (The primary difference between the Mk4 seat and most newer models is the former is not rocket-assisted). It was mooted in the 1980's that the Hunter be upgraded to the Mk10 (Hawk, Tornado, etc.) but this was rejected as the Out-of-Service date at the time was imminent.

Nevertheless, the initial movement was enough to disengage the Scissor and Drogue shackles, deploy the drogue parachutes, and release Hill from the seat. Both he and the seat were thrown clear; he sideways, his trajectory partially determined by the drogues being snagged in trees. The fuselage then ran over the seat. That this aspect of the design worked as intended undoubtedly saved him. As he has no recall, he cannot say what he was thinking. But if he did consider ejecting, doing so in the last quarter of the loop would result in almost certain death, as it would be outwith the seat operating parameters.

Ejection seat servicing

No maintenance records had been provided to Weald when contracted to maintain G-BXFI. This meant it was not possible to determine when the ejection seats had been installed in G-BXFI, only that a private individual serviced them in a 'servicing bay' he had built in his garage. This arrangement had no formal authorisation from the CAA; but nor was there any objection. While the AAIB noted the maintainer was a former RAF armourer, it did not draw linkages with the ongoing Cunningham case; where it had been demonstrated, and admitted by MoD, that its armourers were no longer trained on ejection seats. Thus, the maintainer's past training should have been examined and reported on. So too that of his superiors who signed-off the work.

The AAIB did not address the question of who was now responsible for maintaining the seat Build Standard. Yet this had been a critical factor in the Cunningham case, and it is unlikely the AAIB remained ignorant of what was going there, if only out of professional interest. (Bearing in mind their new Chief Inspector would, or should, have been intimately familiar with the case, as he had until recently been an officer in the Military Aviation Authority). At what point must the AAIB and/or MoD ask to be involved if they identify common factors? And if neither see this as part of their role, whose is it and to whom do they report their concerns?

Cartridges

The AAIB noted that the installed life of the cartridges was two years, and the shelf life six. The latter was *'included as a limitation in the Approval Note, which formed the basis for its certification'*. Yet Weald adopted a six-year installation life. This extension had *'not been documented in accordance with the maintenance organisation's procedures, nor had it been approved by the CAA'*.

At the time of the accident the two-year installed life had been exceeded by more than 4.5 years, and the six-year total life by more than a year. The CAA did not have a documented procedure for approving such extensions, but stated that applications would be considered on a case-by-case basis, and would only be granted for a short period *'upon proof that new cartridges were on order'*. Is it wise to grant an extension of a lifed item in a Safety Critical Escape System on this basis? What if the delivery forecast was years in the future, or the supplier could not provide one? The CAA required the aircraft to be maintained in accordance with MoD's rules. *They* allow a 10% life extension; but only under exceptional (operational) circumstances can this be applied to a Safety Critical Escape System, where no failure can be tolerated. Moreover, new cartridges were available, which had not been fitted.

Admirably, the AAIB went on:

> *'CAP632 requires the pilot escape systems of swept-wing jet aircraft, such as the Hawker Hunter, to be "fully serviceable". The use of time-expired ejection seat cartridges meant that the ejection seats fitted to G-BXFI did not meet this requirement. The practice was not confined to G-BXFI or its maintenance organisation'.*

That is, this was a systemic failing and not just confined to Hunters, and the responsibility of the regulator, the CAA. In summary, the continuing airworthiness requirements could not be met. Given the lack of support, the operator was faced with grounding the aircraft or making the decision to (e.g.) extend the life of the cartridges without the approval to do so. Damned if you do, out of business if you don't.

Status of 'legacy' Martin-Baker ejection seats

Regarding the *'fully serviceable'* mandate, production of Mk4 seats ceased in the early-1970's, and Martin-Baker have never supplied seats or components directly to civilian operators of ex-military aircraft, only to approved third parties. In February 2015, six months <u>before</u> Shoreham, the company withdrew support altogether for seats fitted to aircraft that no longer operated in their military role, including Hunters, recommending they be made inert. The AAIB correctly noted:

> *'This is contrary to the CAA requirement for ejection seats in swept-wing aircraft to be operated in a fully operational and armed condition'.*

Martin-Baker's reason was that the design data had become obsolete, and what had been perfectly good documentation was now inadequate as the company could no longer guarantee the expertise to support the older design. In taking this decision, they demonstrated an appreciation of the direct link between the design pack and training. Lacking one, the other is useless. This decision was undoubtedly linked to the Cunningham case. If a major customer (the RAF) was completely ignoring the company's recommendations, and the HSE criticising the company for not understanding how their own seats worked (!), the decision was easy. What was the point in continuing? The CAA's view was that if it were to adopt this policy, it would effectively ground the great majority of ex-military jets, with serious consequences for the display community. Safety was apparently irrelevant. An impasse developed, the CAA electing to gamble everything would be okay.

The AAIB stated Martin-Baker had not informed the CAA of this, but omitted that the CAA (as discussed before) did not concern itself with maintaining the Build Standard (which is what we're talking about), and had permitted an unapproved contractor to maintain the seats. In such circumstances, one can expect no less than the manufacturer walking away, as they no longer exert control. I see parallels with the Cunningham case, where Martin-Baker had kept MoD fully informed of all seat matters, but for over 20 years been completely ignored. For example, MoD had declined to upgrade the Mk10B (Hawk) seats to the latest safe standard in 1984; which would have saved Sean.

The AAIB did not note the seat Drawing Pack had been transferred to SES (Ltd), whose responsibility it now was to deal with the CAA. This is a good example of what I discussed earlier. SES are excellent at maintaining legacy ejection seats. They are also able to design minor modifications (design approval). But that is not the same as being a Design Authority, which carries numerous other responsibilities, such as here the seemingly mundane task of closing the loop by informing the CAA.

A philosophical question

The above conflict is unresolved, and deserves discussion…

If an ejection seat is to be made inert there are two main considerations:

First, do you wish to maintain the capability for a manual bail-out via the manual separation mechanism of the ejection seat, or install a static seat and use a conventional parachute? Either way, is there an adequate egress route? Can the canopy be opened or jettisoned to permit the bail-out? (Some aircraft designs require the seat to punch through the canopy). Is there sufficient space to get out of the cockpit, especially at high speed? (Which might limit the physical size of aircrew). Often, one must invert the aircraft above a certain height before bailing out, which requires the aircraft to be under a degree of control. If the cockpit access has not been designed for this, then such an option may not be feasible. And will the act of abandoning the aircraft ensure you will not hit the superstructure? Another issue is that deactivated seats have no emergency oxygen supply, limiting the altitude at which one can survive a bail-out. Through extensive testing this has been determined to be 10,000 feet.

Second, if considering a single-engine aircraft (such as Hunter), is the glide threshold speed low enough to permit an off-runway forced landing following an engine failure? For some aircraft such as the Jet Provost the answer may be yes. For high speed swept-wing aircraft such as Hunter the answer will probably be no. So, if the glide speed is too high, and a safe egress route for a manual bail-out does not exist, then flying with an inhibited ejection seat would, in my opinion, be foolhardy. In these circumstances why wear a parachute? Again, it might be thought that taking such risks for recreational flying is not justifiable.

To remove an ejection seat from the design of any aircraft would be a major and very expensive undertaking, and require significant re-assessment of the Safety Case. Who would pay for this? Is there a 'Hunter Owner's Club' who share costs? Or are they borne by the major user and the rest get a freebie? Or by the first to raise the issue and require a solution? This dilemma is common in MoD. For example, there were over a dozen Lynx users. As MoD (Fleet Air Arm, Royal Marines and Army Air Corps) was by far the largest, the rest looked to it to fund most of the work, but there was no formal agreement. They'd keep an eye on what MoD was doing, and attend the annual Lynx Users Conference. Only occasionally would a minority user require something MoD didn't want, or couldn't afford, and go it alone.

A current Hunter operator has three options:

1. Fly with the seat live, using non-Martin-Baker approved components and servicing procedures.
2. Fly with the Martin-Baker seat, but disabled. But it is now in a configuration which is uncontrolled, the manuals are incorrect, and unknown hazards have been introduced. How does one teach a student to fly an aircraft where the manual says 'pull this handle', when nothing will happen if you do? The distraction is a classic Human Factors hazard.
3. Remove the seat and try to fit something else. But what, and by whom?

G-BXFI flew with (1), as required. (2) is the current Martin-Baker position and not permitted by the CAA, and (3) is probably prohibitively expensive. The overarching question is the same - *Who would be the Design Authority?*

Yet, for example, in the Jet Provost (1) and (2) were permitted. But that means training and aircrew/aircraft publications must be clear about the resulting changes in form, fit, function and use. I note the incident involving Jet Provost Mk5 G-VIVM at North Weald Airport in 16 June 2021. The AAIB report does not mention if the above mandatory actions were taken when it was converted from live to inert seats.[15]

My view is ex-military pilots would prefer (1), because it is how they were taught to fly. But they form a minority of those flying and displaying these aircraft. On 17 September 2004 Folland Gnat T.1 G-BVPP lost power and landed wheels-up in a ploughed field near North Weald. The seats were live, but despite the Flight Reference Cards requiring an ejection if a safe landing could not be made onto a suitable airfield, the pilots chose to stay with the aircraft, risking their lives, and were *fortunate to avoid a much more serious outcome*. As an important aside, the AAIB's report on this incident contains an excellent summary of the difficulty in maintaining the Build Standard of legacy aircraft. That was 20 years ago, and matters have only deteriorated.[16]

Linkages

For quite separate reasons, it is important to note the AAIB reported:

'The [G-BXFI] scissor shackle was released, indicating that the Barostatic Time Release Unit had operated'.

Later, in the Annex, I discuss in more detail the links to the 2011 death of Sean Cunningham, and the HSE's prosecution of Martin-Baker. The HSE alleged that the company had not provided sufficient information to allow the RAF to service the seat properly, and ensure the shackles released during an ejection (thus deploying the main parachute). They claimed to the Judge, Dame Justice Carr, that the Mk4 seat did not operate in the way described by Martin-Baker and SES (Ltd), and repeated by the AAIB. Specifically, it stated that only the Mk10B seat (Hawk) had a scissor shackle release mechanism. The company were fined £1.1M.

The key issue is that, at the same time the Crown Prosecution Service were considering charges against Hill, the HSE were (a) preparing their case against Martin-Baker, and (b) contributing to the Shoreham report. In that report the AAIB cited the MoD technical publications containing the information MoD denied it had, and the HSE claimed Martin-Baker had not provided. In other words, both the HSE and MoD knowingly lied.[17]

---

15 https://assets.publishing.service.gov.uk/media/6256d465e90e0729f39fafb1/P84_Jet_Provost_Mk_5_G-VIVM_05-22.pdf
16 https://assets.publishing.service.gov.uk/media/5422fe82e5274a131400094f/Folland_Gnat_T_Mk_1__G-BVPP_8-05.pdf
17 'Red 5' (David Hill, 2019).

It is difficult to separate MoD's decision to (a) act jointly with the HSE in the prosecution of Martin-Baker, and (b) act jointly with the AAIB against Andrew Hill. In both cases it succeeded in defeating the ends of justice. Legal authorities knew this. Behavioural trends emerge.

The *g*-meter

The *g*-meter, or accelerometer, gives a visual indication of acceleration forces imposed on the aircraft's structure during flight, in the direction of the Z axis (i.e. upwards and downwards along the line of flight), by means of three concentrically-mounted pointers. One indicates instantaneous g, the others the maximum positive and negative *g*-readings. It can be reset by means of a knob on the instrument case. (Figures 4 & 5).

Figure 4 - G-BXFI's starboard instrument panel, with relocated *g*-meter (top). The readings, +8.25*g*, -4.5*g* and +2.1*g*, are outwith the limits set out in the Aircraft Maintenance Manual (+7*g*, -3.75*g*, 1*g* on the ground).

Figure 5 - Mk2 Accelerometer

I mentioned earlier that G-BXFI's *g*-meter was unserviceable. The AAIB:

'Examination indicated that the internal mechanism was loose, and it was therefore not possible to test the unit. Disassembly revealed that the control cord which centres the weight was broken and it was free to move unrestrained on the guide shafts. The lower pulley, around which the cord is normally routed, was loose, as was the grub screw which holds it in place. It is unlikely the grub screw and lower pulley were loose because of the impact, but the loose pulley may have altered the tension in the cord and the degree to which the weight could move. This could explain the unserviceability of the g-meter prior to the accident'.

What really happened to cause the unserviceability is central to the entire issue of maintaining airworthiness...

When MoD's Hunters were sold they required an avionic upgrade, including new VHF radios. The Air Traffic Control frequency band had expanded, and it is likely the RAF either (a) had not modified aircraft they knew were leaving service, or (b) retained what were new and expensive radios, which had military features not needed by civilian users. (Either is likely - having bought the new equipment, the RN cancelled their scheduled upgrades to the Hunter GA.11, T.8C and T.8M). Publications were not updated, pilots told to overlook the original Aircrew Manual and Flight Reference Cards (thus breaching the terms of the Permit to Fly) and work it out for themselves. Again, this is a Human Factors hazard, a distraction requiring extended thinking time when intuitive action gained through training, based on correct manuals, is assumed.

The Federal Aviation Administration describes the Hunter T.7 cockpit layout as *'cluttered and unergonomic'*, which is fair comment. In all Hunters the *g*-meter was located in the top left-hand corner of the centre instrument panel (directly in front of the left hand control column). From the Aircraft Maintenance Manual:

> *'This instrument is <u>not shock-absorber mounted</u> as this would have a damping effect on the operating mechanism'.*[18]

Elsewhere, an instruction is given that an indicating accelerometer shall be *'mounted on a rigid part of the aircraft structure'.*[19]

When put to prosecution witness Chris Heames, a pilot in the RAF for 40 years and Canfield Hunter Chief Pilot, that it was a *'critical instrument you would expect to find immediately forward of the pilot's head for the most easy vision'*, he agreed.

But when another prosecution witness, former RN pilot Jonathon Whaley, was asked:

> *'Do you have any concern about the g-meter not being operable?'*
>
> *'No, I don't'.*

He had been partly responsible for the new layout, the *g*-meter moved to make room for the new VHF controllers. The CAA approved its relocation to a <u>spring-mounted</u> sub-panel on the right-hand side of the cockpit, slightly to the right of the right-hand seat occupant. (Figure 4). *'An inconvenient place'*, said Mr Heames. Crucially, the new vibration characteristic, which the instrument was not designed to cope with, meant it not only read incorrectly, but failed regularly. A device critical to recording the Fatigue Index of the airframe was rendered useless.

Why did the CAA approve this new design by Jet Heritage Ltd? This gets to the root of the problem. The modification was not done in accordance with good engineering practice or principles. Specifically, one must always assess the effect of vibration. But the matter was swept under the carpet, and not mentioned in the AAIB report. A cascade of failures had been created, perfectly illustrating the cumulative effect of unofficial and uncertified changes in aircraft configuration.

The basic process is that the instrument designer/manufacturer will state in an 'installation memorandum' how it should be mounted, whether location is

---

18 AP4347N, Volume 1, Book 2, Section 5, Chapter 2, Group 3D, paragraph 3.
19 AP1275A, Volume 1, Section 12.

important relative to other equipment (such as the minimum distance which a device may be installed from a magnetic north seeking device - the 'compass safe distance'). Hence, the note in the Aircraft Maintenance Manual. Individual aircraft manufacturers and Design Authorities then design installations for different aircraft types.

The same applies to all equipment, with avionics subject to Radio Installation Memoranda (RIMs), which can double as Interface Control Documents. But in 1991 the RAF decided, as part of their *savings at the expense of safety* policy, to stop issuing RIMs or maintaining the existing ones. Thereafter, anyone designing a modification installation could not know if they had up-to-date information to underpin the design. There's a reason why the regulations mandate the production, upkeep and use of these memoranda. But the RAF instructed staff (and hence Design Authorities) not to heed them. This had nothing to do with Weald Aviation, Canfield Hunter or their predecessors. Almost certainly the RAF did not inform the CAA of this policy - their own staff only finding out when inundated with complaints from front-line about deficient designs and equipment failures.

No competent Design Authority would have signed-off such a poor installation design, given they would be expected to underwrite the installed performance. *So, who underwrote it, and did he understand he was now legally liable?*

The AAIB reported:

> 'Video evidence showed that the g-meter fitted to the aircraft was defective during the accident flight and in September 2014. No related defects had been reported or recorded, and the maintenance organisation stated that it was not aware of any'.

And, as discussed earlier:

> 'The Airworthiness Approval Note and Permit to Fly required the fatigue state of the aircraft to be recorded after each day's flight. The maintenance organisation read and recorded the fatigue state once each year; between these readings, monitoring of high fatigue inducing events relied on the pilots reporting high loads seen on the g-meter'.

At Hill's trial in 2019, a maintainer at Weald Aviation stated this unserviceability would not be apparent to him if not reported by the aircrew. Under cross-examination by the defence, he agreed that in military service the g-meter was checked after every flight, in accordance with the servicing instructions. But when checking the accident aircraft it was subject only to a 'cursory glance'. Shown images of the *g*-meter, he confirmed it was not reading correctly (so was 'apparent').

One must assume he understood the installation issues (i.e. had read the manual). Given the new location of the instrument, and the inevitably wrong readings, would he question the point of recording them? But the matter was left there, which is unsatisfactory. The investigation should have dug deeper, asking how this design <u>defect</u> had come about, and remained; and why Weald did not, apparently, report the issue and propose a solution. The engineer was the one who had to cope with this. The people who placed him in this position - belonging to a design organisation, not a Design Authority - were never asked to explain.

My gut feeling here is that Weald Aviation appreciated all this, and I would not be surprised if the aircraft had (say, aerobatic) restrictions applied to it that have not been revealed.

I appreciate going into such detail can be counter-productive in court, as one does not want to confuse the jury. The defence's point was made - the instrument was unserviceable, the installation design unairworthy, and the Permit to Fly could not be, and wasn't, complied with.

The engine

The AAIB:

> 'The engine was not preserved during periods of inactivity as required by the aircraft's approved maintenance program. Neither the operator nor the maintenance organisation had an approved Alternative Means of Compliance (AMOC) with the Mandatory Permit Directive related to engine life (MPD 2001-001). The maintenance organisation did not have access to the previous operator's AMOC'.

Therefore the basis upon which the Airworthiness Approval Note was issued was false, once again rendering it invalid.

> 'The maintenance organisation submitted a proposal for an AMOC to MPD 2001-001 to the CAA which in turn requested this be resubmitted to include additional tasks detailed in CAP562 Leaflet 70-80. (Guidance Material for Ageing Engine Continuing Airworthiness, issued following a number of accidents and incidents involving the serious failure of high calendar time engines or their accessories). However, no further application to the CAA was made by the maintenance organisation'.

> 'Engine rpm exceedences occurring during a test flight in 2011 were not

reported or investigated. There was no formal or documented monitoring of engine performance, either during engine ground runs or in flight, which would enable engine performance deterioration to be identified'.

The manufacturer, Rolls Royce, no longer supported the Avon engine, but were able to provide the AAIB with analysis based on archived information and expert knowledge of jet engine performance in general. This related to a static engine under stable test conditions. Inevitably, it could not take into account performance losses associated with being installed in an aircraft, or dynamic performance.

So, Rolls Royce were no longer the Design Authority, but the AAIB did not offer who was; the nearest indication (to the uninitiated) again being the CAA's claim it was the RAF. This is indicative of the sheer difficulty faced by AAIB investigators when a legacy aircraft has crashed. It also goes some way to explaining the time taken to investigate, as there were so many important unknowns that were impossible to check. Unknowns equate to doubt.

The CAA-approved manual for the Avon 122 engine (AP 102C-1512 to 1517) details the requirements for engine storage or periods of non-operation:

'Up to 1 month. Apply anti-corrosion fluid to compressor. Fit engine covers and blanks. Spray engine with lanolin resin temporary rust prevention.

Up to 6 months. As up to 1 month and, in addition, ground run every 30 days and repeat application of anti-corrosion inhibiting fluid to compressor. If the engine is not to be ground run, drain engine oil, inhibit fuel system, apply anti-corrosion paper. Grease the control and inlet guide vane ram linkages'.

The aircraft records from July 2012-on revealed five separate occasions where it did not operate for a period of more than 30 days, with no evidence of engine runs completed at 30-day intervals. In that period the engine had been inactive 43% of the time, and this had been the case since it left military service in 1994. This was said to be typical of civil-registered Hunters, but was atypical of military aircraft. The main failure noted by the AAIB was:

'Information included in a previous AAIB report indicated that there had been several cases involving the type of engine fitted to this aircraft where an <u>uncommanded reduction in engine speed</u> had occurred and subsequent engineering investigation did not establish a clear cause. This investigation was unable to determine whether a reduction in engine speed recorded during the accident manoeuvre was commanded by the pilot. The investigation found that defects and exceedences of the aircraft's operational limits had not been reported to the maintenance organisation,

and mandatory requirements of its Airworthiness Approval Note had not been met'.

With this, the AAIB uncovered a root cause of what was, at first glance, a Weald Aviation failure - they did not hold a CAA-approved Alternative Means of Compliance (AMOC). But in April 2014 Weald had contacted a CAA surveyor to obtain an update on the progress of its AMOC for MPD 2001-001, which was passed to the General Aviation Department of the CAA. The AAIB was *'unable to identify'* any response from the CAA, it agreeing there was no AMOC. The CAA was not asked to explain this.

The AAIB added that a flight test had been conducted on 26 June 2011 as part of the Permit to Fly revalidation process, during which engine speed was recorded as having exceeded the limit of 8,100 ±50 rpm several times - 8,250 rpm on three occasions, 8,350 rpm once. There was no evidence of this being reported in the technical log, or of any inspections or remedial action being taken, and the flight test was signed-off by the pilot as *'airworthy and functionally serviceable to the required standards'.*

Put another way, the AAIB noted a culture of shortcuts (savings) at the expense of safety. If an ethos exists that permits one shortcut, then the regulator must consider the likelihood of wider failings.

High Pressure Fuel Pump

There were two distinct *'atypical power reductions'* during the ascent into the loop, and it could not be demonstrated who or what caused them.

The engine and airframe manufacturers' documentation required engine removal after 450 flying hours for inspection, and an overhaul after 900 flying hours. Records indicated that the engine's last workshop visit, to carry out the 450 hour regime, had been 25 years before in 1990 and, at the time of the accident, the engine had completed 846 flying hours.

The log card for the high pressure fuel pump, part of the Engine Change Unit (the engine itself plus ancillaries, designed to facilitate a fast engine change and to minimise operational failure and technical risks), showed the pump had been overhauled in 1988 and had operated for 269 hours at the time of that inspection in 1990. There was no additional information available to identify any other associated maintenance activity. Asked to examine the pump, Rolls Royce reported:

'The fuel pump governor diaphragm...showed significant signs of distress. The degradation of the rubber on both faces of the convolution, due to the effects of age, loss of flexibility and chemical interaction with fuel, have

resulted in a diaphragm that has exceeded the known predictable functional capability of the design. Its continued integrity would be severely affected by the degraded condition'.

The AAIB concluding:

'The extent of this degradation meant it was <u>not in an airworthy condition</u>. The Alternative Means of Compliance approved for a previous operator of the aircraft did not include routine inspections of the condition of engine fuel systems. This inspection regime, continued by the current maintenance organisation, did not identify the degradation of the diaphragm'.

In other words, instead of referring to <u>time</u> the technical manual being used assumed a certain <u>flying rate</u>, which (typically) would mean at least once every two years during Service use. This serious and inexplicable error was effectively hidden as the military flying rate meant the pump was overhauled regularly. But when sold into private hands this flying rate plummeted, and in interim the aircraft had not accumulated enough hours to require a fuel pump governor diaphragm check. But that passage of time the diaphragm had deteriorated to such an extent it was unairworthy.

The AAIB claimed that Rolls Royce didn't consider this to be relevant to its performance. <u>Rolls Royce said no such thing</u>. The AAIB chose to ascribe a conclusion to something Rolls Royce themselves had avoided.

Peeling back this layer revealed the invalid Airworthiness Approval Note, which said the RAF were responsible for maintaining these instructions.

Incomprehensibly, every Hunter operator the AAIB spoke to claimed not to understand the effects of fuel degradation. The AAIB was too polite. It cited the Air Publication that spelt out the requirement, and numerous violations in the three years preceding the accident, but did not comment on this apparent inability to understand plain English.

The obvious question is if, when Hill demanded power (more fuel flow), the fuel pump/engine responded correctly. Due to crash damage this cannot be known, and the AAIB report should <u>not</u> be taken as a statement that the power plant operated correctly. But that is how many chose to interpret it. I wonder if the jurors drew links in their mind between *'reduction in power'* and *'unserviceable and unairworthy fuel pump'*, and recognised doubt?

Recurrence

On 5 June 1998, Hunter F.4 G-HHUN, fitted with the same engine type, crashed at Dunsfold Airfield in Surrey, killing the pilot. The AAIB conducted a Field Investigation, noting:

> *'During the examination of the fuel and air systems, staining of the fuel pumps was noted and also minor deterioration of the diaphragm. The split in the P7 pipe and the deformation of seals in the Bleed Valve Control Unit were probably due to <u>age-related material deterioration</u>. In RAF service these components had lives in terms of flying hours which would represent extremely long periods of calendar time in current, much reduced, civilian utilisation.*

<u>Recommendation No 99-27</u>

In view of the <u>marked reduction in flying utilisation</u> of ex- RAF Hawker Hunter jet aircraft which have been acquired for civilian use and the related <u>greatly increased calendar time between scheduled overhaul</u> of the fuel and air system components on their Avon turbojet engines it is recommended that the CAA, in conjunction with Rolls Royce, consider the <u>introduction of appropriate calendar time overhaul periods for such engine systems, the serviceable condition of which can be calendar time dependent due to component material "ageing" affects'.

I note this omits a warning in the Federal Aviation Administration (FAA) Hunter Airworthiness Certification memorandum, issued to assist FAA field offices in airworthiness reviews, that the Avon 100-Series is prone to:

> *'Faulty Bleed Valve Control Unit diaphragm, causing compressor stall as the throttle opens'.*

The FAA added that the temporary obstruction effects of internal debris from degraded sealant may have caused a malfunction, and then cleared itself due to airflow purging. This might also have caused the unexplained power reduction incidents on the Avon 122 engine, where the act of ground running to diagnose the problem may have served to clear it, making it difficult to reproduce. I will refer to this FAA memorandum again, because at 181 pages it is infinitely more detailed than anything the CAA has released, and was not mentioned by the AAIB.[20]

Once again, a recurring theme is failure to maintain the Build Standard. So, why was this 1998 recommendation not accepted (or not implemented) by 2015, especially in the light of other power reduction incidents in Hunters with the Avon 100-Series engine?

Indisputably, the Shoreham report is rendered <u>even more</u> incomplete, flawed

---

20 Federal Aviation Administration memorandum 'Hawker Hunter Airworthiness Certification', 11 January 2013.

and deficient by:
1. Omitting mention of this recommendation from 1998, meaning anyone reading the report would believe 2015 the first occurrence.
2. Failing to make the same recommendation, implying a safety critical device being unserviceable and unairworthy was of no consequence.
3. Omitting that this was a serious failure of the regulatory and safety management process.

The G-HHUN report also stated, and this time the Shoreham one repeated:

'In addition to these accidents, records kept on a computerised database between 1980 and 1992 showed 22 cases involving the Avon 122 engine where engine speed had dropped and subsequent engineering investigation had not established a clear cause. In most cases the aircraft had returned safely and the subsequent RAF engineering investigations, including related engine ground runs, had failed to identify associated causes or to reproduce the symptoms'.[21]

Never mind *'most cases'*. What needs to be known is what happened to the others that did not return safely, and what action was taken following the investigations. What became of the MoD database? For example, was it transferred to the CAA to maintain and update? Unlikely, given G-BXFI's Airworthiness Approval Note stated the RAF were responsible for these activities.

There are certain things hammered into first-year apprentices; and then again at regular intervals with a bigger hammer. One of them is the reason behind inspection regimes; another is the way safety critical components must be managed. Deficiencies must be reported, and corrected, as part of maintaining the Build Standard. The process called up in the Airworthiness Approval Note was that supposedly run by the RAF. This smacks of the CAA washing its hands of the entire process.

I do not claim this unserviceable and unairworthy fuel pump caused the lack of power. What it certainly does is introduce serious doubt, and reveals a slack maintenance regime. Far worse, it was a recurrence from a previous fatal accident, and an AAIB recommendation had not been implemented.

---

21 https://assets.publishing.service.gov.uk/media/5422f5f0ed915d1374000589/dft_avsafety_pdf_502233.pdf

Hazardous substances

'The aircraft was fitted with underwing drop tanks made from phenolic asbestos. This hazard had not been identified'.

The COSHH regulations (Control of Substances Hazardous to Health) do not require an asbestos assessment, because it has its own specific regulations (Control of Asbestos at Work Regulations 2002(3)). These are far stricter than COSHH due to the high-risk nature of the substance, which has been fully banned in the UK since 1999. They cover a wide range of duties, from the need to identify and manage asbestos, to the licensing, notification and prevention of exposure, and emergency arrangements. Irrespective of which regulations apply, any Design Authority is required to record the existence of hazardous substances, conduct a risk assessment, and have an agreed mitigation plan. That is, either MoD approved the retention of asbestos in Hunter, or it never knew, meaning the Aircraft Design Authority didn't tell it. Once again, the issue of who was actually responsible for this on Hunter arises.

All I can say is that MoD was very good at such matters. For example, in response to the Montreal Protocol of 1989 we (Technical Agencies) were immediately required to have Design Authorities update Design Packs to list several groups of halogenated hydrocarbons (that lead to the destruction of stratospheric ozone). But, as I said, by 1993 the vehicle for such work had been shut down as a savings measure. In August 2018 a Defence Information Notice was issued, informing former Sea King personnel, serving and civilian, of rising concerns caused by past exposure to asbestos. The following year MoD admitted:

'It is now clear that Asbestos Containing Materials have not been properly identified and tracked across a range of equipment platforms.'

This was disingenuous, the message being *Look how clever and proactive we've been*, when heads should have rolled over the RAF's directive to cease such basic safety work.

I am particularly sensitive to this issue as my former boss, Rear Admiral Ron Holley, died in retirement in 2010 from asbestosis following a single exposure while serving. Had he been in charge when these violations occurred, he would have been apoplectic.

Summary

The foregoing has expanded upon serious failings noted by the AAIB, which, given the fragmented nature of Hunter design control, should have forced a comprehensive review of every design and maintenance organisation under

CAA oversight, and prompted notifications to its equivalents in other countries. Regardless of whether or not the failings were thought to be a direct factor in the accident, an aircraft that is poorly maintained and/or not airworthy is a critical safety risk. G-BXFI, indeed any UK civil-registered Hunter, should not have been flying.

The AAIB Inspectors did very well to identify these failings, but serious questions must be asked as to why there was no follow-up. Plainly, the AAIB understood the impact; but once published its report was not subject to rigorous engineering scrutiny, authorities concentrating on (what they thought was) the easy target - airmanship. As the CAA was part of this process, it is a clear case of being allowed to judge its own case - a recurring theme.

To quote one of Hill's defence barristers, writing on a public discussion forum:

'In court (and in the AAIB report) it was shocking to hear/see the laissez-faire oversight of a failing CAA department; and, the appalling lack of supervision and management of others, all of whom should have performed better with their supervisory and oversight duties. So, it is convenient to steer the families' anger and blame towards the pilot - who screwed up so massively that there's obviously much more to it, as evidenced in court - rather than to call out the tragic failures of the stakeholders. In the Coroner's court, those who benefitted by deflecting from their own (personal and/or organisational) failures were the only ones invited to give evidence. Such a wasted opportunity'.

No fair-minded person, having read the evidence, would disagree. The only thing I'd say is that a number wasted opportunities had arisen, and been rejected, many years earlier. But the point was well made.

NO TRUTH

AAIB test flights (2015)

The AAIB report includes, at Appendix H, partial details of data gathering sorties flown at RAF Scampton on 19 October and 4 December 2015. They were commissioned by the AAIB and contracted to Hawker Hunter Aviation (HHA), themselves under contract to MoD to provide Dissimilar Air Combat Training with an aircraft MoD students would not normally encounter.[22]

The aircraft, a military-registered ex-Swiss Hunter T.58 (ZZ190), essentially an upgraded FGA.9, owned and operated by HHA, was flown by a former RAF pilot, now a professional test pilot. The aim was to gain an understanding of the accident manoeuvre, with four objectives:

- To determine if, having reached the apex, it would have been possible to fly an alternative escape manoeuvre.
- To determine if, having reached the apex, it was possible to have continued the pull through, as attempted, and avoid a collision with the ground.
- To find out what influenced the speed and height achieved at the apex.
- To determine if a Bent Loop manoeuvre could be flown safely if entered with a different combination of airspeed, pull-up technique and power.

AAIB, MoD, HHA and Scampton personnel were in attendance. The AAIB's Appendix H was prepared by its Operations Advisor (the test pilot) and provided to MoD before the final report was issued.

The pilot made an error similar to the one Hill made, almost failing to get out of his loop. The AAIB omitted this in its report, and a mandatory safety occurrence report was not raised. Unable to interview Hill while he was recuperating, it would seem it was *assumed* the accident manoeuvre, and what he intended to fly on 22 August, were one and the same. In fact, the test pilot flew the *intended* one. The AAIB came to accept this:

> 'Where Appendix H refers to a "bent loop", this is the manoeuvre <u>as understood</u> by the test pilot and not necessarily as intended by the pilot of G-BXFI at the time of the accident'.

The AAIB implied <u>it</u> had taken *'ground-based video'*, and was of no value.

---

22 As of 15 September 2017, MoD stated it had no contracts with HHA. The company's website tended to contradict this.

Over three years later, just before Hill's trial, it was revealed it was taken by the Red Arrows' film unit, and MoD and the AAIB held copies (one wide-angle, one narrow and focusing on the aircraft). Also, cockpit video was taken. These videos had not been disclosed in evidence, and have never been released; but events can be gleaned from...

Air safety occurrences - reporting and management

Supporting MoD's overarching Safety Management System, the Air Safety Information Management System (ASIMS) is a software tool used for the reporting, management and exploitation of air safety occurrence and investigation information. It is a dynamic system allowing the most up-to-date information to be recorded as it becomes available, and has the functionality to submit reports anonymously under the Defence Confidential Occurrence Reporting Scheme (DCORS), to improve the trust and honesty in air safety reporting.

The downside is that staff may be disciplined for reporting, or taking action to mitigate, safety concerns; the discriminating criteria being the potential embarrassment to the department and/or senior staff. This has been upheld at Ministerial and Cabinet Secretary level.[23]

In accordance with Regulatory Article 1410, a Defence Air Safety Occurrence Report (DASOR) is to be used to report all air safety related occurrences, be it notification of an event which has already occurred or identification of a potential air safety hazard.[24] The primary method for submitting a DASOR is through ASIMS. Typical reasons are:

- Near misses of any type.
- Safety hazards such as those affecting flight safety, airworthiness or health and safety.
- Quality concerns.
- Continuous improvement ideas.
- Organisational failings, and issues that make human error more likely.

Plainly, a DASOR was required to be raised. In turn, this and a trials report would have to be submitted to the police, and later the Crown Prosecution

---

[23] Unreferenced letter from Cabinet Secretary Sir Jeremy Heywood, 28 October 2014.
[24] https://www.gov.uk/government/publications/defence-air-safety-occurrence-report-dasor-forms

Service and defence. But the AAIB and MoD immediately recognised the detrimental effect this would have on any case against Hill. The test pilot was not asked to raise a DASOR, and the matter was quietly buried.

Twisted tales

To analyse matters more fully, we must jump forward to late-2018, just weeks before the criminal trial was due to commence.

It would seem a number of factors meant the defence did not appreciate the significance of the events of October/December 2015. Most obviously, the full details and trials reports had not been disclosed by the AAIB in its final report of March 2017, or by other participants. And in a practical sense, the defence was funded by Legal Aid, restricted in how much work it could do. With so much else to consider, it may at first have accepted this part of the AAIB report at face value; after all, there were other more glaring mistakes and omissions.

It is likely the defence was checking disclosure issues, and comparing what had been received with what could be expected. This is a simple case of creating a timeline, and asking what would be expected of each participant at each event. Given the AAIB report mentioned the test flights, it would be natural to seek actual reports. Also, Hill would realise the test pilot probably recorded the flights on a GoPro, as most do. They knew each other professionally, and it is likely he asked him if he knew anything; to be told yes, he was in fact the pilot and the flights were filmed. The cat would be out of the bag. Frankly, given the rules of disclosure, and in the almost certain knowledge Hill would work it out, it is difficult to conceive how anyone could think this attempted cover-up could succeed. Yet there are many examples of MoD doing so in other accident investigations.

At this point the test pilot contacted the police to make a statement. The police took possession of the video, then disclosed it to the defence, who had a decision to make. Escalate to legal authorities, or write to the principals seeking information. They chose the latter, and in late-December, a few weeks before trial...

AAIB

First, it is important to appreciate that while the AAIB report was inadmissible in the criminal case, discussion of Appendix H was permitted as it had been served as a standalone expert witness exhibit by the test pilot, who was to appear for the prosecution at trial.

In reply to a series of questions, the Chief Inspector stated that Appendix H contained the pilot's full report (singular), and the event did not require an Occurrence Report; omitting that the AAIB were party to the decision not to raise one. The motive behind this claim must be questioned. He would be expected, indeed required, to know that (as above) Regulatory Article 1410 required all air safety related occurrences to be reported. Later, the MAA had little choice but to disagree with him.

Informed of further disclosure from Sussex Police, in which the test pilot was now named, the Chief Inspector was requested to review his response. During the Xmas break the Principal Inspector overseeing the investigation issued a holding response, adding that the AAIB was not permitted to identify witnesses (true), pointing to Article 14 of Regulation EU 996/2010 listing the types of information the AAIB is not permitted to disclose.

The AAIB claimed it was unaware of what the test pilot said in his police statements, omitting that he was working as an advisor to the AAIB throughout the process, and in this capacity had written its Appendix. In fact, related correspondence to him was addressed to AAIB HQ in Farnborough.

With this being a holiday period, and the defence under a strict deadline from the High Court (the next hearing being on Tuesday 8 January), there was little else could be done. Meanwhile, the phone lines would be hot between the AAIB, MoD and HHA. *Oh crap… We're in it.*

Ministry of Defence

In parallel, a Freedom of Information request was submitted to MoD asking for any Occurrence Report, a copy of the investigation report into the event, and its findings. The Defence Safety Authority replied on 18 December 2018, stating none had been raised. Like the AAIB, it did not mention that they were party to the decision not to raise one. To reply inside a week is extraordinary, and indicative of extreme concern over the perilous legal position the MAA had placed itself in. MoD's default position is to breach the 20-working day reply period, then deny and refuse, and then delay again when asked to review. Often, it never answers at all. But this time it knew the High Court would be told immediately, and take a dim view.

Hawker Hunter Aviation

Asked the same questions, HAA replied on 2 January 2019. Having spoken to the CPS, it had been *'agreed'* that the event was of *'no relevance to the criminal case'*. They added that because the flight trials did not yield any data used by the AAIB, or in any of the test pilot's reports (plural) to the Crown Prosecution Service (CPS), they therefore had not yielded any admissible evidence.

This was nonsense; not least because the reply ignored that the AAIB report *in toto* was inadmissible, but data that had been omitted was not covered by the High Court order. Moreover, it was not for HHA to say what was admissible in the High Court. In the event, the Judge ruled it was admissible, the test pilot examined at length on the precise details of his flights, most of which was not in Appendix H.

The reason why the AAIB did not use the data was because the pilot had made an error that MoD and the AAIB wanted to conceal. And if the test pilot later wrote more than one report for the CPS, surely the AAIB report would have to been reviewed for consistency? It was not, and at that point became even more incomplete...

As with the AAIB and MoD, HHA omitted to say why a DASOR was not raised; or that the AAIB report gave no indication of the seriousness of the error; or that the flight had been recorded. But they went further than the others, revealing the latest date at which the CPS were aware. The implication is that, hitherto, the CPS were told little more than what was in the AAIB report, probably did not view the videos, and did not realise how damaging to the prosecution case it would be when the jury was told a far more experienced Hunter pilot had made the same, or worse, error when flying a briefed, specifically approved test profile, knowing it was being videoed and would be forensically analysed. And, it was important for the CPS and police to understand why such an experienced joint team managed to get almost everything wrong - and compare and contrast this with Hill's actions.

Finally, given their contractual position, it is likely HAA cleared their response with the MAA.

Timeline

It is clear that much discussion/panic ensued between the HHA reply of 2 January, and the MAA decision of the 14th to raise a DASOR. Related correspondence would indeed be interesting, especially on how it dealt with the HHA/CPS's fatally flawed 'agreement'.

It can now be seen that the police were aware of at least the general issues, and the defence's concern over lack of disclosure, by late-November 2018; and at this point they acted correctly. It must be assumed they then advised the CPS - failure to do so would be gross misconduct.

It cannot be known who contacted the CPS first, the police or HHA. Either way, only a fool would believe an error, undertaking essentially the same manoeuvre, was not significant. The CPS knew, well before trial, their case was compromised; and they certainly briefed their Counsel of events. And they would understand the potential impact the truth would have on the jury.

DASOR Hawker Hunter Aviation\Hunter\15\335 - Misflown Manoeuvre

Now that the truth was out - or at least some of it - the test pilot was asked to retrospectively raise a DASOR. The MAA (part of the Defence Safety Authority) issued it on 14 January 2019. It is structured as follows:

1. Reporter's Section (test pilot)
2. Technical Section (HHA Flight Operations)
3. Occurrence Manager Section (HHA Flight Operations)
4. Comments (test pilot)
5. Actions (HHA)

Attachments:

a. Approval for AAIB tasked Flying - G-BXFI Investigation, dated 2 October 2019, relating to first test flights.

b. Approval for AAIB Tasked Flying - G-BXFI Investigation, dated 27 November 2015, relating to final test flight.[25]

Note: Sections 2, 3 and the attachments are signed by the same person, who held a more senior position in 2109. One must be careful interpreting the DASOR; and remember it was raised in January 2019, the attachments in late-2015. The casual reader might think they were written at the same time, which would be misleading. The crucial issue is that the eventual raising of the DASOR required the AAIB report, and its formal position (that one wasn't required) to be amended. It was not, so the report remained incomplete...

Analysis

Reporter's Section

I think it best to simply cut and paste the narrative, written by the test pilot:

'The sortie was the final one in a series of three flown to gather data on

---

[25] Defence Air Safety Occurrence Report Reference Number asor\Hawker Hunter Aviation\Hawker Hunter Aviation\Hunter\15\335 - Misflown Manoeuvre.

specific aspects of Hunter performance for AAIB. One manoeuvre was flown specifically to gather video recording from the ground of the first, upward half of a "bent" loop (which essentially is a quarter clover in other parlance). The aim was solely to attempt to develop a means of identifying flap setting from external video recordings; no other data was required.

It was commenced from 200 feet MSD [Minimum Separation Distance] *and 300 KIAS* (Knots Indicated Airspeed) *with 15° of flap (1 notch) and full power (7,850 RPM) with a pull up in light buffet throughout; a 90° loaded roll was performed passing the up vertical. The plan was to terminate the manoeuvre at the apex with a rolling escape manoeuvre whilst simultaneously reducing power to 6,600 RPM.*

The manoeuvre was flown as planned to the apex at which point, contrary to the plan, I then noted the Indicated Airspeed and altitude and transmitted them whilst maintaining the pitch rate. As I released the transmit button I realised immediately that I should have flown a rolling escape manoeuvre at the apex, but by then I was then close to the down vertical line. I continued to maintain the maximum instantaneous pitch rate wings level and regained level flight at what I considered in-cockpit was approximately 500 feet. I realised what my mistake was and continued with the sortie as planned. After landing I debriefed the sortie, including this error, with the HHA, AM(MF), HHA, Flight Ops and the AAIB sponsor for the task.

This event occurred over three years ago and a request has been made to submit this DASOR retrospectively. I cannot recall the specifics of any discussion that may have taken place at the time regarding submission of a DASOR but I do recall being very aware of the sensitivity of the AAIB investigation for which data from these sorties was to be used. With hindsight I accept that I should have submitted a DASOR when this event occurred.

Overall, I consider the risk associated with this to be low because for a 200-Series Avon engine Hunter the manoeuvre was planned and flown in such a way (full power, roll flown passing the up vertical line) that even following an error such as the one that I made the exit height should not be lower than the entry height'.

The pilot estimated he was '*approximately*' 500 feet above ground level when he achieved level flight. The videos showed this to be nearer 100 feet. The significance is that he admitted an error that was very similar to Hill's. The principals <u>must</u> have realised this completely undermined their case. In fact, it is likely they thought the Judge might dismiss the case there and then -

which I think he should have. Related to this is mention of a '200-Series' engine, but not that G-BXFI was fitted with one of lesser power. The pilot later clarified this to the police.

The severity of the incident was claimed to be 'Category C - Low'.

Worthy of note is that the test pilot wore a number of hats. In addition to being pilot of an HHA aircraft and AAIB Operations Advisor, he was HHA's Independent Safety Advisor and a pilot at the Empire Test Pilot School. It is inconceivable that the requirement for an Occurrence Report was not discussed with the AAIB at the December trial debrief. (Noting the general requirement that AAIB Inspectors hold, at least, a Private Pilot Licence, and would be all too aware of the need to raise a report).

The AAIB incorporated his report, which mentions very little of the above DASOR statement, as Appendix H. It gives the distinct impression of uneventful, successful test flights totalling 2 hours 20 minutes. All concerned knew this was highly misleading.

Technical Section

This reports *'no maintenance required'* on the aircraft, and no MoD Form 765 was raised. (An Unsatisfactory Feature Report; for example relating to aircraft/aircrew publications). This demonstrates HHA were using MoD procedures, begging the question *Who would they send a 765 to?*

Occurrence Manager Section

This is headed:

> 'An HHA Error Management Observation has been raised to investigate why this incident wasn't reported at the time of the occurrence'.

Nowhere in the DASOR is this question answered.

The investigator was an RAF Flight Lieutenant. Disagreeing with the test pilot, he rated the severity of the incident as 'Category B - Medium'. His justification for this was: *'The minimum approved base height for this series of manoeuvres was breached'*.

Comments

The report was *'automatically accepted'* by the test pilot, logged as being at midnight on the same day the DASOR was raised, 14 January 2019.

Actions (in sequence)
- Commentator (the test pilot) - *Submit report.*
- Maintenance (HHA) - *Complete the technical tab.*
- Occurrence Manager (HHA) - *Accept report.*
- Occurrence Manager (HHA) - *Send for investigation.* Returned 15 January 2019.
- Internal - Recipient (test pilot) - *Notified*, 15 January 2019.
- Occurrence Manager - *Close Investigation*, 15 January 2019.

Note: The HHA employees are *'anonymous'*.

It would seem from the timing and lack of detailed comment (with the exception of the test pilot's), the DASOR was hastily written, 'investigated', and waived through within a few hours; tending to confirm the impression HHA were reluctant participants and probably wary of being drawn in. With the exception of the test pilot and the HHA Flight Operations Manager, it cannot be known if recipients were involved in 2015.

2015 Approvals

The Approval for HHA tasking relating to the first two test flights was raised on 12 October 2015, five days before. As I said, it was sent to the test pilot at AAIB head offices in Farnborough, as well as an AAIB Inspector; the text suggesting they were an AAIB team. It was copied to a senior HHA manager, Station Commander RAF Scampton, Officer Commanding the Red Arrows, the Senior Air Traffic Control Officer at RAF Scampton, and an officer in the MAA's Contractor Flying Approved Organisation Scheme office. The latter had been a Test & Evaluation Officer in his previous post, commanding 41 Squadron, so well qualified to offer advice and provide regulatory oversight.

It is well written, setting out criteria such as the Authority for the trial, pilot currency, weather minima, aircraft configuration, deconfliction, and planned manoeuvres. It required the pilot to carry out 'work-up flying', noting this has already been done on 16 September in the same aircraft (ZZ190); meaning the tasking had been agreed very quickly.

Importantly, a comprehensive Risk Assessment was carried out by the HHA Flight Operations signatory, with the test pilot acting in his role of Independent Safety Advisor. My only comment here would be to question why there was no independent signature, especially for a test flight replicating a fatal accident manoeuvre. However, I accept this specific scenario may not actually be covered in the MoD's regulations. Nevertheless, worth mentioning given the outcome. A second approval, essentially the same as the first, was raised on 27 November 2015 covering the final test flight.

Analysis and discussion

Should the pilot have automatically raised a DASOR himself? I think the position he was in - wearing so many hats - would confuse matters. The ex-RAF part of him knew a DASOR or equivalent had to be raised. But he was now a civilian, and should have been guided by the sponsor (the AAIB, whom he was working to) and MoD (as the air safety incident occurred in its airspace, in a military-registered aircraft operated by its contractor). If I seem defensive of him, it is because in this sense he is 'only' the pilot. It is the conduct of higher echelons that is disturbing.

The reason for his error is not the important thing. Infinitely more serious is the process by which all this was hidden by the principals, and then no action taken against them when the plot was revealed. This had easily foreseen consequences, encouraging MoD to continue its practice of lying to Inquests and courts. It had already done so recently at the trial of Martin-Baker, and would do so again in 2021 at Jon Bayliss's Inquest. The Judge and Coroner, respectively, knew they had been lied to, but took no action. Worse, they issued rulings as if the lies were fact.

This highlighted a recurring question. *Is an AAIB investigation bound to report evidence it uncovers that may affect the decision to prosecute?* The answer is clearly *Yes*, because accident investigation protocols demand every uncovered anomaly is reported and dealt with, regardless of its direct effect on the accident. If not, *they* become the adjudicators, not the CPS. The concept of a separate 'confidential' report is not mentioned in the regulations, meaning the main report must set out these events, and any follow-up.

Here, and for the most part, the AAIB reported the anomalies it uncovered, but was only permitted to make recommendations. There was very little accompanying analysis. It was not the judge of whether these had been dealt with correctly, and so those responsible for this became an integral part of the investigation. This aspect - follow-up and follow-through - is direly lacking in all investigations I have looked at. But here, a system that was lacking became one that was violated. The test pilot's error was accidental. The cover-up intentionally obstructed justice, serving to facilitate the decision to prosecute Hill. It rendered the AAIB investigation and report, upon which the police, Crown Prosecution Service and later the Coroner based their decisions, incomplete, flawed, and deficient.

Legal implications

Sussex Police will not discuss the matter, so the extent of their involvement or knowledge cannot be known. If their Air Operations Unit was engaged, as they probably should have been, then they would know that some form of incident report was required. But they later claimed ignorance, implying they were not present; and therefore the CPS would, initially, be unaware. This is reinforced by them having to ask the High Court for access to the trials report. They were relying almost entirely on the AAIB, but that does not mean they should have stepped back to such an extent they had to resort to the High Court. This certainly bears further examination, because the CPS, in turn, had to rely entirely on the police report and recommendations. How could the police know their report was complete and accurate, when they had to ask the High Court for disclosure of basic evidence?

When the decision to prosecute was made in March 2018, the failure to notify the police, and hence the CPS, became conspiracy to pervert the course of justice. That is, *the act of two or more persons agreeing to prevent justice being served*. It doesn't matter whether or not the acts result in a perversion. The offence is committed when acts tending and intended to pervert are done. Factors that can aggravate the seriousness of the offence and lead to harsher sentences include:

- The wider and more complex the conspiracy, especially involving multiple parties or spanning a long duration. (Here, over three years).
- The emotional, psychological, and physical impact on any victims involved directly or indirectly in the case.
- If the individuals were in positions of authority or trust (in which case they face stricter sentences).
- The severity of the crime associated with the conspiracy.
- Actions that significantly hinder major investigations.
- A defendant's prior criminal record, particularly similar offences. (While MoD has no criminal record as such, it is a matter of record that staff have conspired to conceal evidence and lie to courts. The prime examples in recent years are aforementioned Red Arrows fatal accidents in 2011 and 2018; noting an overlap in the MoD/RAF departments involved in this case).

I exclude the test pilot from this, for the reasons given. No action was taken against the other participants.

Despite this new and significant evidence, the CPS decided to proceed with the prosecution; but was it too late to demand that the principals answer questions in court? A bigger question is: *Why does the law permit such a case to proceed knowing that exculpatory evidence cannot be heard in court?* And perhaps the biggest of all: *What of those who the AAIB <u>actually</u> criticised?* Perversion had drifted towards corruption.

Quite separately, a pilot at RAF Valley wrote to me in August 2019, after Hill's trial:

> *'When the DASOR was circulated at Valley people obviously queried the recent date and gradually the story came out. As with Sean Cunningham* [killed in 2011]*, Jon Bayliss* [killed in 2018]*, and the incident when they lost power over the Irish Sea a couple of years ago* [30 August 2017]*, all at Valley and Scampton have been told to keep quiet'.*

The AAIB don't tell MoD staff or contractors to 'keep quiet'. But MoD does.

At this point, most MoD personnel would be wondering what possessed it to get involved. I've been in this position, tasked to assist an AAIB investigation into a fatal accident caused by a shattered gearbox in a civilian Chinook. You stand back and let them get on with their job, and help when asked. In my case, commissioning and operating new transmission rigs. Being asked to do anything illegal was unimaginable. But, as I said, those days of integrity seem long gone. *Who or what has changed?*

Governance and oversight

Regulatory Article 2370 requires governance of trials by Suitably Qualified and Experienced Persons (SQEP). MoD 'Duty Holders' are required to endorse and approve the trials plans, establishing an Approval Board comprising SQEP for the activity. As this involved aerobatics not normally undertaken by the RAF, that would be 22 Group within which (at the time) sat the Red Arrows. Which would be convenient, because both HHA and the Red Arrows were based at RAF Scampton. And hence, the ease with which it would be arranged that the Red Arrows' film unit recorded the flights. But also, the ease with which the information could be contained. The Approval Board must include:

- Design Organisation
- MoD Test and Evaluation
- Continuing Airworthiness Organisation

- Flight Operations

...requiring the direct involvement of at least MoD, RAF, AAIB and HHA. A Combined Test Team would be formed, comprising the same.

The Air System Safety Case, or equivalent Safety Argument, must be up-issued to reflect the trials activity. At the very least one would expect the AAIB to note this was done correctly, and approved. But by whom, given the audit trail for the Safety Case was wholly compromised by the CAA error regarding the Hunter Design Authority. HHA hold MAA approvals to conduct tests and trials, although it remains unclear if this extended to aerobatics, and it can be seen they did much of the Safety Case preparatory work. I consider it more than satisfactory.

The MAA were the lead MoD branch; not only because they were the regulator, but because contrary to what the CAA claimed there was no MoD Hunter Project Team. If this had been an In-Service aircraft, the platform project team would have played a major part, not least because it would be paying for much of it.

The role of the AAIB Chief Inspector bears further examination. He was head of the MAA Accident Investigation Branch in August 2015, was then head of the Defence Accident Investigation Branch when the trials took place, and in January 2017 took over at the AAIB. That proximity must surely be undesirable, especially now we know both his old and new Branches concealed evidence, and he later condoned it. Also, the MAA and his test pilot Operations Advisor came to disagree with the him over whether a DASOR was required. Regardless of any direct involvement in 2015 (and it is likely he knew exactly what was going on), he would know the importance of that information; and it is inconceivable he would not be closely involved in these machinations in run-up to the trial.

The AAIB's report - the Appendix written by the test pilot - discusses a small part of the process. Given its comprehensive reporting of other activities, and even if a DASOR wasn't raised in 2015, the minimum one might expect is the Chief Inspector insisting on a full trials report being included. It is clear RA2370 (Test and Evaluation), and the AAIB's own procedures, were not complied with.

Irrefutably, the AAIB and MoD colluded to conceal both the error, and that it was filmed. It is implausible to believe that once Hill was charged they didn't realise the crucial importance to the criminal prosecution. That, the very mention of the incident introduced so much doubt, the standard of proof could not possibly be met.

An unknown is the point at which the CAA became aware. Certainly, it too should have noticed the AAIB report was deficient, and asked that the trials report and Occurrence Report be included.

When the truth (as far as we know it) was revealed shortly before trial, the CPS should have immediately called a halt and reassessed the decision to prosecute. That in itself would create doubt, and it would be entirely reasonable to conclude that a prosecution could no longer succeed. This would be bad PR for legal authorities, but all they needed was to be honest. *We've been deceived. The AAIB and MoD acted in concert. It doesn't matter who was the principal, and who was the accomplice. They sought to pervert justice and are equally guilty.*

To place all this in context, the final trial was conducted on the same day Hill was interviewed for the third time by the AAIB; his first interview being in November 2015. That is, the AAIB were at both, and it is fair to ask if this was a case of Hill being deliberately kept away from the trial, despite his input being crucial. (And remember, at this point he had not been charged. His status would be that of a first-hand witness). Surely it would have been wiser to wait until he had been spoken to, and have him present? (His first police interview was late-December 2015, and the CPS were not involved formally until much later).

Summary

What happened when the AAIB and Sussex Police decided it would be a good idea to conduct these data gathering trials? (And it *was* a good idea). Let us assume the AAIB was the 'lead' sponsor, as the police do not seem to have been closely involved. This will have been a procedural courtesy, their investigations initially proceeding in parallel until the police paused, awaiting the AAIB's conclusions.

Plainly, a Hunter was needed. If not a T.7, then a Mark with the same or similar flying characteristics, in a similar configuration. But all civilian-registered Hunters had been grounded by the CAA immediately after the accident.

Would the AAIB ask the CAA to 'unground' one aircraft for a trial? Perhaps, but it would be a difficult decision. Easier to look at military-registered aircraft, and approach MoD and HHA. (Or perhaps HHA suggested this to the AAIB...?). From a professional standpoint, HHA would be keen to understand if there was anything to be concerned about. From a commercial viewpoint, it was extra business and kudos.

Where to fly to test flights? HHA were at RAF Scampton, and permission would need to be sought from MoD. First, from those who managed Hunters, and also the Military Aviation Authority, the regulators. So, who to approach?

This is where it would get interesting.

It is likely the AAIB spoke to close contacts in the MAA. One of the first questions would have to be - *Can we get your RAF Hunter Design Authority on board, because our Certification Inspector has to write a report on the airworthiness status of the accident aircraft, and the Airworthiness Approval Note is based on the premise that the RAF are the Design Authority?*

Very quickly, a huge penny would drop. *We've never been the Design Authority and... oh, that means you can't demonstrate G-BXFI was airworthy.*

Both would then ask: *If this was the premise underpinning G-BXFI's Approval, are all UK civilian-registered Hunters the same? Are military-registered Hunters the same? Do we need to ground them?*

The initial decision would be made by the Director General Defence Safety Authority, and it may be that one influencing factor was the effect on fast jet pilot training; which was attracting poor publicity due to its poor implementation.

If this, or something similar, didn't happen, the investigation was incomplete, flawed and deficient. If it *did* happen, then it was still incomplete, because the AAIB report didn't mention it.

The grounding was lifted by the CAA on 6 July 2017:

> 'This action is a result of the CAA concluding there were no airworthiness issues relating to the Hawker Hunter aircraft that caused or contributed to the accident. This is based on our own extensive review and the AAIB's final accident report. All aircraft of this type will have to comply with enhanced maintenance and inspection requirements and, following normal practice, secure all relevant permits and other approvals before they are allowed to fly again. The restriction on aerobatic manoeuvres by ex-military jet aircraft, now including the Hawker Hunter, at overland airshows remains.

The contradiction, indeed deceit, was the AAIB report had confirmed that, due to CAA failings, the aircraft was neither serviceable nor airworthy - and therefore should not have been flying. The CAA was in denial.

JUDICIAL TRUTH

A legal quirk, and High Court rulings

The status of evidence given to the AAIB

The AAIB's aim of preventing recurrence is deemed sacrosanct, allowing witnesses the freedom to relate their version of events without fear of prosecution. An important principle is that they provide information on the understanding it will remain confidential.

The Civil Aviation (Investigation of Air Accidents and Incidents) Regulations set out the powers of AAIB Chief Inspector. These include provisions for access to the accident site and to the debris, and to the flight recorders and any other recordings. They confer the power to examine witnesses, for which purpose he has the powers to issue summonses and to require the persons summoned to answer any questions. These interviews are not carried out under caution. The opposite is true for the police, who interview under caution but cannot compel answers.

There is a strict delineation between evidence the AAIB obtains during its investigation, and what may be used in a criminal prosecution. The regulations state:

'The report of an investigation into an incident shall protect the anonymity of the persons involved in the incident; and where appropriate contain safety recommendations. A safety recommendation shall in no case create a presumption of blame or liability for an accident or incident'.

(Please don't get hung up on 'accident' and 'incident'. They have quite different meanings to different organisations involved here).

The essential issue is that the purpose of an AAIB interview is to obtain the fullest possible information, in order to prevent recurrence; contrasting markedly with the purpose of a police interview, which is to elicit evidence which may be capable of being used at a subsequent criminal trial. There is nothing to prevent the police interviewing the same witnesses; although that is not to say they would ask the same questions or elicit the same statements.

Legal authorities may use the AAIB interviews as the basis of a prosecution. By way of contradiction, the entire AAIB report is available to the public, but may not be used or referred to in court. This sounds bizarre, even unfair, and it is. However, a legal caveat exists whereby such information can be used on a case by case basis if it is believed there is an overwhelming public interest. This requires an application to the High Court by the entity wishing to use the information, and is usually opposed by the State and the information gatherer. The former, especially, believes very little to be in the public interest.

The danger, to the prosecution, and what certainly occurred here, is that witnesses who provided a statement on the assumption of anonymity may change their minds when exposed to the witness stand, and realisation dawns that they may be about to incriminate themselves. And, that a juror who has read the report will notice this. The legal process waltzes round the scenario, as the law makes it impossible to avoid; and later it will become clear that most of the prosecution witnesses gave evidence that fatally weakened the prosecution's case. Plainly, their statements - which the AAIB report merely paraphrased - would have been very different if they thought they would be made public. The challenge, to write a full and independent report, revealing the whole truth, is insurmountable.

The legislation the AAIB adhere to can be found in an international treaty: the Convention on International Civil Aviation, signed at Chicago on 7 December 1944 (Treaty Series No. 8 (1953)) (Cmd 8742), often referred to as the Chicago Convention. Of particular importance is Annex 13, 'Aircraft Accident and Incident Investigation'. Paragraph 5.12 states:

'Non-disclosure of records

The State conducting the investigation of an accident or incident shall not make the following records available for purposes other than accident or incident investigation, unless the appropriate authority for the administration of justice in that State determines that their disclosure outweighs the adverse domestic and international impact such action may have on that or any future investigations:

a) All statements taken from persons by the investigation authorities in the course of their investigation;

b) All communications between persons having been involved in the operation of the aircraft;

c) Medical or private information regarding persons involved in the accident or incident;

d) Cockpit voice recordings and transcripts from such recordings;

e) Recordings and transcriptions of recordings from air traffic control units;

f) Cockpit airborne image recordings and any part or transcripts from such recordings; and

g) Opinions expressed in the analysis of information, including flight recorder information.

These records shall be included in the final report or its appendices only when pertinent to the analysis of the accident or incident. Parts of the records not relevant to the analysis shall not be disclosed'.

Thus, the intent is clear *(shall not be released)* but the decision is left to the court.

EU regulations expand on this; for example the following are also protected:

- The identity of those giving statements.
- Material subsequently produced during the course of the investigation such as <u>notes, drafts, opinions written by the investigators, opinions expressed in the analysis of information</u>, including flight recorder information.
- Covering letters for the transmission of safety recommendations from the AAIB.
- Occurrence reports.
- Drafts of preliminary or <u>final</u> reports or interim statements.

The EU legislation goes much further than *Chicago*. The inclusion of the underlined parts can be, and is, interpreted as referring to the <u>entire AAIB report</u>.

High Court rulings

Crucial to understanding the legal aspects of the case are two High Court rulings of 2016 and 2022, plus precedent. To ease understanding it is best to deal with them in one chapter, and refer back to them later as necessary.

The basic issues are:

1. Admissibility and dissemination of evidence gathered by the AAIB.
2. The application of any ruling to (a) the criminal case, (b) the Coroner's Inquest, and, potentially (c) subsequent civil proceedings.
3. Whether the Coroner can or should investigate matters the AAIB has already looked at.

Historically this has been a grey area. Uncertainty has been fuelled by the conflict between the requirements underpinning accident reports, and the desire of claimant or the accused to use such reports to make their case. This is particularly important if the report is flawed, yet has been used as the basis of the decision to prosecute. So, while the law says one is innocent until proven guilty, what it actually means is that you may start off as innocent, but the law will do its best prevent you proving innocence, despite the onus being on the prosecution to prove guilt. Exactly what happened here.

Civil cases

While, ultimately, there were no civil proceedings taken out, let us deal with this first as its sets the scene.

In a landmark case, in March 2014 the English Court of Appeal affirmed the High Court's decision in *Rogers v Hoyle* that accident reports prepared by the AAIB are admissible as evidence in civil proceedings.[26]

The case involved an aircraft accident, in which Mr Rogers was a passenger in a vintage Tiger Moth bi-plane piloted by Mr Hoyle. Mr Rogers was killed and Mr Hoyle seriously injured. The AAIB report was published in June 2012 noting, amongst other things, that a loop manoeuvre:

> 'Was carried out at too low a height for the pilot to be able to recover from the subsequent spin. [Mr Hoyle] *did not have sufficient knowledge or training on the Tiger Moth's correct spin recovery technique, and it is probable that he would not have been able to recover from an unintentional spin, especially given the limited height available'.*

Mr Hoyle made an application that the report be declared inadmissible. Mr Justice Leggatt, sitting in the High Court, held that it was admissible, both as evidence of the facts stated therein, and as expert opinion evidence.

Mr Hoyle's appeal was heard by Lord Justice Clarke, who ruled:

- The defendant's submissions that the AAIB report was unsuitable as evidential material was rejected. That, insofar as the report contained statements or reported statements of fact, it was, in the view of the court, *prima facie* admissible.
- The AAIB was not, in producing its report, acting in a judicial or quasi-judicial role, reaching decisions on disputed issues of fact. The report was instead a document containing expert statements of opinion (which the AAIB was qualified to make) on statements of fact.
- The procedural rules for expert evidence did not preclude the admissibility of the report. Instead they regulated the use of a particular category of

---

26 https://www.hfw.com/insights/Landmark-English-Court-of-Appeal-decision-accident-investigation-reports-March-2014/

expert evidence, namely of experts who had been *'instructed to give or prepare expert evidence for the purpose of proceedings'*. They did not therefore exclude the admissibility of other expert evidence, such as the AAIB report, prepared for other purposes (e.g. preventing accidents).

The court also rejected the notion that the admissibility of AAIB reports was so likely to prejudice the interests which the AAIB serves, that its reports should generally be excluded from evidence; noting, *inter alia*, that AAIB reports are available to litigants and can be used as the foundation for a claim or defence, and this has not had any apparent adverse effect on the AAIB's work.

The court noted the challenge faced by many litigants to advance claims without access to the relevant information submitted to the investigators, and/or in financing independent evidence. But it stressed that nothing in its judgment *'should be taken to mean that anything in the* [AAIB Report] *is to be treated as conclusive or prima facie conclusive of anything'*. That is, there was no compunction on courts to regard the AAIB report as accurate. (This becomes important later).

This ruling, that AAIB reports are admissible in civil cases, and are not necessarily accurate, did not apply to criminal cases or Inquests; not because of an actual ruling to that effect, but simply because those scenarios were not part of the application. Nevertheless, the ruling ran contrary to *Chicago* and EU legislation.

The court's decision was not appealed further and, accordingly, now stands as the most definitive statement on the admissibility of AAIB reports in civil proceedings in England and Wales.

High Court ruling - 2016 (Criminal cases)

In September 2016 the Chief Constable of Sussex Police made an application to the High Court for disclosure of evidence. It covered materials in the possession of the AAIB and gathered as part of their investigation; mostly witness statements and cockpit video footage. That is, the application referred only to one small part of the investigation and report.

The application was opposed by the Secretary of State for Transport (i.e. the 'boss' of the AAIB and the CAA) and the British Airline Pilots Association (BALPA). The hearing was held on 15/16 July 2016, the High Court informed this was the first application of its kind to be made in England and Wales.

The Secretary of State submitted that disclosure of the material would have a significant and adverse domestic and international impact on future safety investigations; something the Court was required to weigh against the public interest in an effective investigation, and detection of crime by the police. That, disclosure would *'have a detrimental effect on the AAIB's ability to carry out its functions'*.

BALPA submitted:

> *'Should cockpit and image recording be passed to the police, pilots may be inhibited in what they say and do during emergency situations. Should records of the flight which are made by the pilot of his own volition be passed to police the pilot may be disinclined to carry such equipment which may otherwise provide useful information to the accident investigation bodies'.*

It can be seen these repeated the State's unsuccessful argument in the *Rogers v Hoyle* case of two years before, but was now testing criminal law.

The first stage of the hearing was conducted in the normal way in open court, with members of the public and the media present. However, there came a point at which this was no longer appropriate, and henceforth only the two parties were represented. This, to avoid prejudicing any future criminal trial.

At a third stage the Chief Constable was also excluded. In effect the court had to conduct a hearing similar to an application for public interest immunity. Consequently, confidential matters were set out in a Confidential Annex attached to the judgment, and made available only to the Chief Constable and Secretary of State. (Note: not BALPA).

The judge, Lord Thomas of Cwmgiedd, Lord Chief Justice of England and Wales, was of the opinion that the material sought by the Chief Constable fell into three broad categories:

1. Statements made in response to interviews or discussions by Hill.
2. Contemporaneous evidence from the flight itself which was not the product of any human action. The only material in this category was video footage.
3. Material that was not contemporaneous, but subsequently produced by various others. For example, experiments conducted and tests done on various aspects of the accident.

The judge rejected (1) because there would be a *'chilling'* effect which would deter people giving evidence, and on grounds of unfairness because *'the powers of the AAIB, unlike the ordinary police, are such as to permit the compulsion of answers to questions'*.

Regarding (2), he did not find the State's and BALPA's arguments '*persuasive*'. He stressed that the footage was unlike cockpit voice and flight data recordings, which normally have to be created as a matter of legal duty by those operating aircraft. But there was no such duty in the present context, and therefore distinguishable from other case law. Furthermore, it was significant that the cameras were installed not only on a voluntary basis, but for leisure and private commercial reasons. Indeed, it appeared to him that the intention was to use the video footage as part of a broadcast. He was not, therefore, persuaded that pilots would be deterred in the future from installing such equipment on a voluntary basis.

Regarding (3), the other material, he noted that the scope of the police request had narrowed during the course of the hearing. In private, it was confirmed that the Chief Constable would not pursue his application for disclosure of speed calculations or the report of the Health and Safety Laboratory (HSL); the Judge noting this would be made available to the public when the AAIB report was issued. The Judge pointed out the police could carry out their own investigation (which, some might argue, is an unnecessary waste of time and money, especially to cash-strapped forces).

This left two requests to be considered; reports of the test flights flown at RAF Scampton in 2015, and engineering reports on the mechanical state of the aircraft. He refused these requests, but the reasons were set out only in the Confidential Annex. What was it about these two aspects that meant the public could not be told about why the Judge refused them? *Who benefitted?* The answer is clear.

It cannot be known if the Judge was told the extent or significance of the data from the 2015 test flights. Highly unlikely. Either way, the effect of the ruling was to encourage the AAIB and MoD to continue their concealment.

On 28 September 2016 the application was dismissed, with the exception of the G-BXFI cockpit video footage which the Judge allowed to be released to Sussex Police, the Crown Prosecution Service, and Hill.[27] He set the following conditions:

'(1) The material set out in the Schedule attached herewith is to be disclosed to the Chief Constable of Sussex for the purposes of his criminal investigation into the circumstances surrounding the crash of the Hawker

---

27 High Court of Justice Divisional Court - Approved Judgment Case No: HQ16X01053 (Chief Constable of Sussex Police v Secretary of State for Transport (AAIB) and British Airline Pilots Association (BALPA), 28 September 2016)

Hunter T.7, G-BXFI piloted by Mr Andrew Hill;

(2) The Chief Constable of Sussex will retain overall responsibility for the material until its return to the AAIB;

(3) The material that is disclosed to the Chief Constable of Sussex shall not be further disclosed by him save that he may disclose the material to:

(i) Experts instructed by the Police in the furtherance of their investigation.

(ii) The Crown Prosecution Service for the purposes of advising him and pursuing a prosecution.

(iii) Mr Hill and any other Defendant prosecuted as a result of the investigation into the crash of the Hawker Hunter T.7, G-BXFI and any Solicitor or Counsel engaged by them for the purposes of ensuring that he receives the required procedural safeguards by way of disclosure.

(4) The results of any analysis and any subsequent opinion as a result of the expert consideration referred to in 3(i) above shall be treated on the same confidential as the rest of the material.

(5) The material in the Schedule shall be returned to the AAIB at the conclusion of any criminal proceedings'.

The ruling is now known as 'Sussex'.

Five months later, on 3 March 2017, one could simply download the AAIB report - serving to confuse everyone. It appears that Hill (who at this point had not been charged) had to abide by the EU legislation - he could not refer in any correspondence to the AAIB report. This restriction went far beyond the intent of the application.

Regarding (5), Sussex Police were later found to have retained copies of the cockpit video, and were forced to apologise to the Coroner:

'The High Court's (2016) Order granting the police permission to use the footage, required them to return the footage to the AAIB at the conclusion of the criminal proceedings. Whilst they did return the footage, they retained copies of the original footage. The first defendant, the Chief Constable of Sussex, accepts that this was a serious breach of that order. The Chief Constable has apologised to the court for the failure to abide by the terms of the order of this court; and has provided assurances in evidence that processes have now been put in place to ensure that such a

*breach does not occur in the future'.*²⁸

I wonder if the legal system would have accepted a mere apology had others been in breach? There is a similarity with the death of Corporal Jon Bayliss in 2018, where North Wales Police removed evidence in the form of Jon's GoPro and phone, examined them, extracted personal data, and failed to maintain the chain of custody, but did not disclose this to the court or return them to the family. No action was taken.²⁹

High Court ruling - 2022

Vital to the conduct of any Inquest is how much duplication of effort is permitted. That is, under what circumstances may the Coroner investigate matters which the AAIB have already investigated?

Where interested parties already have materials which provide the findings and conclusions of prior investigations - for example by independent experts or other suitably qualified bodies - Coroners have been judicially discouraged from (re)investigating the cause of the accident (i.e. the wider circumstances). In *R (on the application of Secretary of State for Transport v HM Senior Coroner for Norfolk & British Airline Pilots Association)* (an Inquest into the deaths of four men in a helicopter accident), a report had been produced by the AAIB. In the weeks running up to the Inquest, the Coroner issued a number of notices requiring the AAIB Chief Inspector to disclose the cockpit voice and flight data recorder and/or a transcript of the recording. He refused, the Coroner twice fining him for non-compliance with the notices.³⁰

The subsequent High Court ruling, commonly known as *'Norfolk'*, established there was *'no public interest in having unnecessary duplication of investigations or enquiries'*, unless it could be demonstrated that the official investigation *'is **incomplete, flawed or deficient'**.* (Hence my emphasis of this phrase). Only then may an investigation or Inquest be re-opened. This assumes *(inter alia)* the Coroner has the wherewithal to identify incompleteness, flaws, and deficiencies.

Various Coroners and MoD have cited this as reason not to hold Inquests into military deaths at all. For example, the Senior Coroner for North West Wales has refused to hold a mandatory Inquest into the death of Flight Lieutenant

---

28 https://vlex.co.uk/vid/hm-senior-coroner-for-896165228.
29 'A Noble Anger' (David Hill, 2022).
30 https://www.hendersonchambers.co.uk/2021/01/19/alerter-by-tim-green-elizabeth-tremayne-reflections-on-maughan-disclosure-in-inquests/

Hywel Poole, who died in a Tornado mid-air in 2012, saying the RAF's Service Inquiry was sufficient. This ignored that Service Inquiries and the AAIB seek to establish cause of the accident, the Coroner cause of death - which were different. Another good example of divergence is the death of Sean Cunningham, in 2011; where, but for the RAF's violations, he would have survived the accident. Moreover, by definition Service Inquiries are <u>always</u> incomplete, and hence flawed and deficient; primarily because they are entirely one-sided, with no representation permitted for the bereaved. In fact, *Norfolk* has little or no relevance in military deaths; and likewise civil accidents where (like here) the AAIB has not been entirely truthful or diligent. Plainly, it needs amending.

The Senior Coroner for West Sussex, Ms Penelope Schofield, had been given wide-ranging evidence that the AAIB report was deeply flawed. However, in her application to the High Court on 21 April 2021 she chose to confine herself to a paper written by Dr Christopher Mitchell, submitted in September 2020, in which he advanced a theory that Hill suffered a particular mechanism of Cognitive Impairment resulting from cerebral hypoxia during the flight.[31] She sought:

- Disclosure of the split screen cockpit Go-Pro footage which was created for comparison purposes and used at the criminal trial.
- Disclosure of defence and prosecution expert reports addressing issues related to Cognitive Impairment, produced and/or relied upon in court.
- Permission to consider and use transcripts of the expert and factual evidence given during the criminal trial, in so far as that evidence described or relied upon protected material, including the cockpit footage.

Her position was that:

'Dr Mitchell's paper presents a <u>credible suggestion</u> that the AAIB's investigation of the Cognitive Impairment issue was incomplete'.

She declared that, if given permission, she would seek to further investigate matters within the AAIB's reports. The families of three victims supported the application, each emphasising the *'importance of a full, fair and thorough investigation'*.

Hill also supported it, but made a broader submission arguing the AAIB's investigation was <u>actually</u> incomplete, flawed and deficient. The Coroner did not investigate his claims (perhaps because she knew them to be corroborated

---

31 At no time was Dr Mitchell's Christian name mentioned.

by separate, independent submissions); simply passing them to the AAIB for comment, knowing it was unlikely to criticise itself. And it didn't.

Using the same argument as before, the AAIB resisted the application on the grounds *'there is no public interest in re-examination of a matter which it has already considered'*, overlooking that while much had been 'considered', it had not been reported on; and much had not been considered at all. Also, while both the Coroner and AAIB were required to make recommendations on prevention of recurrence, the AAIB's were far from comprehensive - which the Coroner was fully aware of. Again, BALPA supported the AAIB. As ever, one might ask why the resistance? As such events unfold, it is always wise to go back to the source and re-read the report to place matters in context. Hitherto benign or easily overlooked comments suddenly took on huge significance; the main area being the 2015 test fights, of which there was very little detail.

The High Court refused to entertain Hill's submissions, saying it was *'not an appeal court for the AAIB'*, which rather neatly avoided one of the cardinal rules of natural justice, *Nemo judex in causa sua* (no-one should be a judge in their own cause), and that there was no other means of appealing.

Noting the Coroner sought further guidance on the protected status of the cockpit video footage, the court considered *Norfolk* and *Sussex*, and also an application made by the BBC in 2019 to use the same footage.[32] It noted the position of the Coroner and families was that *'both the Sussex and the BBC cases were decided in error'*, adding:

> *'It is wrong in principle for the Coroner to seek protected information before determining that there is at least credible evidence the AAIB investigation was incomplete, flawed or deficient'.*

A play on words. The Coroner had determined, via the Mitchell paper, there was a credible *suggestion*. The Court required *evidence*. The problem she caused herself was citing only Dr Mitchell's work, when firm *evidence* was not only before her, but staring everyone in the face following the criminal case. Moreover, the High Court ruling meant it was acceptable for the AAIB and MoD to conceal the full evidence, and it was up to Ms Schofield to identify

---

32 Secretary of State for Transport v Senior Coroner for Norfolk [2016] EWHC 2279 (Admin) (the *Norfolk* case); Chief Constable of Sussex Police v Secretary of State for Transport, British Airline Pilots Association [2016] EWHC 2280 (QB) (the *Sussex* case); and BBC v Secretary of State for Transport [2019] 4 WLR 23 (the *BBC* case).

what that evidence was. Once again the law was inadequate, rather assuming nobody would attempt concealment. I think the answer is to sanction the AAIB and MoD over attempting to perverting the course of justice. That would soon put a stop to this scheming.

In short, in a lengthy 35-page ruling issued on 4 February 2022 the High Court refused the Coroner's application, ruling there was:

- No public interest benefit in disclosing the protected material for use by Dr Mitchell or other experts who may be appointed by the Coroner to reinvestigate the Cognitive Impairment issue.
- Neither credible evidence nor (even adopting her approach) a credible suggestion that the AAIB investigations were incomplete, flawed or deficient on the issue of Cognitive Impairment.

It is difficult to find a word other than injudicious. No public interest? Eleven members of the public had been killed. But the criteria for public interest is not the interest of the *public*, but protection of those who are meant to serve the public. The ruling went far beyond any sensible interpretation of the law, strengthening it beyond the intent of *Norfolk*. Who benefitted? Certainly not the families, now contemptuously dismissed to protect Departments of State.

But, infinitely worse was this. Ms Schofield's application, and hence the court's ruling, only applied to there being no credible evidence of the AAIB investigation being incomplete <u>on the issue of Cognitive Impairment</u>. But she was now ordered to treat the entire report as 100% accurate. There were unintended, almost laughable, consequences. She was now required to heed the AAIB's confirmation that:

1. Hill was given an unairworthy and unserviceable aircraft.
2. The CAA failed in its duty.

It could be said she breached the order, in that her later finding (of Unlawful Killing) could not be reconciled with the High Court ruling. Was she in contempt of both courts, just the High Court, or just her own?

The 'Mitchell paper'

While Dr Mitchell was derided by Ms Schofield as a non-expert, to a layman such as myself I must say I find his report extraordinary and well-researched. It is more comprehensive that anything produced or discussed at trial, subsequently by the AAIB, or in what we know of MoD's work. It would not surprise me if MoD draws on it.

The Coroner and High Court both made a point of emphasising that Dr Mitchell was a friend of Hill's, the implication being this coloured his professional judgment and integrity. The same comments were not made regarding AAIB and MoD staff, who knew each other and colluded while acting for the prosecution. In fact, a feature of his paper is an immediate caveat that it is based on limited evidence, and must be used as a starting point for further investigation. In other words, it agrees with RAFCAM. At no time does it purport to be definitive. Contrast this with the prosecution's claims.

Quite why the Coroner seized on the paper, and took *it* to the High Court instead of the firm evidence she was sitting on of the AAIB investigation being deficient, only she can say. Taken with the derogatory comments, and the fact she never spoke to Dr Mitchell or followed-up on his suggestions for the next steps, I'm afraid the impression is she was going through the motions. But it may not be as black and white as that. Having described Dr Mitchell's views as *'credible'*, she later changed her mind - or was told to change it - but without offering a reason. We'll probably never know the truth, but her original belief, stated to the High Court, was obviously incompatible with her later finding of Unlawful Killing.

It must be said she was under enormous time pressure over the Inquest, and to make a wider and more relevant submission on incompleteness would probably have brought sanction upon her, the High Court perhaps seeing it as an attempt to reopen the investigation through the back door - effectively, asking it to rule not only on the AAIB's report, but also the offences committed by MoD and the AAIB, and the CAA's violations. Put another way, had the AAIB investigation and report been complete, and witnesses lived up to their oath to tell the whole truth surrounding the 2015 test flights, it is unlikely the High Court would have felt able to make the same order. In fact, matters wouldn't have got that far.

Summary

This situation, whereby criminal, civil and Coronial cases are subject to different interpretations of the same principles, is a job creation scheme for lawyers and courts, and a great waste of AAIB, police and court resources. In the interests of efficiency and fairness, it is crying out for a single, rational ruling. The solution, I believe, is to ignore the EU 'amendment' and allow all courts to use AAIB reports, but by all means grant anonymity. If a witness is found to have lied, then anonymity is lost anyway. (And the very fact this possibility is acknowledged in law calls into question the order to regard the

AAIB report as wholly accurate).

One might also apply this principle to the assumption of the AAIB's total independence, which the rulings are predicated upon. *Was the protected status of their investigations negated by their collusion with MoD?*

But above all else, there is a huge difference between not permitting the use of a few pages of specific witness evidence gathered by the AAIB, and binding the Coroner by law to accept the <u>whole</u> 452-page report as complete and accurate. In some circumstances this might be irrelevant, but it is surely inappropriate when used to effectively make a criminal judgment. That is too big a leap. Strictly speaking, within the confines of the law, the Judges may have been correct. But the law is often a complete ass. The rulings were not right or fair, nor did they further justice, knowledge of the accident, or prevention of recurrence. They were a direct attack on the families.

Finally, and worthy of note, in military cases subject to civil legal proceedings (Inquests, and in Scotland Fatal Accident Inquiries) matters are even more complicated. The report of the Service Inquiry, which the AAIB may have contributed to, is permitted in court, and the Branch may be called as a witness. Also, MoD will often release witness statements, but may withhold those that are detrimental to its case (which is usually against the pilot), and may alter those it does release. As with Inquests, there is no obligation to disclose evidence, and it is normal for evidence to be removed from the scene and concealed before investigators arrive. It is up to the bereaved to conduct their own investigation, and unearth any such evidence. The best-known example of this is the loss of RAF Chinook ZD576 in 1994 on the Mull of Kintyre. It took 17 years for the public 'investigation' to succeed, and have the Gross Negligence (manslaughter) findings against the pilots quashed.

Sussex Police Investigation

The role of the police is to gather evidence and make recommendations to the Crown Prosecution Service (CPS). It is for the CPS to assess this evidence and make a decision as to whether it is admissible, obtained fairly, and whether it is sufficient to bring a criminal case before the courts with a reasonable chance of obtaining a successful prosecution. This is made less straight-forward by the political dimension.

On 3 March 2017 Sussex Police received the final report from the AAIB, and began its investigation in earnest, using *'independent experts'*. It was dubbed 'Operation Bowdell'. Detective Chief Inspector Paul Rymarz:

'We have been waiting some time for this report and it will take us some time to review. Our progress has been dependent on this final report, and as a result of the ruling in the High Court much of the material contained in it has not been seen by the investigation team until now. We hope to do everything we can to submit a file of material to the CPS in advance of the Pre-Inquest Review on June 20'.

The High Court order of 28 September 2016 prevented the AAIB showing evidence to the police, even that which was not included in the report. And what information had been shared between 22 August 2015 and 28 September 2016? Could any police investigation be complete?

As the police report to the CPS is not in the public domain, I can only offer general observations:

- Regardless of who their 'experts' were, the police did not have the expertise to investigate such an accident; and certainly not the Hunter being unairworthy and unserviceable. Not a criticism, just fact. And given Hill's lasting amnesia, it is unlikely they gleaned further information from him. Were they capable of making a full and fair assessment of the AAIB report given it omitted so much?

- Like every other reader, the police could not help but notice that it was the CAA who was criticised, the AAIB reproducing hard evidence of systematic and systemic failings, and refusal to correct them. It revealed the CAA as negligent, not Hill. It is inconceivable they did not point this out to the CPS.

- In 2019 they should have written again to the CPS recommending action against MoD and the AAIB for conspiring to conceal evidence and perverting the course of justice.

Not having sight of the report, I believe it is fair to reproduce an internet post made by one of Hill's defence barristers, offering insight into how the police proceeded:

> *'Commentators may be interested to know that the police trawled through social media aviation sites and had screen shots of (e.g.) PPRuNe [Professional Pilots Rumour Network] and Flyer forums, etc. Sadly, in cases such as this defence lawyers are no longer paid by the hour for preparation, otherwise they would have been paid for reading endless pages of PPRuNe disclosed by the police. The police had actually contacted some of the "experts" on those threads in the hope that they were, indeed, experts. They received a wide range of opinion ranging from some well-informed guesswork through to the positively barking - there was one suggestion that the crash had been caused by alien involvement'.*

On 17 December 2015 the police sought to interview Hill under caution. He made no comment. On 1 June 2017 he was interviewed again, and again made no comment; but did provide a 10-page prepared statement. In summary:

- He had no memory of the event, and so could offer no insight as to why he made the errors he did.
- He could not understand why his engine speed had varied or why he had not applied full throttle in the run in to the loop, which he said would be instinctive. (There is no evidence that he did not apply full throttle). He could offer no explanation other than to say that *'It appears probable that I sustained a Cognitive Impairment for reasons that need further exploration'*.
- He provided police with a second prepared statement on 3 August 2017, setting out his normal practice before displaying, and that he had *'Never suffered a blackout, although had suffered the odd grey out since beginning aerobatic flying'*. In an attachment to this statement, he provided answers to questions posed on 1 June.

On 30 November 2017 he provided another statement, further discussing his normal practices and, having been able to view bystanders' video, expressed a belief:

- His entry speed to the manoeuvre was lower than it had been on previous flights.
- He had rolled out of the turn and approached the Bent Loop from the

perfect position.
- The *g*-forces experienced by him may have been a factor.
- Cognitive Impairment did not require that there was a total absence of control input by the pilot. (A statement of fact).

These statements were made only after he was able to read the AAIB report; hence, some are a reaction to the supposition it contained. It is likely his legal representatives advised him not to comment before this. At this point he had not been permitted to view the cockpit videos he had taken. There is a procedural subtlety here. It is a feature of criminal proceedings that the police can interview/question prior to charging, but once charged there is no more interaction; so they could not show him the video. Whether the AAIB or CPS should have is another question. He was criticised in some quarters for apparent lack of cooperation. But how was he to comment on accusations of poor airmanship, if he was not permitted to see and assess the alleged evidence? I believe this prejudiced media reporting.

The police engaged two RAF officers to advise on Cognitive Impairment. One was a cardiac specialist. The second was also an advisor to the CAA and AAIB, and the prosecution's expert medical witness at trial - the defence proving the key aspect of his evidence incorrect. Therefore, the police report was similarly flawed if he gave them the same advice. That apart, they would not have seen anything in the AAIB report suggesting grounds for a prosecution of Hill. Also, as I have explained, much evidence was concealed, and it is likely they at least suspected this. Above all else, it would certainly be obvious, even to non-aviation experts, that the AAIB report was incomplete.

The decision to charge

The test applied by the Crown Prosecution Service [33]
There are two tests to satisfy before a prosecution will take place:
1. The evidential test - the realistic prospect of conviction. That, in the view of the CPS, a jury is more likely to convict than not. It must assess the evidence as credible and reliable; and be satisfied of its sufficiency, or if more could be obtained through further reasonable lines of inquiry.
2. The public interest test, which takes into account:
   - The seriousness of the alleged offence.
   - The level of culpability of the accused should he be found guilty.
   - The circumstances of and the harm caused to the victim(s).
   - The suspect's age and maturity.
   - The impact on the community.
   - Is a prosecution a proportionate response?
   - Do sources of information require protecting?

Together, this is termed the 'Full Code Test'. In limited circumstances, if it is not met a Threshold Test is applied. It has five elements:
- There are reasonable grounds to suspect that the person to be charged has committed the offence being considered. (Indeed, has there even been an offence?) The assessment must consider the impact of any defence or information that the suspect has put forward or on which they might rely.
- There are reasonable grounds to believe that the continuing investigation will provide further evidence, within a reasonable period of time.
- The seriousness or the circumstances of the case justifies the making of an immediate charging decision.
- There are continuing substantial grounds to object to bail.
- It is in the public interest to charge the suspect.

It cannot be known whether the CPS thought the Full Code Test was satisfied, or if it proceeded to the Threshold Test.

My view is that the content of the AAIB report meant the very first hurdle was

---

33 https://www.cps.gov.uk/publication/code-crown-prosecutors

not cleared, the realistic prospect of conviction. Any knowledgeable, independent examination of the known facts, <u>arrived at by the CPS's own advisors</u>, would conclude this. That of course would not, at that stage, prove innocence (or guilt), but that is not the issue.

It cannot be known which test the CPS took the decision to charge against. But of one thing there is no doubt. Between August 2015 and the trial in January 2019, the case was extensively analysed by people vastly experienced in aircraft accidents and their investigation, and the precise outcome predicted. Perhaps the CPS were just too close, and needed to stand back and look at similar cases. For example, their correct decision not to prosecute Martin-Baker in the Sean Cunningham case, where many of the same issues and evidence were exculpatory.

The CPS had ample time to consider whether the Test(s) could be met. Between September 2016 and March 2018 they knew of the High Court order prohibiting the use of the AAIB report, despite it being fully available to the public (and potential jurors). And while the Tests are well-intentioned, the rules rather assume the prosecution's advisors (the AAIB and MoD) will not actively conceal evidence that would cause the evidential test to fail. They also assume the CPS has the knowledge to assess and understand the nuances of what, here, was highly specialised evidence relating to Technical, Airmanship, Legal and Medical aspects; and that the AAIB report is complete.

One can only conclude the CPS were relying on the High Court denying the court *all the circumstances*. A risky strategy. This is a difficult area. If the AAIB report had *not* been released, the cry of 'cover-up' would have boomed. So, while it would have provided Hill with an obvious defence, having been actively prevented from advancing it meant Cognitive Impairment was his only practical route. This would be fairly obvious; and in any case it was made known before trial, so the CPS should have asked its own 'experts' if they could absolutely refute the defence's position. Their answer would have been an unequivocal *No*, which was later their sworn position in court.

Of equal import, the CPS should also have confirmed its advisors, and the witnesses it intended calling, could substantiate their allegations against Hill. When later placed under oath, they could not.

Notwithstanding, on 21 March 2018 the CPS charged Hill with:

1. Eleven counts of Gross Negligence Manslaughter, and;
2. Endangering the safety of an aircraft contrary to Article 137 of Air Navigation Order 2009. *('A person must not recklessly or negligently act in a manner likely to endanger an aircraft, or any person in an aircraft').*

What should have been considered here is that, as a pilot, he relied on others who, unknown to him, had consciously suborned the regulations they were bound by. Yes, the CPS would have some difficult questions to answer, but that comes with the territory if you are going to ignore serious offences by your own advisors. Better to be honest and transparent. One way out of this dilemma would have been to recommend a public inquiry.

Negligence

There is a distinction between Negligence and Gross Negligence. That is not the *kind* of negligence, but *degree* of negligence.

- Negligence is commonly defined as *'the inadvertent taking of an unjustifiable risk'*.
- Gross Negligence is *'a conscious act or omission in disregard of a legal duty and of the consequences to another party'*.[34]

In other words, degree relates to appreciation of the risks involved, together with serious disregard or indifference. The outcome (in this case death) is not a factor in determining degree.

If a risk to life is properly notified by experts in the field, along with the mitigation required to reduce the risk to As Low As Reasonably Practicable, and this notification is rejected, it follows a conscious decision was made. But that does not necessarily constitute an offence due (for example) to the principle allowing a Cost Benefit Analysis. But, if the rejection is accompanied by a false declaration, especially if self-serving, that would be clear evidence of intent. Rather, the question to be asked is:

'Having regard to the risk of death involved, was the conduct of the defendant so bad in all the circumstances as to amount to a criminal act or omission?'

Particularly relevant here is that inexperience cannot equate to negligence.

The *Misra* decision is important in determining grossness and mistakes, the key test being whether a reasonably prudent person would have foreseen a serious and obvious risk of death arising from the act or omission. The Court of Appeal ruled:

'Mistakes, even very serious mistakes, and errors of judgment, even very serious errors of judgment, are nowhere near enough for a crime as serious

---

34 Ormerod D. Smith 8 Hogan's Criminal Law (11th edition). Oxford University Press, 2005.

as manslaughter to be committed. The defendant's conduct must fall so far below the standard to be expected of a reasonably competent and careful (person in the defendant's position) that it was something truly exceptionally bad'.[35]

Again this refers to intent. Knowingly permitting recurrence is a key element, and one need only prove the effect was notified. The breach does not have to be the only cause of death, nor even the principal cause; but it must have more than *'minimally, negligibly or trivially'* caused it. It is not for the jury to evaluate competing causes or choose which was dominant, provided they are satisfied that the defendant's actions (or in this case those of others) could be said to have been a significant contribution to the victim's death.

Hill's final actions (or lack of) were undoubtedly a significant factor; but so too were those of other parties identified by the AAIB, made worse by being conscious violations. It was the duty of the legal system to explore these and have the parties explain them. The High Court ruling ensured it would not.

Manslaughter

Manslaughter is primarily committed in one of three ways:

1. Killing with the intent for murder but where a partial defence applies, namely loss of control, diminished responsibility or killing pursuant to a suicide pact.
2. Conduct that was grossly negligent given the risk of death, and did kill. (Gross Negligence Manslaughter).
3. Conduct taking the form of an unlawful act involving a danger of some harm that resulted in death. (Unlawful and Dangerous Act Manslaughter).

The term 'Voluntary Manslaughter' is commonly used to describe manslaughter falling within (1); while (2) and (3) are referred to as 'Involuntary Manslaughter'.

Where an unlawful killing is done without an intention to kill or to cause grievous bodily harm, the suspect is to be charged with manslaughter not murder. Apart from the absence of the requisite intent, all other elements of the offence are the same as for murder.

Unlawful Act Manslaughter

The prosecution must prove an intentional act (not omission); that the act is

---

35 *Misra* (2004) EWCA Crim 2375.

unlawful; and it is an act which all sober and reasonable people would inevitably realise must subject the victim to at least some risk of harm.

Again, a well-known example of this is the RAF Chinook ZD576 case, when 29 were killed on the Mull of Kintyre in 1994. An conscious and illegal decision was made by a senior officer to tell aircrew the aircraft was airworthy, when he was under mandate that it was not to be relied upon in any way whatsoever.[36] No action was taken, the offender not even interviewed.

Gross Negligence Manslaughter

This is committed where the death is a result of a grossly negligent (though otherwise lawful) act or omission. The elements of this offence are:

'The breach of an existing duty of care which it is reasonably foreseeable gives rise to a serious and obvious risk of death and does, in fact, cause death in circumstances where, having regard to the risk of death, the conduct of the defendant was so bad in all the circumstances as to amount to a criminal act or omission'.[37]

The most common case law is *R v Adomako [1994]*, whereby the defendant, Mr Adomako, was an anaesthetist during an eye operation during which the patient was required to be placed under a general anaesthetic. During the operation, and whilst under Mr Adomako's supervision, a crucial tube became disconnected from the ventilator and the patient suffered a fatal cardiac arrest. Mr Adomako was convicted of manslaughter by breach of duty, and his appeal subsequently dismissed.

The Judge must impress upon the jury the high threshold for gross failure, and that duty of care has no time or geographical limit. The jury is permitted to take into account any other factors which it may consider relevant; for example, the following constitute *prima facie* evidence of grossness:

- Failing to act following 'near misses' or occurrences.
- Failure to follow the organisation's written, mandated procedures and regulations designed to prevent recurrence.
- Indiscriminate cost cutting.
- Ignoring or concealing evidence of any of the above.

All of these apply in this case - to others, not Hill.

---

36 Lord Philip, Mull of Kintyre Review, paragraph 2.2.8.
37 *Rudling [2016] EWCA Crim 741*

TWISTED TRUTH

The Trial (16 January - 6 March 2019)

Regina
v
Andrew Hill

As I said, my aim is to explain why Hill was acquitted. It will be clear by now that, to achieve this end, it is more important to discuss evidence that was <u>not</u> given, was undisclosed, and prohibited. The latter is possible because the AAIB report remains in the public domain. Despite the High Court ruling being explained to them, it is likely the jurors realised that without direct AAIB and CAA evidence it was impossible to come to an informed judgment; especially as the CAA had received severe criticism (in addition to the AAIB being proven wrong). They may also have noted that AAIB reports are not subject to a standard of proof; the decision on what to claim and publish, and on what evidence, lying with the Chief Inspector, who was never required to justify a report which the CPS relied upon. Similarly, the Health and Safety Executive were not called, their evidence being harmful to the CAA and organisers, not to Hill.

The practical difficulty this posed both jury and defence was, while evidence led may have been truthful to the best of a witness's ability, recollection, or the constraints he was under, it was <u>not the whole truth</u>. Each swore under oath to tell the whole truth, but in fact this should have been qualified with '*as far as I am permitted*'. Once again, this speaks to the politically motivated decision to prosecute. I cannot help but conclude this, because the CPS had recently reviewed similar evidence in the Sean Cunningham inadvertent ejection case, and correctly and sensibly decided not to prosecute Martin-Baker. In both cases false declarations were made to the pilot. Both had been let down by their regulators. The only difference was the public horror of Shoreham.

One difficulty in writing about the trial is that extensive use was made of visual aids (mainly model aircraft), hand gestures indicating flight manoeuvres, and a plethora of lengthy videos; none of which I can reproduce in a narrative form. So, to take you through all the witness testimony would, I think, be mind-numbingly boring. Rather, I think the aim will be better served if I constrain myself to discussing the key elements of the testimony that had a direct effect on the verdict.

The trial transcripts were not released until the Coroner sought a court ruling, paid for them, and distributed them to interested parties on 25 June 2019. I did not attend the trial, but am grateful to one good friend who did, and for access to his extensive notes. My normal practice is to seek, as far as possible, independent corroboration. Here, the press reporting was misleading and mostly incomplete. Much of it was taken from the prosecution's opening statement - which it had distributed to all and sundry beforehand in a 53-page document. The (perhaps natural) result was the media regurgitating large chunks of it over the next two months as if it were 'live' reporting and factually accurate; despite much of it being proven inaccurate in court, and the jury directed to ignore the parts most important to the prosecution case. During that period, their readers were led to believe the verdict was not in doubt. When Hill was acquitted there was outrage; but no attempt to explain why, because that would reveal their reporting was plain wrong.

However, my task is made easier by the prosecution witnesses, almost to a man, acting as superb defence witnesses. I have to emphasise this, otherwise you will be utterly confused by what follows. A major question that must be asked is this. *Could such a scenario have been foreseen by the CPS?* The answer is categorically *Yes*; and the AAIB report contained the necessary supporting information.

The Judge, and conduct of a trial [38]

The trial took place in Court No.8 at the Central Criminal Court of England and Wales, commonly referred to as the Old Bailey after the street on which it stands in central London. The Crown Court sitting there hears major criminal cases from within Greater London. In exceptional cases, trials may be referred from other parts of England and Wales. As with most courts, trials are open to the public; they may take notes, but may not record proceedings.

All Judges sitting in the Old Bailey are addressed as 'My Lord' or 'My Lady' whether they are High Court, circuit judges or recorders. The Judge appointed to the trial was Lord Justice Edis (The Right Honourable Sir Andrew Edis), at the time a Presiding Judge for the South Eastern Circuit and a member of the

---

38 https://www.judiciary.uk/about-the-judiciary/our-justice-system/jurisdictions/criminal-jurisdiction/

Investigatory Powers Tribunal. In October 2022 he was appointed Senior Presiding Judge for England and Wales; succeeding Justice Sir Charles Haddon-Cave, who took on the Afghan Unlawful Killings Inquiry.

Criminal cases come to court after a decision has been made by, usually the CPS, to prosecute someone for an alleged crime. Other bodies who may prosecute include the Health and Safety Executive (HSE), the Civil Aviation Authority (CAA) and the Post Office. Readers will be all too aware of the Post Office scandal whereby over 700 postmasters were unfairly prosecuted, the abuse of power so great that it will be interesting to see if it is stripped of these powers. I've already mentioned the Martin-Baker case, where the HSE took over the prosecution when the Crown Prosecution Service (CPS) declined to proceed. The CAA's powers are set out in the Civil Aviation Act 1982, but this does not extend to manslaughter prosecutions. It is therefore likely discussions took place between the CAA and CPS. Had the latter not proceeded with Gross Negligence Manslaughter, the CAA would probably have done so with endangering the aircraft.

(On 19 June 2019, Dorset Police announced that they had arrested a man on suspicion of manslaughter by an unlawful act in respect of the death of footballer Emiliano Sala, who had been killed when the light aircraft he was travelling in crashed into the English Channel. On 11 March 2020 it was reported no further action would be taken against him by the CPS. However, in October 2021 he was prosecuted by the CAA and found guilty of arranging a flight without permission or authorisation and of endangering the safety of an aircraft).

The vast majority of cases (over 95%), are heard in the Magistrates' Court, either by a panel of three Magistrates or by a District Judge. They hear the evidence, and make a decision on guilt or innocence. If the defendant is found guilty, the Magistrates or District Judge will decide the sentence, or send the case to the Crown Court for sentencing if they believe a custodial sentence beyond their powers is appropriate.

More serious criminal cases are heard in the Crown Court, usually by a Circuit Judge or Recorder sitting with a jury. In the most serious, the case may be heard by a High Court Judge sitting with a jury, which is what took place here. The jury is responsible for deciding whether the defendant is guilty. In England and Wales it consists of 12 members (15 in Scotland). They are permitted to ask questions of clarification and seek guidance on matters of law. They are not permitted to discuss the case after the event - ever - whereas in the USA, for example, they frequently write books about their experience.

Before the trial starts, the Judge will familiarise himself with the details of the case by reading the relevant case papers. These include the indictment setting out the charges on which the defendant is to be tried, witness statements, exhibits, and documentation on applications to be made by any party concerning the admissibility of evidence. Plainly, this process assumes that what is placed before the Judge is true, and doesn't mislead by commission or omission.

Once the trial commences, he ensures all parties are given the opportunity for their case to be presented and considered. He plays an active role, controlling the way the case is conducted in accordance with relevant law and practice. As it progresses, he decides on legal issues.

Once all evidence has been heard, he will sum up. He sets out for the jury the law on each of the charges made, and what the prosecution must prove. At this stage he refers to notes made during the course of the trial, and reminds the jury of the key points of the case, highlighting the strengths and weaknesses of each side's argument. He then gives directions about the duties of the jury before they retire to the jury deliberation room to consider the verdict.

If the jury finds the defendant guilty then the Judge will decide on an appropriate sentence. Imprisonment is not the only one that may be imposed; a community punishment or fine may be deemed more appropriate. He will be influenced by a number of factors: principally the seriousness of the offence, the impact that the crime has had on the victim(s), relevant law - especially guidance from the Sentencing Council - and take into account the mitigation and any reports and references on the defendant. He will also consider how a particular sentence may reduce the chances of an individual re-offending. Only once he has considered all of these factors will the sentence or punishment be handed down.

The standard of proof in criminal cases is *beyond reasonable doubt*, whereas in a civil matter it is *balance of probabilities*. In the Coroners Court it is a mixture of the two, something that becomes important later. If a jury is hung, the judge may accept a 10-2 majority.

Witness testimony

Witnesses are first examined-in-chief by their own side, followed by cross-examination by the opposing barrister. This is usually the critical part, where the barrister adds new elements, or tries to disrupt the organised examination-in-chief. Finally the first barrister re-examines. He is not supposed to introduce anything new, but clarify (or try to rescue) evidence from the cross-examination.

Oral witnesses are split into two categories; expert and non-expert. Only expert witnesses may offer their opinion on a set of facts, and they have to comply with certain court rules about being objective and having a duty to the court. Witnesses who are not called as experts may only give factual evidence, not their opinion. I ask you to remember this subtlety, because some non-expert prosecution witnesses deviated and offered unsupported opinion; often as if it were fact. (In much the same way the AAIB report did). At one point, this caused the Judge to shut down prosecution examination-in-chief. This is why Counsels are often aggressive towards witnesses who are not what they profess, or who seek to offer more than permitted. When selecting expert witnesses, one must be careful to ensure they truly are expert, and that what they are asked to give opinion on is uncontested fact. This, too, became relevant.

It would be confusing to follow the strict order in which witnesses appeared, so I have grouped the evidence into categories; however within each category I have addressed the evidence in sequence:

- First Response
- Airshow Organisation
- Operations
- Flying
- Image Analysts
- Medical

The first three are essentially background, and none were expert witnesses. Of the ten Flying witnesses, only the last five were called as experts; as were the two Image Analysts. All three Medical witnesses were experts. When I say 'expert', that is in the specific subjects they were engaged on.

A ruling of law

On the first day, a joint application was made to the Judge by the BBC and the Press Association, who sought to broadcast the cockpit footage as part of their coverage of the trial. They cited a long-established legal principle of open justice, and the desirability of being able to broadcast material seen by a jury as part of responsible and well-informed reporting of an important criminal trial. The British Airline Pilots Association (BALPA) became aware of this application the day before it was due to be heard, and immediately opposed it. The Judge agreed to allow BALPA to take part, and gave all parties seven days to submit evidence. This culminated in a day-long hearing on 23 January 2019.

BALPA argued that allowing cockpit footage of an aircraft accident to be released to the media, thereby putting it permanently and indelibly on the internet, would undermine confidence in the AAIB and discourage pilots from creating such footage, which is of obvious potential value to accident investigators. You will appreciate that essentially the same argument was being raised yet again.

The Judge agreed, and refused the application:

> 'I am not satisfied that the benefit of disclosure outweighs the adverse impact on future safety investigations it will have. It is a matter of real importance that the international air investigation world accepts that the UK complies with its obligations under [EU Regulation 996 and supplementing UK regulations], and treats those obligations seriously'.[39]

Once again, the ruling went beyond the intent of the law. Had he cited potential upset of the bereaved I would have been more accepting. I would have applauded had he laughed at the very thought of the BBC in London attempting 'responsible and well-informed reporting'; especially a mere seven weeks after providing the HSE a platform on which to repeat their lies to the Judge in the Martin-Baker/Cunningham case.[40]

The proceedings

After the jury was sworn in, but before the prosecution opened, one juror was discharged. He had admitted to staff he knew of the accident before he had learnt any details about the case from court, remarking that he was *'never going to find anybody guilty'* because it was an accident, and *'they could say what they like but [I am] never going to change [my] mind'*. (It is likely he had read the AAIB report). The Judge called this a *'clear statement of bias'*, saying it was the bias that caused concern, not that he favoured the defendant. He was replaced. This event could only be reported after the trial finished. While I understand the Judge's concern in isolation, anyone reading the report would realise the would-be juror had made fair comment.

---

39 https://d15khrjun3ryw0.cloudfront.net/2019/02/BBC-PA-v-SEC-ST-FOR-TRANSPORT-FINAL.pdf
40 'Defenders UK', Season 1, Episode 8, broadcast 5 December 2018.

On 29 January one juror fell ill and was taken by ambulance to hospital. She was excused further jury service, leaving seven women and four men.

Given the High Court ruling, no accident investigator, nor anyone from the CAA, appeared to explain their work. The jurors were told the AAIB report would not form part of the evidence and should be disregarded. I believe this created a huge problem in their minds, not least because the prosecution case was built entirely upon selected extracts from it - mainly the incomplete and deficient parts. For its part the defence would have heavily relied on it, as it revealed prior failings and root causes not of the pilot's making. If it did not quite exonerate him, it demonstrated that if blame were to be apportioned, others were more likely candidates.

But that did not prevent the content being discussed, because the prosecution and defence were free to mount their own investigations and lead this in evidence. They could interview the same witnesses, but if their evidence differed from that given to the AAIB this could not be revealed in court. This is a good example of where the Judge must exercise close control over his court, and Justice Edis proved himself adept. It is also a good example of where money talks - it being prohibitively expensive for most defendants to re-run an investigation, especially when not permitted to know who actually gave evidence first time around.

The proceedings were interspersed with a number of legal argument sessions. In addition to video disclosure to the press; non-AAIB video, newly submitted witness evidence, anonymity of witnesses, the agreed facts and historic video from previous airshows, defence expert reports, and disclosure of further AAIB material.

Also, 24 witness statements were read out in two lengthy sessions, over two days. This was deemed 'uncontentious' evidence, and is normal. Additionally, 14 character witness statements were read; including a past leader of the Red Arrows, a former director of the Empire Test Pilot School, and a pilot to the royal families of the UK and Jordan who was a former RAF fighter pilot. They spoke of Hill's high personal standards and his awareness of regulatory, operational and aircraft limits. One mentioned his *'superior intellect and ability to project ahead, identifying potential errors or hazardous situations and mitigating them'*. Another spoke of his *'threat error management'*. Yet another said, *'Compared to his peers, Andy Hill's situational awareness was excellent'*. Of course, none of this precludes error, their point being he was not the reckless cowboy painted by the prosecution.

Prosecution opening (Mr Tom Kark QC)

Mr Kark was not just hired for the 2019 trial, having been advising the CPS from summer 2017, prior to the charging decision. He began:

> 'The Hunter crashed because Andy Hill had not reached a safe gate height, he was quite simply too low at the top of the loop. There are three possibilities we suggest:
> 1. He checked his altimeter and must have realised he was low, but he thought that by lowering some more flap to give the aircraft some extra lift he would be alright and could get away with it;
> 2. He simply failed to check his altimeter with sufficient care and somehow misread it, or;
> 3. He simply did not bother to look at his altimeter because he was judging his height by eye and experience.
>
> Whichever version is right, once he committed the aircraft fully to the descent, he and all those below him were in extreme danger, because he was going to crash'.

This pointedly excluded possible incapacitation. He added:

> 'Until the moment that it crashed, there was nothing wrong with the flying capabilities of that aircraft. It was in excellent working condition'.

Mr Kark knew the AAIB had already proved this untrue - and later his own witnesses would confirm it as untrue. I note that the Crown has adopted the same tactic in other cases, such as Chinook ZD576, Nimrod XV230, Sea Kings XV650 & XV704, Hercules XV179, Hawk XX177. (61 killed in just those accidents, and there are more). Occasionally, the lie is identified immediately (e.g. XV179). But more often the defence or families lack the necessary expertise, information or resources to challenge. In fact, Mr Kark had himself been a victim of this, when representing the Cunningham family in the XX177 case; only finding out during the 2014 Inquest that MoD had lied and withheld exculpatory evidence. He declined to put this to the Coroner, it being left to the public. Again, the evidence of the lie was in the accident report.

He continued, saying *'The jet...had a valid Permit to Fly'*. But it was not valid. Immediately, the impact of the High Court ruling of 2016 was evident. The truth was not only being concealed, but blatant untruths being put to the jury. Also, it was the prosecution's case that because the aircraft flew in July 2015, and the pilot on that flight did not report any faults, it was therefore serviceable some weeks later at Shoreham. This has no logical basis. (Try challenging an MoT failure on the grounds your car passed last year). It was also implied that cockpit and ground footage was a valid substitute for a Flight Data Recorder.

It might be wondered why the Judge didn't interrupt and instruct the jury to ignore these claims. This is not as fanciful as it sounds. At the Chinook ZD576 Fatal Accident Inquiry in 1996, Sheriff Sir Stephen Young immediately challenged the Crown's QC when he told a witness to ignore a critical airworthiness issue. (Aircraft Icing restrictions). Similarly, Oxford Coroner Andrew Walker rejected the Crown's statement in the Nimrod XV230 case that airworthiness was *'irrelevant'*, halted proceedings, and demanded that MoD produce copies of the regulations.

Defence opening (Mr Karim Khalil QC)

Mr Khalil's opening was brief. He reiterated that his client was seriously injured in the accident and had no memory of events, and for that reason would not be questioned on this.

He agreed Hill had made errors, and not only at Shoreham; but had dealt with them in a respectful and professional manner, his aim being to prevent recurrence. He then escalated matters by telling the jury:

> *'You will hear of a particular mistake made by a prosecution expert, even as he conducted his investigation in this very case. You will be able to judge his explanation, and you will be able to contrast how he conducted himself in its aftermath'.*

At this point he did not mention this evidence (from the test flights) had been withheld by the AAIB and MoD for over three years. Given the disclosure timescales, it is possible he/the defence had insufficient time to assimilate and truly appreciate the scale of the gift that had been handed to them.

He summarised the prosecution case, saying it:

> *'Alleges it can all be explained by pilot errors - most importantly, that Andy Hill <u>deliberately</u> flew in the way that led to the fatal crash; also, that he <u>deliberately</u> failed to take evasive action while he still had time'.*

He said he would be challenging the allegation of deliberate act, adding:

> *'This case may not be about pilot error at all; because Andy Hill may not have been in full control of all he was doing. We will present evidence he may have been suffering from Cognitive Impairment'.*

He described the symptom succinctly, introducing the concept of g-forces. He emphasised his use of *'may not have been in full control'*, reminding the jury that the defence did not have to prove anything, it was for the prosecution to prove Hill did <u>not</u> suffer impairment.

First response

The only first responder who appeared was Anthony Kemp, a senior lecturer of medical education at the University of Bedfordshire, and an examiner for the Royal College of Surgeons in Edinburgh. On the day, he was a volunteer immediate responder for the South East coast immediate care scheme; his job to keep people alive until they reached hospital. He saved Andrew Hill's life.

Mr Kemp was most impressive, recounting that when the crash occurred he was attending to a lady who needed assistance, on the flight line close to the A27. He was tasked to go back to the main first aid centre, which was the combined operations control and hospital area for the airfield.

There, the communications officer contacted the South East Coast Ambulance Service by radio, who had already received a number of 999 calls. Dispatched to the scene, he picked up two doctors on the way who were attending as spectators, Marianne Jackson and Karen Eastman. (All three were recipients of Royal Humane Society awards, presented by Princess Alexandra the following May). Upon arrival they were told by a police officer the pilot was alive. A swift assessment of each other's specialisms meant Dr Jackson went to tend the severely injured.

Mr Kemp and Dr Eastman worked their way across an 8-foot wide ditch and through a wooded area, the terrain underfoot made difficult by broken trees and bushes; and the ever-present danger of the dry scrubland being set ablaze by the raging fires caused by aviation fuel, which were no more than 20 feet away and being blown towards them by a 15 knot wind. Such was the dense smoke and noxious fumes, the two firefighters there were using breathing apparatus, but the medics didn't have any.

They found Hill in the scrub, lying parallel to the cockpit area, which had detached from the main fuselage. His helmet was off, and he was not in his seat. Still armed, this was lying under wreckage. Mr Kemp's initial impression was that Hill, his eyes closed, was unconscious. There was a lot of noise and he couldn't hear if he was trying to communicate. It became apparent he was semi-conscious and able to respond, albeit slowly.

He and Dr Eastman assessed his injuries as serious. Hill was obtunded (diminished responsiveness to stimuli, often due to a state of reduced consciousness), wasn't complying with basic commands to lie still, kept pushing the oxygen mask away, and struggling against what they were trying to do. He was having difficulty understanding what was being said to him; he would eventually say he understood, and then not remember, and the medics would have to repeat. He was bleeding profusely from a head injury, his face covered in blood, and this was initially thought to be the main problem.

His breathing was fast, with a fast radial pulse (in the wrist, just below the thumb). At that point he was compensating quite well, but the medics were wary of evolving injuries as this scenario is quite common in the very early part of an accident. It was difficult to check for pelvic injuries normally associated with high impact events, and they quickly became aware there was something critical going on in his chest.

His breathing became more laboured, and suddenly collapsed very seriously, very rapidly, to the point where he was about to have a cardiac arrest. He had a life-threatening punctured lung (tension pneumothorax, which distorts the heart). Rapid intervention was necessary; a needle was inserted in his chest to take the air out, and he responded quickly.

50mg of Ketamine was administered intravenously, a very strong dose. This immediately sedated him and he lost consciousness. Ketamine is a dissociative anaesthetic that has some hallucinogenic effects. It distorts perceptions of sight and sound and makes the user feel disconnected. Larger doses cause amnesia. If or when memory returns, recollections are often jumbled or inaccurate, and hence unreliable. It is also well known as a date rape drug; not only to facilitate the rape, but wipe out the memory.

Had Hill not received this treatment he would have died at the scene. He was placed in an induced coma, recovered well albeit with amnesia, and eventually discharged home on 9 September, almost three weeks after the crash.

The above events were recorded by one of the cameras in the cockpit, which was still operating. The video showed just the cockpit, so only audio was played in court.

Airshow Organisation - The first turning point

Rod Dean (Flying Display Director)

Mr Dean explained his role; in this context being responsible to the CAA, and being the person who communicated any *stop* call to the pilots. He said the sole function of the Flying Display Committee was to *'act as his eyes and ears, monitoring safety in action'*.

He had conducted two pilot briefings that day; at 0945, and 1245 for those displaying in the afternoon. Hill's had been by telephone. Also, they had spoken two weeks before at Blackpool, with him having no concerns over the display flown there, describing it as *'well performed and very smooth'*. He agreed Hill was *'less of a show-off'* than himself.

The 1245 briefing meant he had to leave for the south end of the airfield shortly before the Hunter display. He was further diverted by displayers voicing concern over the weather forecast, and the need for their model aircraft to be on the ground before the Hunter displayed. He saw the Hunter's first pass, which he recalled as *'fine'*, but was speaking to others when it crashed.

In reply to Mr Khalil for the defence, he confirmed there are no set ways of flying routines, with individual pilots having developed their own. Specifically, some may feel confident approaching a loop at a lower speed. He confirmed his own target at pull-up would be 300-350 knots. (Hill was at 310 ±15 knots), saying 20° of flap would give the aircraft around 1g more pull, and make it more stable. Finally, he confirmed he had *'no problems whatsoever'* with Hill's display at Shoreham the previous year.

Dave Evans (Flying Control Committee)

Mr Evans was the member responsible for flying standards and disciplines, appointed by the FDD. He had previously been a Display Evaluator and Display Inspector for the CAA. There was an immediate contradiction: Mr Dean had said every committee member carried a radio - Mr Evans hadn't.

He stated he had watched the Hunter display and *'nothing made me think anything was wrong'*. Realisation set in when he saw the aircraft nose *'go below the horizon'*. He saw the wings rock, an indication of stall onset.

To Mr Stephen Spence for the defence, he described the procedure whereby a *stop* call would be initiated, and what would follow. He agreed that on the day it had taken him *'a while to work out what was going on'*.

Derek Davies (Flying Control Committee Chairman)

Mr Davies was a former RAF pilot and instructor, teaching aerobatics and formation flying, and then became airline pilot. He had chaired the committee for 15 years.

On the matter of the radios he confirmed Mr Dean's evidence, that all members had (or should have had) one. He stated that any member of the committee could issue a *stop* call (assuming they had access to a radio).

He said *'It all looked normal'* at the apex, but he became concerned over the apparent slow speed from the moment the descent began, as he heard no power being applied.

> 'It continued waffling down at about 150 knots, at about a 45° angle, and when it got to about 100 feet it did a violent pitch up at about 30° or more. He was not pulling back as if trying to miss the ground. I think that at 100 feet there was probably some recovery, I think his eyes suddenly opened, or he saw something, and instinctively pitched up'.

He stated he had not watched any videos of the accident until 19 months later when the AAIB issued its report.

Cross-examined by Mr Spence, he confirmed he thought the speed correct at the apex. Asked if the aircraft was high enough, he said *'Yes'*. At this point the court was emptied while the Judge heard from the prosecution. It was clear Mr Kark didn't expect his witness to say the aircraft was at the correct height and speed at apex, which was the entire substance of his case. Mr Spence characterised this as *'the first curiosity'*. The first turning point.

This ended the evidence from airshow staff. I remain puzzled over why these witnesses were selected by the prosecution. It's as if they were not taken through their evidence, or the prosecution didn't understand that it wholly undermined their case - under prosecution questioning! The defence had nothing to do save have them repeat it. That is the problem the prosecution faced. It <u>had</u> to produce witnesses. I cannot imagine what the jury thought. *That's all you've got? But they've just contradicted your opening remarks.* They weren't poor witnesses. They were honest and extremely helpful. Just not to the prosecution. If this were a John Grisham courtroom thriller, the book would end now with the Crown dramatically withdrawing all charges and everyone going down the pub.

Operations

Two maintenance engineers from Weald Aviation Services appeared for the prosecution; but no management, nor the owner or operator.

<u>Fran Renouf</u>

Mr Renouf was the Deputy Chief Engineer at Weald, and had worked for their predecessors from 2000. Prior to that he had been in the Royal Navy for 14 years working mainly on Sea Harriers. His main role was to support the Chief

Engineer in the running of the maintenance side of the business, ensure all work was carried out in a satisfactory and safe manner, and that records were updated regularly.

Mr Renouf confirmed he was involved in the revalidation of the Permit to Fly. Asked if the aircraft was serviceable every time the Permit was renewed, he stated it was. (The question avoided that to be declared serviceable it first had to be airworthy). He explained the maintenance regime, which was standard. The main difference between his RN experiences and now was having to seek the owner's permission to spend money every time work was required.

Asked if there were any faults prior to the accident flight, he stated the Aileron Trim Gauge was inoperative; but this did not have any bearing on the safety of the aircraft, and that G-BXFI was in very good shape.

Charlie Selwyn

Mr Selwyn joined Weald in 2013, having been employed as a plumber. His training was on-the-job, starting with odd jobs, progressing to maintenance, then servicing, and general tasks on the aircraft. He stated he had now served an apprenticeship as an *'engineer'*, but in 2015 was allowed to work on aircraft only under strict supervision. Asked about the ejection seats, he confirmed they were included in his inspections. If he had a problem, he would *'report to my Chief Engineer to come and inspect'*.

He had carried out the final pre-flight check on G-BXFI the previous morning. This was done in accordance with Air Publication 101B-1300-5B1 (Flight Servicing Schedule), and took between 2-3 hours. (The defence had provided the publication to the prosecution). Cross-examined by Mr Spence, he confirmed the first edition of 5B1 was issued in September 1977, but it was not stated what edition Weald had. Nor that the AP was not listed in the Airworthiness Approval Note.

Moving to the after-flight checks, Mr Spence pointed out that the AP required a check of the g-meter to *'Observe maximum readings +7 and -3.75'*, and then a reset. He simply made the point, not mentioning that Mr Renouf had instead said he took a *'cursory glance'*.

Observations

1. It would appear an apprentice was permitted to work alone on ejection seats, the level of supervision being he could go to the Chief Engineer with any problems. That remoteness is not 'supervision' when dealing with a

safety critical escape system that employs explosives. Nor does it align with MoD practices, as required by the Permit to Fly. (Although, it must be said, the Cunningham case proved MoD's practices had regressed).

2. Why did the defence have to provide the Flight Servicing Schedule? Why wasn't Weald's copy produced and examined; and compared with a certified and maintained copy obtained from the Design Authority? But according to the CAA that was the RAF. What confidence could there be that the AP series was up-to-date? Who was contracted to do this work? Under what process was it ensured that privately owned Hunters received all updates? Unwittingly, I believe, the defence were just a little *too* helpful. They should have asked for disclosure to see what the prosecution came up with.

3. There is a world of difference between a 'cursory glance' and 'observe', when strict numerical limits are given. And there is an obvious omission - what to do when the 'observation' is that the instrument is unserviceable, in an incorrect location, and/or the readings anomalous?

4. It was implied that because G-BXFI was (allegedly) serviceable it was also airworthy. This tainted the entire case, MoD's Military Aviation Authority routinely making the same mistake in all accident reports.

None of these observations were made by either side. This is explained by it being the AAIB report that confirmed G-BXFI was not airworthy, and the defence being aware that citing it would breach the High Court order.

Regarding publications, the AAIB recommended that:

'The Civil Aviation Authority define a minimum amendment standard for the technical publications for each ex-military jet aircraft type operated on the United Kingdom civil register. Following the publication of FACTOR F1/2016 Issue 2 the CAA's response is as follows:

"Working in conjunction with industry, the CAA will establish a minimum amendment standard for the technical publications for each individual ex-military jet aircraft operated on the UK civil register. The established standard will be recorded in the Airworthiness Approval Note (AAN) for each aircraft. The CAA will complete this work by December 2018".

The AAIB has categorised the CAA response to Safety Recommendation 2015-44 as "Adequate - closed".[41]

---

41 AAIB report, 4.4.

The jury raised the same points, so this bears some examination:
- *'A minimum amendment standard...'* How about up-to-date and verified, as required by the Permit to Fly? If they are not, the ability to demonstrate airworthiness and serviceability, verify aircrew currency, and operate the aircraft safely, degrades rapidly.
- *'Working in conjunction with industry...'* and *'recorded in the Approval Note'*. This gets to the root of why no Hunter could be airworthy in August 2015. Now, but without admitting the error in the Approval Note, the CAA agreed that it was 'industry' who must be engaged.
- *'Adequate - closed'*. The above errors are bad, but easily explained and fixed. But the notion that a promise from the CAA that it will now do its job properly, when it has already stated (e.g. by signing the Approval Note) that it has been done properly, is remotely 'adequate' does not instil confidence. It is unhinged. What was needed in the AAIB report was a Compliance Matrix to illustrate at a glance (for example, with a 'traffic light' system) the degree of organisational failure. (It would be a sea of red). What is now needed is an appointed authority to police the CAA, and ensure recommendations are prioritised and implemented as soon as possible. In MoD, the relevant mandated airworthiness policy says safety critical work must be carried out *'irrespective of delay, scrap or downtime involved'*. I agree with this. The CAA seemingly does not, despite mandating it upon operators.

To give you an idea of the scale of this work, and how quickly publications can become out-of-date, in 1976 the Hunter T.7 Topic 1 (Leading Particulars) had received 161 amendments.

I don't intend going through all 32 of the AAIB's safety recommendations in such detail. Suffice to say, their report describes 26 as *'Adequate - closed'*. This may be sufficient for the AAIB's purposes, but *it* is not required to accept and implement the recommendations. The CAA, which, after all, has the same line management chain as the AAIB, should have been instructed to prepare a safety statement for the report, to make it clear that progress was <u>not</u> adequate, and why. And, like MoD must do, provide a named individual responsible for overseeing implementation.

Having praised MoD's official policy in this matter, what of the reality? Essentially, we are discussing risks. These must be reduced to 'As Low As Reasonably Practicable'; and a Duty Holder <u>must</u> sign to say he has satisfied himself they are. However, in recent years the MAA have given a name -

'ALARP (Temporal)' - to the long-standing policy whereby it is sufficient to have *identified* the risk without any kind of plan to *mitigate* it. I first came across this in 1999. I was instructed not to mitigate a critical risk on my helicopter, but wait to see if it materialised. (That is, was shot down or suffered a mid-air collision). I ignored the order and directed that the aircraft be made safe; but my decision was overruled by an administrative superior. Under his direction the aircraft was made unsafe and unairworthy, and seven aircrew were killed in a mid-air. He had been given full warning of the likely outcome, making this a prime example of Unlawful and Dangerous Act Manslaughter.[42]

A further example is Collision Warning Systems in fast jets where, despite a series of fatal mid-airs, the risk status remains ALARP (Temporal). In another case, a promise was made to the Senior Coroner for North West Wales after the 2018 death of Corporal Jon Bayliss, to modify the Hawk T.1 ejection seat system to make it ALARP. (MoD admitted that had the modification been embodied, Jon would have survived). Upon the Inquest closing, the head of the MAA promptly rejected the modification on affordability grounds (which is strictly forbidden). You may wish to think of this the next time you marvel at the Red Arrows.

A risk can only be ALARP if mitigated correctly. In practice, a risk to life can only be borne when MoD and the government accept 'military risk' in times of conflict. (And if the risk was foreseen, but not mitigated, by definition that is a catastrophic failure of the Safety Management System). In my opinion this cannot apply to a recreational pursuit, conducted in the vicinity of tens of thousands. This is entirely an airworthiness matter, not least because its formal definition includes the safety of those whom the aircraft overflies. In other words, the reasons behind Shoreham boil down to assessment of whether risk was managed to the ALARP principle.

I believe this entire concept was lost on the CAA. *We don't want to make the aircraft safe? Get rid of the policy that says it must be.* I'm not being flippant. I'm actually summarising the entire thrust of the Nimrod Review.

Flying

Tom Maloney (Former Jet Provost display pilot)

Mr Maloney had acquired G-BXFI from MoD in 1997. It was sold two months later to Fox-One Ltd, and housed, maintained and operated by Jet Heritage Ltd based at Bournemouth International Airport. There, it was refurbished

---

42 'Breaking the Military Covenant' (David Hill, 2018).

and flown again. His business was still based at Shoreham Airport, and he had been keen to watch Hill's display. He stated that all seemed normal until the ascent commenced, which he described as *'fairly slow'*. Mr Kark had to stop his witness there, as he was offering opinion when not allowed to.

Not long into Mr Spence's cross-examination, the prosecution raised a point of law. Upon resumption, Mr Maloney's evidence finished quickly.

Squadron Leader Dan Arlett (RAF pilot)

In August 2015 Squadron Leader Arlett had been officer in charge of advanced training on Hawk at RAF Valley. He had displayed Tornado F3 for the RAF, and a host of jet aircraft at airshows, including Hunters. He had flown with Hill in Team Viper until around 2012, describing him as *'probably the most diligent of all the team'*.

He related how the Shoreham area was challenging; the runway smaller than it looks, presenting oculogravic illusion. That is, it looks further away than it is. *'I've made some hard landings at Shoreham'*. He described the 400 foot hill to the north east, and significant built-up areas to the south and south west, setting out the flying restrictions these imposed.

He then demonstrated the accident flight with a model aircraft and by reference to images (and all I can do is refer you to Figure 1), describing it as *'normal and graceful'* until it pitched up when *'it did perhaps look a bit slower than I was expecting'* and he didn't hear the usual noise as the throttle opened up.

He noted that his and Hill's Hunter displays were deliberately similar to these performed in Jet Provost, the reason being they wanted to memorise the sequence to avoid having to look at notes during the flight.

Cross-examined by Mr Spence, Squadron Leader Arlett went through the 'active g-strain manoeuvre' whereby one clenches muscles to offset the effect. He emphasised: *'If you haven't flown a high-g manoeuvre for a month, you're back to square one'*, losing tolerance very quickly.

He described a looping manoeuvre as:

> *'Pitching up at the prescribed g, which in the Hunter is simply a minimum of 4g, then you go over the top. Check your height, that you are okay'.*

This elicited no comment, but the AAIB had claimed a maximum of 2.7*g*, and the prosecution later claimed 2.4*g*.

While applying full power into the ascent, he said:

> *'The stick would come back to pull to a certain pitch, which can be*

coordinated using the g-force and the g-meter'.

It was not mentioned that the *g*-meter had been moved out of clear sight of the left hand pilot, and was in any case unserviceable.

Chris Gotke (RN officer, pilot)

In 2015 Mr Gotke was a serving RN pilot, having flown Sea Harriers and, very early in his career, Hunters. Also, Hawk and Jaguar.

He opined G-BXFI seemed slow when starting its ascent. But he believed the power applied was *'sufficient to conduct the manoeuvre'*, adding that *'a loop is not circular, it's like a teardrop'*.

His evidence was impressively descriptive; and on flying matters essentially repeated that of Squadron Leader Arlett.

Chris Heames (Retired RAF pilot and Air Traffic Controller)

Mr Heames had been an RAF Air Traffic Controller for eight years, and then retrained as a fast jet pilot, flying Phantoms, Lightnings and Tornados. He began flying Hunters in 2001 as a display pilot, and had flown G-BXFI extensively. In 2010 Team Viper, of which he was leader, purchased the aircraft; disbanding in 2012 when it became financially unviable. The new owner, Graham Peacock, invited him to be Chief Pilot.

Mr Heames made the important point that, while the pilot is responsible for the safe operation of the aircraft, it was Weald Aviation who certified it serviceable. In a telling remark, he said G-BXFI was his favourite aircraft *'as it flew so frequently'*. Given the evidence of G-BXFI's relatively low hours since 1994, this said much about how *infrequently* these vintage jets fly.

(The Judge reminded Mr Heames: *'You are not here to give your opinion, you are here to tell us what you actually need to'*).

Asked about what constitutes an aerobatic manoeuvre, he said:

> *'The Air Navigation Order is woolly. It talks of abrupt changes of flight path and gives examples of manoeuvres. The consensus is that any manoeuvre involving more than 60° of roll or 30° of pitch is aerobatic'.*

(This is actually laid down by the Federal Aviation Administration).

Mr Heames explained that his apex would be 3,500 feet above his start height, the first time it had been expressed this clearly; the aim always being to come out of the loop at no less than 500 feet, the authorised minimum. He described the gate height as:

'The height at the top of a manoeuvre which you must be above to commit the nose down, to continue'.

...and an escape manoeuvre as:

'The most height efficient way of getting out of a manoeuvre and recovering the aircraft into level flight. For every manoeuvre the escape manoeuvre would be different'.

He described Hill's performance of the manoeuvre in training as *'textbook'*, adding that his *'preparation was second to none'*.

Regarding *g*-forces, and consistent with Squadron Leader Arlett, he said:

'During a looping manoeuvre, I would pull to achieve approximately 4g'.

Cross-examined by Mr Khalil, Mr Heames said:

'You never fly a perfect mission. It is the same as driving your car to work. You make mistakes but hope they won't be critical'.

Asked about the accident flight, he said:

'I was asked by the AAIB to watch cockpit video from two GoPros'.

The Judge immediately intervened:

'The AAIB material is not admissible in these proceedings. The witness is not to tell you anything about it. He cannot opine on how Mr Andy Hill conducted his display. The complicating factor is he clearly is an expert'.

Thereafter, he could only answer in general terms.

Ben Watts (Airline captain)

Mr Watts, a pilot with Ryanair, was a trainee Hunter pilot, and related how he flew with Hill during a practice sortie at Duxford in 2014. This became more relevant later, when the prosecution's allegations were systematically refuted. Asked by Mr Spence for the defence, *'With regard to his display flying, would you say he had a cavalier attitude?'*, he replied: *'In my experience he had the absolute opposite'.*

Jonathon Whaley (Pilot, and first expert witness)

Mr Whaley had joined the Fleet Air Arm in 1965, flying Jet Provost, Hunter and Sea Vixen; later becoming a Display Authorisation Evaluator for the Civil Aviation Authority, and flew as a display pilot. He was Managing Director and Chief Pilot at Jet Heritage Ltd, who had operated G-BXFI. He had been partly responsible for redesigning and fitting out the cockpit.

Asked to explain a number of theory of flight principles and the operation of jet aircraft in general, and the concept of stall, he used videos. He described in detail the application of airshow display rules; touched on 'risk assessment' (but not management); and spoke at length on practical aspects of display flying and use of the primary flight instruments.

Towards the end of what was a benign session, Mr Whaley was asked about the operation of the aircraft's flaps, and if he agreed evidence offered earlier by Mr Heames. He replied: *'I disagree, utterly disagree'*.

On that note, a disagreement between prosecution witnesses, his evidence finished. As this session was just groundwork, and he was later recalled, the defence did not cross-examine.

Peter Younger (National Air Traffic Services)

Mr Younger was Head of the Surveillance Analysis Team for NATS, and previously a research analyst in their Systems Performance Team.

He described the radar plot he had created from Primary and Secondary radar returns from G-BXFI, giving excellent explanations to both Counsels regarding the calculation of groundspeed from the data, and the important difference between groundspeed and airspeed. He confirmed G-BXFI's Secondary Radar did not transmit airspeed data, only barometric altitude.

Dave Walton (Aviation consultant, flying displays)

Mr Walton was a director of TSA Consulting, who provided services to assist in organising air displays. As part of his role he had been engaged as the Flying Display Director at Southport airshow in 2014, and had been for a number of years. He was not a pilot.

He related how, in poor weather, Hill had erred by breaching the lateral separation and height limits. Mr Walton called *'stop'*. He said that Hill had immediately acknowledged his error to both he and the Flight Control Committee, and they permitted him to display the following day. In his written debrief, Hill stated:

'I was slightly too slow and too close to the display line to successfully complete the manoeuvre prior to crossing the display line. The error occurred because, in taking into account and adapting for the prevailing cloud, visibility and "goldfish bowl" conditions [whereby there is an indistinct, misleading or lack of visible horizon], *I did not correctly judge the effect on this one manoeuvre. I successfully abandoned the manoeuvre and*

halted the display'.

In response to Mr Spence, and upon studying a video of the event, Mr Walton now agreed Hill had stopped his display <u>before</u> the *'stop'* call. Another prosecution mainstay had been disproved by its own witness.

Jonathon Whaley (recalled)

Before examination-in-chief began again, the Judge took Mr Whaley through a number of questions submitted by the jury. These related to the oxygen system, panel lighting, and flap settings. Mr Whaley was unable to answer fully, but it was perhaps a little unfair expecting him to be able to recall such precise details. I imply no criticism, and nor did the court. The Judge was content.

The final question was: *How could the seat be ejected without the ejection button being pressed or lever pulled?* Mr Whaley replied that the Hunter had two handles above the pilot, and one between his legs; and that these were the only way to initiate ejection. Mr Kark interjected, probably realising the jury's question was about how Hill's seat had 'ejected' without him making a deliberate action, saying this would be dealt with later.

Note: The Mk4HA seats fitted to G-BXFI had a B-Handle above the pilot's head, as distinct from the older D-style, the 'B' often being confused as two separate handles. Given *g*-forces were a significant factor in the case, it is important to note that pilots were instructed to use the B-handle in normal use, but if positive-*g* prevented use of the B, to use the crotch handle.[43] The practical impact is that when using the crotch handle one did not benefit from the protection of the face screen that is pulled down with the B-handle.

Mr Whaley was asked to explain a comment by Hill in a police interview:

'My display typically involved two loops and two and a half Cubans'.

Both Mr Kark and the Judge became frustrated at how long this took. My feeling here is that Mr Whaley understood his target audience was the jury; not Mr Kark, who probably had an inkling of what the answer would be. The jury, less so. This is a perennial issue in jury trials, where the jurors are expected to grasp complex concepts that 'experts' take years to master.

There was an interruption, and the court was adjourned. Upon returning, the Judge told the jury that a third party (not the prosecution or defence) had

---

43 AP101B-1302 & 3-15, Part 4, Chapter 3.

applied for GoPro footage from the accident *not* to be shown in court. *'Somebody else who has some control or influence may have been seeking to prevent that'*. He had ruled that it *could* be shown.

Mr Kark turned to a practice flight conducted at RAF Duxford in 2014 (discussed earlier in the evidence of Ben Watts) and GoPro footage taken; reiterating his opening statement when he had said:

> *'It is clear from the video that Hill did overfly what would have been the crowd line. The Duxford minimum height when overflying the M11 was 500 feet, but he overflew it at about 250 feet on one occasion and 200 feet on another. He played fast and loose with the rules which are designed to keep people safe'.*

Later, under cross-examination by Mr Khalil, Mr Whaley was asked:

> *'Now I've taken you to the additional documents, do you accept that at the time of the practice the crowd line was not as you have drawn it?'*

> *'I do accept that'.*

> *'You told us that it was a 500 feet minimum over the motorway. Would you look at the bottom of page 10B? It's underlined in bold type and it says 200 feet?'*

> *'You're quite right'.*

Mr Khalil went on:

> *'There is a need sometimes to appreciate whether a witness is saying "I am an expert in this" or "I am simply able to look things up and do my best". You're the latter of those, aren't you?'*

> *'Yes'.*

My opinion... If you're going to accuse someone of reckless endangerment, and quote a minimum height and position, it is wise to check it really is the minimum height, and are able to prove what height he was at, and where. The impression was of hearsay, Mr Whaley accepting this as true, and the prosecution assuming its expert was correct. This is the danger of calling an 'expert' witness. If he errs, that is what the jury will remember.

After a break Mr Kark continued... but had to start again because either (a) they'd forgotten to recall the jury, or (b) it had lost the will and absconded. The Judge made a comment about going into overtime.

Moving on to Shoreham in 2014, Mr Whaley described Hill as performing a *'high energy, good display'* and making *'good use of the limitations of Shoreham'*. Yet another video was shown, the focus again on throttle settings and engine speed, and flap settings at various points.

The prosecution had alleged Hill overflew Lancing College, which is forbidden. Mr Whaley, clearly expected to say he did, was honest and said he was unsure. Mr Kark took him through his extensive analysis of the throttle movements which were claimed to be detectable in the video footage of both 2014 and 2015. In such analysis it is crucial to know the height at any given time. A GoPro does not record this.

The prosecution played a video. The view was over the pilot's right shoulder, Mr Whaley asked to speculate on what he was doing out of sight of the lens. He couldn't be sure. He was then asked:

'The Airspeed Indicator is now showing at 178 knots. Is that fast or slow at this point in the manoeuvre?'

'You can't tell, because you can't tell what the pitch angle is'.

Once again, Mr Whaley was in an invidious position. What possessed the prosecution to ask him of something that required a visible reference point, such as the horizon? Was there no preparation?

Cross-examined by Mr Khalil about the effect of *g*-forces:

'As pilot you may not know something's wrong, but someone else might be able to trigger you to start correcting the situation?'

'Yes'.

And finally, to the crux of the matter - the prosecution's position that Hill didn't experience *g*-forces above 2.4-2.9g. Mr Khalil quoted Mr Whaley:

'"I believe Andy Hill performed this turn at various g-levels between 2.5-2.9g and no higher, and for no longer than 23 seconds". Do you stand by that?'

'I do not'.

'Do you accept that the 4-5g proposed by Mr Cubin [a later defence witness] *would be about right?'*

'I can't say'.

It transpired that the online 'calculator' used by Mr Whaley did not take account of air density, 1g Earth gravity, wind speed or direction. He agreed that another party, Mr John Jeffrey, who was not a witness, had produced a figure of '*4.8g, followed by a varying 2.5-3.25g*', and that he now agreed with that.

He also conceded that his height estimates were taken from the Height Encoding Altimeter (Mode C Transponder data), but that the instrument had not been checked for accuracy. Correctly, and without prompting, he noted that the Encoding Altimeter is a separate instrument, not in the cockpit. That is, there could be no correlation between the altitudes shown on the cockpit altimeter(s) and the Encoding Altimeter. This served to undermine other prosecution claims.

Mr Whaley spent almost four days on the stand, an interminable time and undoubtedly stressful and wearying. A great deal of this was spent analysing videos which, as I said, I cannot possibly describe to you. However, I feel the need to comment on this, in rather strong terms. My belief is that there is something inherently unjust about the prosecution being allowed to dissect videos, more or less frame by frame, with a running commentary by a witness for the prosecution; especially when in real time the aircraft is flying at ~400 knots. *('Stop there. Can we go back a couple of frames? Okay, stop there')*. In real life a pilot doesn't get to 'stop there, go back...' to reassess and try again. As a number of witnesses agreed, all pilots make mistakes. That is the whole point of practicing. I firmly believe the jurors felt the same, or at least were mentally worn down. They probably suffered Cognitive Impairment.

Mr Whaley had conducted his own extensive analysis of the various displays and practice flights discussed, was given access to footage that was denied Hill, and then produced a number of reports - including one written jointly with two other witnesses. This was, it seems, peer-reviewed very late in the day by one person, who pointed out a number of fundamental errors in *g*-calculations. As did Hill himself. Mr Whaley fully acknowledged these. One report had been issued only two days before the trial commenced, and updated a week later. It is difficult to see how the defence could have time to prepare for this; but in the event didn't need to as the errors were conceded.

On a number of occasions both Mr Kark and Mr Whaley seemed to get lost in the evidence, with it constantly skipping between Duxford 2014, Shoreham 2014, and the accident flight, and each video being very similar. My overriding impression is that the evidence, and the way it was presented, was overly complex, and essentially speculative. Mr Whaley declined - correctly in my view - to offer an opinion on a number of issues; for example, he did not perform bent loops in Hunters. The effect, however, was to undermine his status as an 'expert' - but one cannot be an expert in all things aviation. Nevertheless, the prosecution's first expert witness had expertly destroyed its case before the defence had been heard from.

David Southwood (Pilot)

Mr Southwood had joined the RAF in the early-70's, flying Buccaneers, Hunter, Hawk, Jaguar and Tornado. In 1985 he became a test pilot at the Empire Test Pilot School; where he was now an instructor. One of the UK's most experienced pilots, he had flown approximately 150 types. He had flown Hunters continuously since 1978, logging over 1,000 hours, held comprehensive Display Authorisations, including World War 2 fighters, and was a Display Authorisation Evaluator.

He had been tasked with conducting the test flights, already described. Given the recent revelations, his evidence, while not contradicting his Appendix in the AAIB report, was now more comprehensive. Asked if he made an error in the December 2015 flight, he confirmed he had forgotten to read out speed and altitude data for the voice recorder at the correct point, and should have flown an escape manoeuvre. He realised this about six seconds after apex, and pulled-through at below 200 feet, when the minimum height for recovery to level flight of 1,000 feet for all sorties. The low level pull-through was unplanned, forced upon him by the earlier error - not rolling out after the apex - which was the pre-planned profile. Once the first error was made he had little choice but to minimise height loss and attempt the pull-through, which was executed well. A little cascade of errors, if you like. The essential points were (1) the main error, and subsequent low-level pull-through, were very similar to Hill's, and (2) even the most experienced pilot can make an error.

During these tests g-force had been measured at pull-up as $4.9g$. Despite the AAIB sponsoring the tests and being present, its report said *'the peak g-force calculated for [Hill's] turn was $2.7g$'*.[44] It did not mention any figure experienced by Mr Southwood.

Much of his evidence repeated that of previous witnesses, confirming gate heights, speeds and other parameters. He summarised a key point:

'The gate height is the same for a straight loop or a Bent Loop, but the probability of not reaching your gate height at the apex is greater from a

---

44 AAIB report, 1.18.10.1.

Bent Loop, so there is a higher risk of failing'.

He went through the various gates for different manoeuvres, saying that when he assessed Hill's manoeuvre he had *assumed* his apex was 2,700 feet, because there was no firm data. He actually flew the sorties at 2,600 - 2,950 feet, plus 500 feet for minimum height, plus 1,000 feet safety factor. At this point he referred to *'the data'*, which Mr Kark reminded him was in the AAIB report so not available to the jury.

Cross-examined by Mr Khalil, and asked about Duxford in 2014, he confirmed Hill had <u>not</u> breached the crowd line, and did <u>not</u> fly below 500 feet. Of the alleged overflight of Lancing College at Shoreham in 2014, he confirmed there was *'an element of interpretation as to the definition of Lancing College'*, as the grounds were extensive, with some structures quite a distance from the main building. Asked to estimate Hill's height over Lancing, he said this was impossible, caused by GoPros having a fisheye lens, distorting the image, and was unwilling to speculate. Regarding Southport in 2014, where Hill stopped his display after an error, Mr Southwood agreed with other witnesses that Hill had been *'open and honest'*. Returning to escape manoeuvres, Mr Southwood considered it a *'failing'* that this *'essential aspect of training'* was not taught.

The jury was sent out, discussion continuing between the Judge, Counsels and Mr Southwood regarding concerns Mr Khalil held over evidence disclosure of Mode C (height) data. The problem was that while data was available for the first set of test flights (October 2015), none had been disclosed or provided for the final one (December 2015) in which the height error had been made. Mr Southwood confirmed he had never been in possession of this. The underlying concern was that the details of these test flights, and that they had been recorded, had not been disclosed until just before the trial. The defence had successfully highlighted the potential for a miscarriage of justice, and the Judge agreed. He recalled the jury, and the remainder of Mr Southwood's testimony was answering questions from the Judge, not Counsel; another indication of the former's mounting concern.

I should emphasise that the failure to disclose was nothing to do with Mr Southwood. His job was to fly the sorties. The recordings were seized and retained by the AAIB (cockpit) and MoD (ground).

My impression of Mr Southwood's evidence is the same as when I reviewed Mr Whaley's. Much of it was unrelated to Hill's final manoeuvre. He was asked to recite a huge amount of data which, once again, probably left the jury utterly bewildered. On a number of occasions the Judge had to intervene so *he* could gain understating. None of this was Mr Southwood's fault - he answered the questions, exhibiting superb knowledge, befitting his experience.

Image Analysts

I think it wise to deal with these two witnesses separately, because I believe most readers will wish to understand why MoD was so heavily involved - something that was not reported in the media.

At the request of the AAIB, MoD analysed the imagery to determine speed and positional information. At MoD's request, the Analysts were granted anonymity under a Witness Anonymity Order issued on 3 October, due to the nature of their work. This relates to the data gathered by, for example, Photographic Reconnaissance Units and satellites. It is the data that is classified, not how it is analysed or by whom.

Image Analyst 1

IA1 was a retired MoD civil servant specialising photogrammetry, which is the process of obtaining measurements from imagery. Examined-in-chief by Miss Broome for the prosecution, it was established he had been asked by the AAIB to analyse over 450 ground-based still images, around 20 ground-based videos, cockpit footage, plus some video from 2014. Based on his conclusions, he had produced a diagram of the flight.

Unfortunately, Miss Broome referred to groundspeed when meaning height, and vice-versa. This led to utter confusion, and I can only summarise by saying the height was said to be anywhere between 150 and 250 feet at pull-up (into the ascent), and groundspeed 150 to 310 knots *'plus or minus'*. Estimated height at apex was 2,800 ±325 feet, at impact the aircraft had 14 ±3° degree nose-up attitude, and was travelling at 225 ±20 knots.

IA1 estimated the flap setting just before apex was 11 ±3°, although caveated this and recommended further examination by experts in that field, to include direct photographic comparison and that a *'high fidelity Hunter T.7'* model be created by LIDAR scan (Light Detection and Ranging). His report had been delivered first, and IA2 was tasked with follow-on work. The defence commissioned LIDAR work, it proving inconclusive; but IA2 did not...

Image Analyst 2

IA2 was also a Photogrammetrist, specialising in 3D modelling. He had formerly been an RAF engineer. Asked to ascertain the flap settings, he had selected around 40 images to work from. He concluded between 15° and 23° of flap had been applied during the ascent stage, and 23° of flap on the way down from apex. He regarded this as having a confidence level of 70-90%. He could not say *when* the flaps changed.

Plainly there was significant potential for these prosecution witnesses contradicting each other. To avoid this, it would have to be proven that Hill changed the flap setting at or about apex. (There are eight flap positions, which the pilot changes with his left hand. IA/1 was saying Position 1, IA/2 Position 2).

Under cross-examination by Mr Spence as to how he could be so specific about 23° flap, he replied that he had taken that from the Aircrew Manual, as *'That's all I could go on'*. (The manual says 22°30' for Position 2).[45] That is, he hadn't actually calculated it. (So where did the confidence level come from?).

Asked if he had sought the publications describing the flap system, he said no; and was unaware of the tolerance allowed when rigging the aircraft, or that there was a tolerance in the first place. Despite being a former RAF engineer, he had not approached any MoD department, preferring to use 'blueprints' he had downloaded from a website. Mr Spence:

> *'You work for the MoD. Did it cross your mind to ask "Can someone arrange for me to have the authorised design drawings so I know exactly what the dimensions are"'?*
>
> *'No'.*

Mr Spence summarised - IA2's work was not what IA1 had recommended.

Observations

Expert witnesses act under:

- Criminal Procedure Rules, Part 19 (Expert Evidence).
- CPS Guidance Booklet for Experts - Disclosure Experts' Evidence, Case Management and Unused Material.

IA2 carried out his work as part of his MoD duties, and his report of 8 January 2018 was issued as an MoD document. It appears to me this did not meet the requirements of the above rules and guidance, in that the work was provided to support Sussex Police, not the court. Also, his conclusions did not follow from the report. Had the recommendations of IA1 been taken up, these

---

45 AP101B-1304-1A, Section 3, Chapter 4, Figure 11.

conclusions could not have been arrived at. In effect, IA1 and IA2, although both prosecution witnesses, were acting in opposition. It is clear the CPS took particular note of IA2's report when deciding to prosecute, without assessing the obvious conflicts.

Finally, and as an aside, it would be interesting to know who IA2 would have gone to for a LIDAR scan. (The defence carried their scan out on a Hunter T.7 at Bruntingthorpe Aerodrome and Proving Ground, near Leicester). MoD gave its expertise to QinetiQ in 1999, who in turn made most of the UK's LIDAR experts redundant in 2010 when deciding to downsize that area of business.

Andrew Hill

While Mr Hill was on the stand for four days, he could not speak of the important issue, what happened during the accident flight, because he had no memory of it. For this reason, there is little point regurgitating what was mostly repetition. I think it best to offer a few key points:

- He fully acknowledged his error at Southport in 2014.
- He stated he did not disagree with anything said by Mr Southwood, including some mild criticism.
- Regarding the g-meter, he was not aware it was faulty and the data not being recorded, but was aware that due to its relocation the typical errors were *'enormous'*.

Shown video, he fully admitted errors had been made, he did not know why, and his only conclusion was impairment. Asked:

'Do you accept, that if you were of clear mind, you had an opportunity or opportunities to adjust the flight path of the aircraft?'

He replied:

'More than one. I can identify a point where everything is going well, and the point everything starts being anomalous. I can't understand it. I go off line and the aircraft doesn't accelerate, because I haven't got the power on. If it wasn't increased, that's an omission. It might have been the engine but I have no reason to believe it was. It's not particularly well-flown. The pitch rate over top is too low. It could have been pulled harder and there was a lot more performance in the aircraft available. I could have pulled and I did not'.

Rather than argue with any witness evidence, he spent time, when necessary, explaining and clarifying issues, or placing them in context. My view is that he and his Counsel realised the prosecution witnesses had already destroyed the prosecution's case; that, it was a matter of emphasising his amnesia, and relying on the defence's medical experts to reinforce the overwhelming doubt.

The AAIB came to accept their errors, so clearly Hill's arguments were cogent. He remained sharp throughout. I don't think the prosecution barristers were prepared for this, and he quickly had the upper hand due to their errors and lack of knowledge. He made a good job of emphasising that it needed a pilot to understand the evidence - which was fair comment - but without making the prosecution look foolish, which would be counter-productive.

Andy Cubin (Pilot)

After over a month of prosecution evidence, on 18 February 2019 Mr Cubin was the first (defence!) witness to appear for the defence. He was examined-in-chief by Mr Spence. He told the court he had joined the RAF in 1981, flying primarily Jaguar and Hawk. He was seconded to the Sultan of Oman's Air Force, also flying many missions over Bosnia and Iraq. From 1994-96 he was the RAF's Jaguar display pilot, and in 1997 was selected for the Red Arrows. After completing his 3-year tour, he left the RAF in 2000 and flew as an airline Captain. He had displayed Hunters extensively, including G-BXFI, and had reviewed the records of Hill's conversion to Hunter, which had taken five flying hours. By comparison, and because he was current on fast jets, *he* had taken 45 minutes. He emphasised the difficulty faced by civilian display pilots in retaining currency, for what is essentially a privately funded hobby.

Asked of his *g*-training, he stated:

> 'G-LOC was described in broad terms, specifically to look out loss of colour vision, tunnel vision and then blackout - the precursors to actually losing consciousness'.

He confirmed there was no specific requirement to train for escape manoeuvres, as they weren't applicable at the heights normally flown by operational aircraft. Only the likes of Red Arrows pilots were taught them; so, he had been taught in a Hawk, but not Hunters. Others not at all.

Of Southport in 2014, his opinion was that Hill had recognised his error and flown a correct escape manoeuvre. He had written a report on the incident, saying: *'No action was taken, and none needed to have been'*. Similarly, of Duxford in 2014 he said it was *'impossible'* to determine from video footage if Hill had overflown the museum, which the prosecution had alleged. Moving to the accident flight, Mr Cubin explained how Hill had deliberately changed his routine to avoid any possibility of encroaching over Lancing, describing his plan as *'reasonable'*. He said the first set of manoeuvres were exactly the same as his own display.

Regarding the prosecution claim that g-force did not exceed 2.4-2.9g:

> *'From my experience of flying that manoeuvre hundreds of times, I would never have pulled 2.4g. It would have been closer to double that'.*

He said that Hill was not quite wings-level when exiting the previous manoeuvre (the Derry Turn) so was slightly banked when he began his ascent into the loop. The effect would be some loss of lift. However, this could be deliberate, as the engine has more than sufficient power to achieve gate height. He stated that, when flying these vintage jets, in order to protect the engine full power would not be used during the ascent; whereas in the military this was less of an issue. That is, having applied full power during the run-in to the loop, it would be taken back a little after the ascent began. (It was not asked if this could account for the first power reduction).

The first real problem he perceived was when the aircraft starting to pitch up it immediately started to roll. Then, when coming off the apex, he found it *'incredible'* that Hill did not conduct an escape manoeuvre.

Regarding the aiming point out of the loop, the prosecution had suggested it was the A27 - obviously highly dangerous. Mr Cubin explained that it would have been the runway, and that the aircraft would be blown slightly off course by the prevailing wind. This was unremarkable, and it was normal to apply correction on the way down. He described this as a *'cognitive process'*; as distinct from something that he would do automatically. (This distinction assumes huge import later).

Asked if, assuming he were in full control, there was anything to have stopped Hill from turning away, Mr Cubin replied:

> *'It is my belief that he wouldn't have recognised the aircraft was too low until beyond the point of recovery'.*

Under cross-examination by Mr Kark, Mr Cubin did not disagree with any of the flying techniques described by (primarily) Messrs Whaley and Southwood, only saying there were different perfectly valid ways of flying the same manoeuvres.

Regarding Southport 2014, he said Hill misjudged his range from the crowd, not his height, due to the goldfish bowl effect causing him to believe he was further away than he was. He stated that, while no overflight of the crowd was permitted during a display, it was permitted to do so if abandoning the display. This was explicit in the CAA's rules.

The Shoreham 2014 cockpit video was shown again. It seems Mr Kark did not accept, or had missed, Mr Cubin's explanation about not using full engine power, as he tried to get him to criticise Hill's slightly lower power setting at Shoreham in 2014. Mr Cubin reiterated his previous evidence.

Asked about Hill overflying Lancing, he produced a map showing the building in question clearly <u>outside</u> the prohibited zone. He noted the prosecution's map had been redrawn with a thick, red pen, which encroached on the building; but when viewed on the Display Instructions issued by the Flying Committee the line was much thinner, the boundary more clearly defined. Mr Kark implied this had not been disclosed in evidence, but Mr Cubin pointed out it was reproduced in his report.

Mr Kark: *'Oh, I see'*.

Judge Edis: *'Yes'*.

Game over.

I should say here that I am fully aware of the legal difficulties Mr Cubin found himself in two years after the trial, as a result of Post-Traumatic Stress Disorder following the death of his 14-year old daughter in 2016. While I do not condone what he did, I too have lost a child and I empathise. His name was Andrew Hill, and writing this book has brought back some very dark memories. People react differently. Some cope, some go off the rails. Unless you've walked in their shoes, you cannot know.

Flaps

In his opening statement Mr Kark had said:

> *'The prosecution suggest that Hill adjusted the flaps at or near the apex, and this was a conscious and deliberate control movement. It is obvious when one further notch has clicked into place. This is a deliberate move by the pilot and we suggest could not be done unless the pilot was thinking and alert. Why did Hill extend the flaps before commencing the descent? It is an indication, we suggest, that he realised that he was lower than he should have been and required greater lift to make it around the loop'.*

The Hunter is equipped with hydraulically-operated, electrically-controlled split flaps. They change the profile of each wing to provide greater lift allowing the aircraft to fly more slowly, and they increase the aircraft's manoeuvrability. The Aircrew Manual, under 'Airframe limitations', states that the maximum permitted speed for Positions 1-4 is 300 knots, for Positions 5-8 250 knots. As the AAIB report could not be mentioned, this observation from the report was overlooked:

'The aircraft had been operated with the flaps extended at speeds exceeding the limit for doing so. [It did not say by whom]. *This had not been reported in the aircraft technical log'.*

And quoted the Aircrew Manual:

'If the Indicated Airspeed limitations for the use of flaps are inadvertently exceeded, the flap angle is limited according to the air load to prevent damage, but sufficient flap is extended to create a strong nose-down change of trim. This can result in elevator jack stalling and tailplane actuator clutch slip. In this event not only is longitudinal control lost but the aircraft cannot be trimmed nose-up by either the main or the standby systems. In extreme cases, the air loads may then force the tailplane to move in opposition to the actuator thereby causing an additional nose-down change of trim'.

Hence, the Image Analysts offered by MoD to establish the flap settings. I've discussed the difficulty they had, with IA2 simply (but incorrectly) quoting the Aircrew Manual. Moreover, the prosecution had missed how the flaps worked. There are no locks to keep them at (e.g.) 11° when Position 1 is selected - they oscillate between two micro-switches, so are constantly moving. (Making analysis even more difficult). Perhaps suspecting this might be a key area, Hill had made a model using an actual Hunter flap electrical module to show how much flaps could move.

As the camera looked over Hill's right shoulder, his body and the seat obscuring the flap lever and what his left hand was doing, Mr Southwood had stated he could not say with any certainty what he was actually doing. Before that, Mr Whaley had asserted that, because Hill *seemed* to reach down twice, that meant he had moved through Positions 1 and 2. (Equally, he could have been scratching himself). In short, most of the evidence was speculation.

Jet Pipe Temperature

The prosecution had alleged that Hill had a habit of taking off with the temperature too low, which would affect engine efficiency. It emerged they were quoting the Aircrew Manual, which gave a max/min of 690/580°C. If 580°C was not achieved, one should not take off. He was criticised for taking off at Duxford in 2014 at 520°C, and at Shoreham in 2014 at 540°C.

But Mr Cubin noted the Flight Reference Cards (FRC), used by pilots during flight, did not state there was a *minimum*. (Nor did the Airworthiness Approval Note). Nor was this tested in the Hunter Essential Knowledge quiz when Hill converted to Hunter in 2011.

I've discussed this before. It is a typical problem occurring across Air Publications - the need to ensure consistency. That is why, as far as possible, MoD seeks to put information in a single place. However, this is impossible with the FRC's, their point being to summarise key data. This is one reason why these aircrew publications were managed by a separate and specialist department at Boscombe Down, the RAF Handling Squadron. But, of course, they had had no involvement in Hunter after 1994. It transpired that the set used by Hill was over 40 years old.

Moreover, this same problem was noted by the AAIB in its report into the fatal accident involving Hunter F.4 G-HHUN in 1998, quoting Rolls Royce:

'The texts quoted in the AAIB Draft Bulletin are taken, we understand, from the Pilot's Notes available to the pilot of G-HHUN. They differ substantially from those for Hunter T.7 aircraft which were amended following earlier cases of turbine burn-out resulting from incorrect use of the 'ISOLATE' system...'.

(The High Pressure Pump Isolation switch, which must only be operated with the throttle closed. Even momentary use of the switch with the throttle open will destroy the engine turbine).

Once again the question arises - *Who was the Hunter Design Authority?* - because the regulations require, in the first instance, Unsatisfactory Feature Reports be submitted to them, the process controlled under permanent contract by the MoD Publications Authority. As I said earlier when discussing the unserviceable fuel pump, that mandated contractual process had been abandoned by the RAF in 1993, and the consequent poor state of publications (out-of-date, irreconcilable, incorrect, etc.) had been noted a number of times by the RAF Director of Flight Safety as a critical airworthiness failing. In short, no blame could be attached to any aircrew.

Medical - The second turning point

The effects of *g*-forces

The human body is much more tolerant of *g*-force when it is applied front to back (Gx) than when applied longitudinally (Gz), or laterally (Gy). In general, most sustained *g*-forces incurred by pilots are applied longitudinally, whereas for example in a Formula 1 car the drivers experience Gy. The *g*-thresholds at which these effects occur depend on the training, age and fitness of the individual. An untrained individual can black out between 4 and 6g, particularly if this is pulled suddenly. A trained, fit individual wearing a g-suit can, with some difficulty, sustain up to 12-14g without loss of consciousness.

G-LOC (g-force induced Loss of Consciousness) is caused by a critical loss of oxygen supply to the blood cells (hypoxia), such that the cells 'switch off'. Under increasing <u>positive</u> g-force, blood will tend to move from the head toward the feet. Under <u>negative</u> g, blood pressure will increase in the head, running the risk of the dangerous condition known as Redout, with too much blood pressure in the head and eyes.

Because of the high level of sensitivity that the retina has to hypoxia, symptoms are usually first experienced visually. With higher intensity or longer duration, when progressively applying g the reducing level of oxygenated blood flow means one experiences, in turn:

- Tunnel vision - loss of peripheral vision, retaining the centre vision; the effect being like looking down a tunnel and everything around is grey or black.
- Greyout - a partial loss of vision so that one sees speckling before the eyes, the edges of the tunnel being grey dots.
- Blackout - a complete loss of vision <u>but retaining consciousness</u>. One slumps, and the eyes close as the muscles gently relax. In this situation the eyes have stopped working but the brain is still functioning, so one is vaguely and briefly aware something is wrong and there is a need to do something.
- G-LOC - where consciousness is lost.

In practice, the first three warning signs should be sufficient for the pilot to take action to avoid loss of consciousness, as if cognitive ability is lost one would tend to relax the pull on the controls, thus reducing g.

At this point a serious misconception must be corrected. It was widely reported that Hill had told first responders he had 'blacked out'. In fact, these were the paramedic's words, who emphasised in court that he could not recall exactly what was said. This might seem innocuous but is of huge significance. To a pilot 'blackout' means lost vision but retained consciousness and learned motor functions, such as operating the controls but not always correctly or in time. To the layman, it usually means unconsciousness. The court fully accepted this.

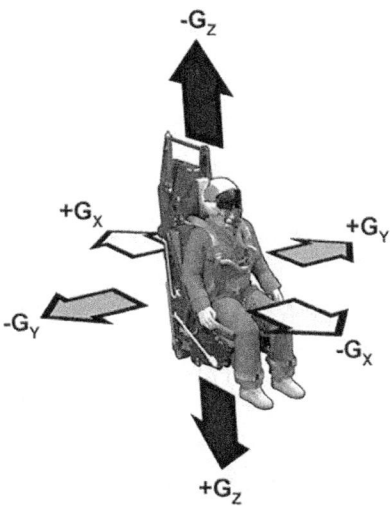

Figure 6 - Gravitational (Gx, Gy, and Gz) axes with respect to pilot

G-LOC relates to g being applied at a high level, and rapidly. The brain has about five seconds of oxygen reserve, so if one pulls $10g$ for three seconds, then relaxes, there should be no issue. However, pull for more than five seconds and the brain, which is not getting more oxygen, suddenly runs out of its oxygen store (not supply). The danger is there is no warning sign.

Absolute incapacitation is the period during which one is physically unconscious, and averages about 12 seconds. Relative incapacitation is the period in which the consciousness has been regained, but the person is confused and remains unable to perform simple tasks. This averages about 15 seconds. Brain oxygenation lags quite significantly behind the recovery of g. That is, the oxygen debt within the brain builds up, the brain gradually becoming more hypoxic with the duration of g exposure. Upon regaining cerebral blood flow, the victim usually experiences myoclonic convulsions (sudden, brief involuntary twitching or jerking of a muscle or group of muscles) and often full amnesia of the event.

Many believe that if the g pulled is not enough to stop blood flow to the head, it might reduce it enough so that the oxygen supply is insufficient to retain higher level function, but enough to retain consciousness. Again, if the g is applied quickly, then the brain gets no warning - it is living off the oxygen store, then suddenly drops to a low supply.

The symptoms are similar to strangulation and any form of hypoxia - even stroke, albeit this is usually measured in the long term effects over days/years, not the immediate seconds.

The point between blackout and G-LOC, when vision is lost but muscle tone remains and eyes are open, is termed A-LOC (Almost Loss of Consciousness). This level of hypoxia is not quite as severe, but the individual is unable to function cognitively. They are generally sitting up and there will be some swaying of the head, but there is no essential response. An MoD witness confirmed that pilots are not taught to recognise the difference between A-LOC and G-LOC, because to them it is irrelevant; and Mr Cubin had confirmed this.

The defence's position was that Hill might have suffered a form of A-LOC, perhaps caused by a combination of moderate g and one or more blood vessels being constricted due to tilting his head. No-one could refute what seemed a logical argument. All witnesses agreed on one thing. There remains a great deal of uncertainty over precisely what is happening, because there is a related debate over what constitutes loss of consciousness.

The terms G/A-LOC (and Cognitive Impairment in this context) were introduced during the late-80's/early-90's when rules and a better understanding around the subject of Human Factors were being established/revised. MoD conducted extensive research, especially after the loss of Jon Egging, and is acknowledged as a leader in the field. Study of medical papers and teaching from the time reveals quite heated debate over the term Cognitive Impairment. Many use it generically to cover different physical and mental conditions which could affect the efficiency of a pilot. MoD routinely used the term in the late-90's, and has on more than one occasion cited it in accident reports to explain a pilot's actions - a recent example being the death of Red Arrows pilot Sean Cunningham in 2011. Self-induced Cognitive Impairment was mooted, brought about by taking an over-the-counter medication. The main concerns were him forgetting a door lock combination, apparently forgetting his helmet visor and mask, and being distracted by a phone call on the walk to the aircraft. The pathologist had said:

'Whilst seemingly trivial in isolation, these events in combination raised the possibility of a degree of Cognitive Impairment'.

Due to this immaturity of knowledge, when Hill underwent his RAF g-training at RAF North Luffenham in the early-90's he was not specifically advised of G-LOC or A-LOC. However, like all pilots he was aware of the adverse effect of g-forces, and fast jets are fitted with an 'anti-g system'. In the

Hunter, this consists of four high pressure air bottles, a filter, an ON/OFF selector valve, a pressure-reducing valve, and an anti-*g* valve to automatically control the air pressure to the trousers according to *g* loads in the Gz axis, when they exceed 2.5*g*. The Aircraft Servicing Manual states:

> 'The use of an anti-*g* suit raises the pilot's blackout level and considerably reduces fatigue caused by repeated applications of *g*, and enables the pilot to carry out "all round" observations at high *g*.'[46]

Severely damaged by impact and being cut away by medics, what remained was tested and deemed satisfactory. (The filter was clean and the anti-*g* valve working). However, quick-release connectors and pipework could not be checked for leaks, security, or correct assembly. These components are particularly susceptible to dust and dirt causing malfunctions, and must only be dismantled/assembled 'under conditions of absolute cleanliness'. (Implying a Clean Room).[47] The AAIB did not say if this had been verified. In court, a prosecution witness said that an anti-*g* valve check, whereby one can press a button on the valve and inflate the suit, was accepted as whole-system check. Most engineers would consider this, at most, a confidence check. This conflation of confidence check and serviceability test had occurred before, in the Sean Cunningham case; pilots believing that 'rattling' the ejection seat shackles proved the main parachute would deploy. (While your car engine may start, you won't get far if the drive shaft is lying on the ground).

When the suit inflates, one's diaphragm is restricted, reducing lung expansion. Low levels of Gz have a pooling effect in the lungs which, coupled with the diaphragm issue, results in less oxygenation of the blood in the lungs. That is, there is a negative side to the anti-*g* system, whereby the lungs are starved of oxygen.

Not only does the suit squeeze, but one can also strain against it - termed *g*-straining - providing an extra 2*g* of tolerance. This involves taking deep breaths and breathing out with a closed throat - so you don't actually breathe out but pressurise the inside of the chest - as well as tensing the lower part of your body, increasing blood pressure. In doing so the blood flow to the brain is improved, and with it the ability to tolerate higher levels of *g*. This has to be trained, and it has to be done intermittently, every three seconds or thereabouts, for it to be effective.

---

46 AP 4374H, N & Q, Vol. 1, Book 1, Section 3, Chapter 13.
47 A specially designed room that removes pollutants such as particles, harmful air, and bacteria from the air; and controls temperature, pressure, airflow velocity and distribution, noise, vibration, lighting, and static electricity.

A person's performance in *g*-straining is improved when trained in a centrifuge, and this was mandated, every five years; the periodicity determined from experience gained by the US. Hitherto, UK training had been at Farnborough, but the centrifuge there was limited to 2*g*. In 2018 a new facility finally opened at RAF Cranwell. So, while I said MoD is a leader in the field, as ever it is constrained by beancounters regarding safety/training as optional, and having got rid of the specialist staff and posts whose role it was to fight these machinations.

The court was also told that pilots would be placed in a decompression chamber, taken to 20,000 feet, told to remove their oxygen mask, and given a series of cognitive tests. After five minutes some would show no effects, others would be severely affected; heavy smokers being most vulnerable.

The basic argument was whether there is a gradual onset, or a sudden switching off. The defence's case was there was gradual onset, so footage showing Hill moving did not necessarily mean he was in full control. This was termed 'low *g*-force syndrome' (below around 4*g*), whereby the subject can continue to function, particularly with regard to learned motor skills, but has reduced cognitive ability and the capacity to deal with abnormal situations. This is because if one hasn't learnt something well, then the brain is more involved in actually trying to do it. This increased brain activity and thinking is impaired by hypoxia, and the effects are much more significant than once it becomes a skill and automatic.

The prosecution's case was that there was no such phenomenon, that Hill was in full control of his faculties, and therefore the aircraft, at all times. This, it said, was based on advice from MoD. But what MoD *actually* said was such a syndrome had never been documented or directly studied. That doesn't mean it doesn't exist; it simply means the generic terms G-LOC and A-LOC were used, and their effects not entirely understood.

This evidence was presented by two defence experts, eminently qualified physicians, and formed the basis of the medical aspects of the case. However, the prosecution's medical witness disagreed, saying A-LOC to G-LOC was:

> '*A very black and white step which is related to this sudden cessation of blood flow, because the veins collapse so they're stuck together*'...

...but later agreed knowledge was immature and more research was needed. As I said, in the aftermath of Hill's acquittal this has ramped up.

Finally, regarding training, while MoD requires aircrew to undergo periodic refresher training on *g* forces, and with it medical checks (pilots from different eras inform me this has varied between 1-3 years), there was no such requirement placed on Hill once he attained his display licence from the CAA. That is, while he was compliant with the medical standards required to display in 2015, MoD would have deemed him out-of-date and not permitted to fly. This raises one of the key questions of the entire case. *Why has the CAA adopted an approach that is the polar opposite of MoD's?* It is the regulator, with almost unlimited authority, but seemingly no accountability or sense of responsibility. Its regulatory failures, involving multiple breaches of the Reason Model defences, were none of Hill's doing.

Video evidence

Prior to seeing the draft AAIB report in November 2016, Hill was advised by first-hand witnesses, many of them pilots, that the accident sequence had all the hallmarks of a A/G-LOC problem. The crucial question was: *When did the medical incapacitation event manifest?* Once the AAIB report was released, what became known as 'Point X' was readily identified by applying the graphs and diagrams to Google Earth. Subsequent study of the cockpit video confirmed this. When Hill was asked about this under interview, he identified that *'everything was right'* until the end of a long, left turn. In response to specific questions, he stated:

'From 12:21:49 [Point X] until 12:22:14, no pilot action, reaction or decision seems to occur in accordance with the likely planned display or appropriate practice. These are an inexplicable series of events, the sequence of errors and absence of any correct or rational actions of no obvious explanation'.

Engine power started to increase, but then reduced abruptly at Point X. Thereafter *'almost everything was wrong'*. If he suffered a G-LOC, A-LOC or cerebral hypoxia problem, the causal event would be 4-6 seconds earlier.

A former RAF aviation doctor viewed the video independently in the following days. Without knowing the wider picture, he pointed to when Hill tilted his head sharply over to the right, saying *'If there was a problem, that was likely when it started'*. He did not know the significance of the timing of his observation, five seconds before Point X. In Hill's view, this confirmed his own thoughts; the tilt being necessary due to the limited view from the Hunter T.7 cockpit following conversion to 2-seater (apparent in Figure 7), combined with the features of the Shoreham display site.

Pressed at a 'joint experts' meeting on 17 December 2018 (held by order of the Judge so that the court could be told of areas of agreement and disagreement), the prosecution agreed this remained to be understood (modifying its previous position of poor airmanship).

Figure 7 - Pilot Andrew Hill's head tilt, just before Point X *(AAIB)*.

In essence, the belief was that this head tilt, under moderate g, restricted blood flow to one side of his brain. This was reduced and/or not fully recombined above the neck, at a time when it needed to be at maximum. That is, if one side is cut-off and some of the brain is starved, other parts continue as normal leading to *partial* loss of consciousness or cognition; which is the current definition of A-LOC. (Sometimes called P-LOC). Notably, there was no research available assessing a tilted head - all centrifuge work was carried out 'head up' (and at nominal g).

This was the uncertainty, the thin line between blackout and loss of consciousness, and only with great difficulty could it be replicated in a centrifuge. This would explain the retention of some automatic motor functions, but errors elsewhere; and Mr Cubin had already emphasised the need to *'consider the separation between motor function and cognitive function'*. However, this was difficult to present as 'evidence', precisely because knowledge was immature; exacerbating the doubt.

Note: It is important to say that under High Court order Figure 7 is prohibited. However, the AAIB breached the order by reproducing this image in its Supplement of 2019, so I'll take the risk. My understanding is that at its greatest extent the tilt was more pronounced to the right.

Expert medical witnesses

The defence produced two experts, Dr Henry Lupa and Dr Stephen Jarvis; the prosecution one, Wing Commander Nicholas Green. Once again, I should explain that the witnesses used visual aids, which I cannot reproduce for you; nor the mannerisms used when explaining them. Under different circumstances this would make an author's task impossible; but as I have said, there is a fundamental and overriding factor here. No amount of aids and expertise could produce hard facts that everyone agreed upon, so there was significant doubt. For that reason the following sections are relatively brief, as I concentrate on the standard of proof and why Hill was acquitted. During evidence, the defence experts' respective reports were referred to, but these have not been released. However, Wing Commander Green wrote, or at least significantly contributed to, the AAIB's Appendix M (RAFCAM report). I invite you to try to put yourself in the jurors' shoes.

(It is likely others, such as psychologists, contributed to the RAFCAM report, but for current purposes it was Wing Commander Green who was named, and was the only prosecution witness on Human Factors).

Earlier, I said only expert witnesses may offer their opinion on a set of facts. The Judge allowed significant leeway here, with the experts offering opinion and hypotheses on matters that were not established as fact. He did not specifically say he was allowing this. Rather, my impression is he wanted the jury to appreciate that no facts had been established at all about low-*g* impairment. Certainly, neither side raised any objections.

To summarise what was lengthy, highly detailed, and repetitive evidence, here are the crucial elements.

Dr Henry Lupa, whose most recent PhD was on 'Some cerebral effects of hypoxia in man', described this as:

'The performance of the brain, essentially the thinking task and logical reasoning, awareness of one's self, one's situation - it covers a wide range of symptoms and signs. There is scientific evidence showing quite significant cerebral hypoxia occurring after exposure to a moderately high level of g...but which doesn't lead to A-LOC. The main problem is that the amount of blood getting to the brain has been reduced'.

He described the current understanding of G-LOC as fairly consistent, but A-LOC variable. Asked if he agreed with Mr Whaley's description of A-LOC, he replied:

'No. There were errors in his understanding'.

The question had to be asked, but it was unfair on Mr Whaley, who should not have been asked to opine on a subject he did not profess expertise in.

Dr Lupa confirmed that he and Wing Commander Green had met to view the cockpit video, and agreed Hill did not suffer G-LOC or A-LOC during the flight. He had then gone on to consider if there was any evidence indicative of something short of A-LOC, but amounting to Cognitive Impairment; and indeed had received a new research paper only two days before referencing other new studies, which he hadn't yet digested, suggesting there *was*.

<u>Wing Commander Nicholas Green</u> was responsible for the *g*-training of all RAF pilots, and advisor to Duty Holders on related risks. He had also acted as the police's 'expert' in order that they get round the AAIB report being protected. That is, lacking balance the police investigation was potentially biased towards the prosecution. Having described G-LOC, he said:

> *'The deeper question as to what is actually going on in the brain, I don't think anyone could clearly answer, because that is a question of what is consciousness. You've lost vision, and then you stop thinking -* <u>*at least from my understanding*</u> *- you're unable to act or move and when you watch people having A-LOC they just stare vacantly ahead'.*

He opined that without G-LOC or A-LOC there was no Cognitive Impairment. (Dr Lupa found this *'very hard to accept'*). However, he agreed that the evidence presented, of research into *g*-forces, would be a good *'signpost for other people to try and explore it'*, including the consequential effects such as Cognitive Impairment. In other words, he agreed research and medical knowledge was immature. The jury would, naturally, construe this as doubt.

<u>Dr Stephen Jarvis</u>, an expert in Human Factors Performance and author of the CAA's 'Flight Crew Human Factors Handbook' (CAP737), had analysed the cockpit and other video, concluding that Hill had made a *'cascade of 8-12 errors'* revealing a form of Cognitive Impairment, in just 23 seconds. That is, they stemmed from an initial error or event, making them very difficult to explain other than by some degree of Cognitive Impairment:

1. Power reduction after a certain point in the flight
2. Continuing to turn beyond that inbound track
3. Failure to notice or act upon the low airspeed
4. Pitch oscillations
5. Entering the manoeuvre too early, away from the crowd

6. Inappropriate pull up into the loop
7. Applying left roll input from early in the manoeuvre
8. Reduction in power in the first part of the vertical
9. Applying and holding further left roll input from the vertical
10. No escape manoeuvre
11. Failure to eject
12. General position of the aircraft

Some are errors of judgment, others known Human Factors issues associated with display flying. Regarding 'failure to eject', this is poorly phrased, implying he *should* have ejected. Any decision not to eject (if he was capable of such unimpaired thought) was irrelevant to the errors that caused the accident. It may be that had he ejected, the aircraft would have taken a different flight path and different people, or nobody, would have been killed. As the aircraft had stalled that behaviour could not be predicted, with little control possible in the final seconds. There are other considerations, such as the seats in G-BXFI were neither serviceable nor airworthy, and their performance could not be guaranteed. I discussed this earlier. The critical one is power reduction, and it is not at all clear this was pilot error, or even caused by him.

He stated that Cognitive Impairment would not stop Hill being able to fly the aircraft:

'Your consciousness is not required for the movements being made in those last 20 seconds. If Cognitive Impairment were the catalyst, once impairment had begun to set in one would expect to see the display continuing but getting a lot less accurate'.

This, he said, would result in an increase in the number of errors being made. Asked by Mr Khalil if there was any explanation for these errors other than Cognitive Impairment, Dr Jarvis replied, *'No, not really'*.

Regarding the prosecution's assertion that the crash was a result of *'extremely bad piloting'* and not Cognitive Impairment, he said:

'I can't really accept that. It just doesn't seem credible'.

Finally, Dr Jarvis reported that, like Dr Lupa, he had received the new research paper in the past few days. This suggested Cognitive Impairment occurred at lower g than required to produce A-LOC and G-LOC, and this had prompted him to strengthen his standpoint.

Summary of expert medical evidence

The debate was not 'won' or 'lost'. The experts merely differed in opinion, and no relative value could be attributed due to the medical conditions not being fully understood. That was not a good basis upon which to seek a conviction when the test was *beyond reasonable doubt*. Add to this the highly specialised nature of the evidence, and I can only imagine the jurors' heads would have been spinning.

At an early stage the AAIB considered g and G/A-LOC:

> 'A study of the available data by the Royal Air Force Centre of Aviation Medicine concluded that a high g load was not present at any point in the left turn preceding the entry to, or in the upward half of, the accident manoeuvre. The peak g force calculated for the turn was 2.7g....'[48]

But there was no balance. Moreover, the AAIB's source, Wing Commander Green, made it clear he was <u>not</u> an expert in g-calculations. So why did the AAIB rely entirely on his figures without checking them? In court, they were exposed as wrong, practically handing the case to the defence.

Notably, the initial g-value used when charging Hill was a direct quote from the AAIB report (maximum 2.7g), and attributed to the AAIB, not Green. But it meant that, in direct violation of the High Court order, the police (and CPS) were seen to be using the AAIB report.

The prosecution spent a lot of time and effort trying to disprove the evidence of its own witnesses. One telling aspect was that, faced with the convincing evidence of Dr Jarvis, it chose not to engage a Human Factors expert to challenge him. (Shortly after the AAIB report was published, Dr Jarvis was engaged as a Human Factors consultant by the AAIB during the investigation into a serious incident at Belfast International Airport on 21 July 2017).[49]

The Judge's legal directions

Background

Given the charge was Gross Negligence Manslaughter, there were five elements the prosecution had to prove against Hill:

1. He owed an existing duty of care to the victim;
2. He negligently breached that duty of care;

---

48 AAIB report, 1.18.10.1.
49 https://assets.publishing.service.gov.uk/media/5bf5148640f0b607875e2877/2-2018_C-FWGH_Lo_Res.pdf

3. The breach of duty must be the cause of death of the victim;
4. The circumstances of the breach were truly exceptionally bad and so reprehensible as to justify the conclusion that it amounted to gross negligence and required criminal sanction, and;
5. It was reasonably foreseeable that the breach of that duty gave rise to a serious and obvious risk of death.

The offence must be 'complete' so, if (1) cannot be satisfied, then the matter is over. *(Adomako)*. The defence has to do nothing save challenge and probe the prosecution's case. The prosecution however has to actively prove its case, and that involves demonstrating that the full definition of the charge has been met. This is a widely debated area of law, and the bar is set high. Indeed, the bereaved families were warned of this by the police. To illustrate this, let us look at test #1...

There is a further 3-fold test to decide if a duty should be held to exist:

1. Whether the damage was foreseeable.
2. Whether the victims were in an appropriate position of proximity to the defendant.
3. Whether it was fair and just to impose liability on the defendant.

In court, Mr Kark had said:

> 'There can be no issue, that he owed all of those below him on the ground a duty of care'.

But clearly there *was* an issue. As per Lord Mackay in *Adomako*, the jury must consider the conduct of the individual or entity against the background of *'all the circumstances in which the defendant was placed'*. Here they were not considered, by High Court order. Also, a number of factors were wholly outwith Hill's control. Primarily, he was given an aircraft that he did not know was unserviceable and unairworthy.

That said, I can understand why the defence would not want to go down this route. It is a difficult subject to grasp, especially when the prosecution, AAIB and MoD, routinely conflate serviceability and airworthiness. It would be easy to get drawn down a rabbit hole, and the defence may have thought impairment easier to present to a jury. However, it would certainly have been interesting if, say, Justice Sir Charles Haddon-Cave had been called as an expert defence witness, and asked his opinion on Hill being charged when his aircraft didn't have a valid Safety Case and shouldn't have been flying. His reply would be short, referring to his Nimrod Review.

With this circumstance in mind, was it fair and just to impose sole liability?

Had <u>all the circumstances</u> been revealed, I doubt very much if the case would have proceeded at all, because in arguing it the prosecution would have to reveal the offences of others who were, in effect, their co-prosecutors. I see no point in the law saying *'fair and just'* if it is not.

But with most of the evidence favourable to Hill not permitted, and the Judge unable to cite the AAIB report, he had to direct the jury that elements 1, 2 and 3 were not in doubt. He told them 4 and 5 were the *'subject of disputes which are for you, and you alone, to resolve'*. He distilled matters further. Given Hill had freely admitted his errors, he stated:

> *'To this extent, it is actually part of Mr Hill's case that the flying was "truly exceptionally bad" and, if you take that view as well, it may be that the real issue in this case is a simply stated one: Has the prosecution proved, so that you are sure, that any cognitive impairment which may have affected Mr Hill was not at such a level that it was a substantial cause of the accident, and that therefore he was responsible for the course of flying which led to the accident?'*

Regarding the allegation that Hill was too low at pull-up, he directed:

> *'There was nothing negligent about starting this loop from a low altitude, but that decision did mean that more power would be required to reach the safe gate height to enable the loop to be completed'.*

He summarised the *'central allegation'* as:

> *'(Hill) arrived at an apex of about 2,700 feet, which was too low to carry out the second downward part of the loop safely, but nevertheless decided to continue with it, rather than flying an escape manoeuvre'.*

The prosecution had alleged this was deliberate; the defence that it was the result of misjudgements caused by Cognitive Impairment, meaning he did not appreciate he was too low. In other words, the jury had to decide:

1. If the prosecution had proved *beyond reasonable doubt* that there was no Cognitive Impairment. If so:
2. It then had to consider if Hill's admitted error amounted to <u>gross</u> (deliberate act or omission) negligence. If not, he was not guilty.

The jury was directed *to 'accept, and act on, the <u>agreed</u> expert evidence';* the Judge naming the witnesses who were to be heeded. There was more, but I will stop. This, I believe, was the key direction. All medical witnesses <u>agreed</u> knowledge was immature, the prosecution's expert recommending further study. That equated to significant doubt.

Prosecution and Defence closing arguments

I think, after the foregoing, there is little point setting out in any detail the prosecution's summing up. It went through the allegations again, almost as if the Judge had not issued his directions, and ignoring what its own witnesses had said. The jury could not help but notice this. For its part, the defence dwelt heavily on the fact the prosecution had not sought to challenge Dr Jarvis. That, it had done or said nothing to counteract his evidence.

The Judge's summing-up

Judge Edis took the jury through the notes he had taken about the evidence of the non-expert witness; the emphasis being on the contradictory data, or no data at all, available to Hill due to aircrew manuals not being aligned.

In an otherwise suitably sober narrative there was a humorous pause when he commenced speaking about Duxford 2014, but using the wrong notes. He apologised for his *'brain fade'*, presumably not wishing to use 'cognitive impairment' lest it prejudice matters.

He then issued several more directives to the jurors:

- They must accept the defence's position on Duxford 2014, and in any case this had no bearing on Shoreham 2015.
- If they believed there was disagreement over Southport 2014, they needed to resolve it. (Where Hill admitted an error in poor visibility).
- The experts substantially agreed about Shoreham 2014 and 2015, the jury having already been instructed to accept this.
- Regarding the error made by the test pilot when performing a similar manoeuvre, the jury was instructed to consider this with care, and reminded that the pilot had described this as an *'unconscious error'*. He had pulled 5.5g, calling the manoeuvre *'an unusual profile, it was at the extreme end of our workload, and every pilot makes errors every time we go flying'*.

RAFCAM's status in the investigation and trial

It would seem RAFCAM were engaged by the AAIB almost immediately, as it did not have its own Human Factors expert.[50] (One was recruited after the

---

50 In RAFCAM's words, they were 'tasked' by the AAIB, implying a hierarchical relationship.

trial). This is not unusual - the CAA and its Confidential Human Factors Incident Reporting Programme (CHIRP) suffer likewise. (Similarly, the UK Airprox Board has no-one qualified to investigate accidents). Although, intriguingly, from 2014 the AAIB had an arrangement with the Rail Accidents Investigation Branch to use their very good expert.

A Puma crash in Afghanistan on 11 October 2015 (seven weeks later) soon diverted RAFCAM, relegating Shoreham's priority. However, they did produce a 'Human Factors Aircraft Accident Report', included in the AAIB report as Appendix M. Much of this simply repeated evidence gathered by the AAIB which they were given access to, such as cockpit video from the accident flight and a *flight trials report prepared by the AAIB Operations Advisor*' - that is, Mr Southwood. It was omitted that he was actually the test pilot, the impression given that he was part of the AAIB team.

Crucially, and candidly, the report does not purport to be complete:

'The results of the RAFCAM analysis should not be considered in isolation, but rather in the context of the wider investigation and other HF issues identified and reported by the AAIB'.

However, the AAIB relied entirely on the analysis, its own brief Human Factors narrative (paragraph 1.18.10) simply referring to it; serving to emphasise that it had no expertise. But also that it sought no independent verification, and didn't carry out basic fact-checking. For reasons already explained, this weakened the prosecution case beyond recovery.

I think this subtlety changes entirely the perception of RAFCAM's role. If the AAIB had its own expert, RAFCAM would simply be an advisor engaged in a very specialised area, which is normal. But for all intents and purposes they (and with them MoD) were now part of the investigative team, 'tasked' with conducting perhaps *the* central part of the investigation, which became the entire basis of the prosecution's case against Hill. Yet, by their own admission, it should not have been 'considered in isolation'. That is, the AAIB report could not be complete until 'other HF issues' were studied and the results reconciled.

But the AAIB accepted the RAFCAM report without question; and hence so too the prosecution (and the High Court). Wing Commander Green was a major contributor, and later the prosecution's only medical/Human Factors witness. The report was not produced as a stand-alone exhibit (in the way Mr Southwood's trials report was), for very good reason. The AAIB and prosecution would not want it led in evidence as the content ran contrary to the charge of Gross Negligence Manslaughter, because human errors are not considered negligence. The AAIB/RAFCAM claimed Hill's <u>errors</u> were within the normal range of human performance, which is why they ignored Cognitive Impairment. The Crown Prosecution Service took the opposite view - Hill did not err, he acted deliberately; a decision making process that must surely have anticipated the likelihood of a Cognitive Impairment defence. As the Crown took a polar opposite view on this to its experts, one must ask why the AAIB and MoD were called as the prime prosecution witnesses. Could it be because the CPS could not find anyone to support their view of deliberate act?

Put another way, the Crown laid a serious allegation against Hill, but made no real attempt to justify it in court. Is that not astonishing?

Wing Commander Green based his evidence upon the report he contributed to, and was wise enough to highlight the main caveat - his work was inevitably and unavoidably incomplete. A number of issues fall out of this. First, there is a strong case for the RAFCAM Appendix M actually being part of the AAIB narrative. Placing it as an appendix was misleading, implying they were wholly independent. Second, while the AAIB was not called as a witness (as its report was prohibited), in effect it *was* called, and its report *was* presented, in the form of and by Wing Commander Green. But the problem the prosecution faced was Appendix M included much that had no tie-in with the main AAIB narrative, and had not been verified.

Moreover, the International Civil Aviation Organisation (ICAO), a special agency of the United Nations, sets out procedures for interviewing witnesses after accidents.[51] Hill was not interviewed by RAFCAM, and so the many obligations placed on the interviewer/investigation could not have been met, such as gathering and reviewing basic information. Thus, its report was one-sided. In effect it admitted this by only listing AAIB-sourced evidence; in turn rendering the AAIB report incomplete. And not only was it one-sided and incomplete, it was wrong; and the prosecution agreed it was.

Thoughts on the trial

The Judge and jury sat through almost two months of testimony, much of it detailed and technical. They watched and listened as the prosecution floundered with the facts, and its inability to mount a case. The jury carefully

---

51 Human Factors Digest No.7 (Cir 240) 'Investigation of Human factors in Accidents and Incidents'.

considered what it was allowed to hear, spent seven hours deliberating, and came to a conclusion.

On *g*-forces, RAFCAM got the basic calculations wrong; and because this work was used by the AAIB and police, so their reports were flawed and deficient. This was not the jury voting if one argument was better than another. This was the prosecution failing to check its own 'facts' before entering court. Frankly, it was inept to think this argument could succeed. Perhaps they were lulled by the High Court rulings in their favour. Either way, the prosecution barristers had little to work with, and were buried under the weight of their collapsing case.

But that is not to criticise the prosecution team in court; although one could ask why they didn't go back to the CPS and say *There's no case*. (Perhaps they did?) What persuaded the CPS to continue? The simple answer, I believe, is perceived public and political pressure to *hang the guilty bastard*. After all, he'd already been found guilty in the media, who had simply quoted the prosecution's opening statement. The case was ill-conceived. One potential juror said so, and wasn't selected. It is likely others harboured the same thoughts, but remained silent.

Andrew Hill perpetrated the final act. He admitted his errors. But, as per *Misra*, intent is important, and the jury is permitted to take into account any other factors which it may consider relevant; for example, the following constitute *prima facie* evidence of grossness:

- Failing to act following 'near misses' or occurrences.
- Failure to follow the organisation's written, mandated procedures and regulations designed to prevent recurrence.
- Indiscriminate cost cutting.
- Ignoring or concealing evidence of any of the above.

None of these applied to Hill. But they most certainly did apply to others who stood against him, in particular the CAA. It was the regulator, charged with protecting the public, but failed to enforce its own rules. It would have been far easier to prove negligence on *its* part.

I therefore believe it incumbent upon the CPS to explain why only Hill was pursued. He was 'merely' the pilot, a human weakness in one of the slices of Swiss Cheese. That was the CPS/AAIB/MoD's most significant failure. They only looked at the final act. The easy target. Any organisation that does that is unfit for purpose.

Would Hill have accepted a sole charge of *Endangering the safety of an aircraft*? This carries a maximum sentence of five years imprisonment, whereas Gross Negligence Manslaughter can be life imprisonment, although that is rare. Perhaps a moot question, as a decision was made in late-2018 to drop it to focus on the manslaughter charges, and not distract the jury. The defence was Cognitive Impairment, and if successful would have also offered a complete defence to that charge as well.

In my view four issues made the jury's decision easy:

- The prosecution was unable to disprove Cognitive Impairment, to the point of actively assisting the defence.
- Evidence was actively concealed and falsified.
- By disallowing fundamental evidence, the legal system left too many unanswered questions; exacerbated by the AAIB report being available legitimately on-line for almost two years prior to trial.
- The fundamental unfairness of a selective prosecution, when collective responsibility was required.

As defence barrister Karim Khalil, wrote:

'(Our) successful defence exposed serious failings in the investigation conducted by the AAIB, together with shortcomings in the medical data base and knowledge relating to cognitive impairment in pilots'.

And his colleague, former RAF fast jet pilot Stephen Spence:

'Did I think he screwed up? I vehemently did. But after watching the evidence in court, it convincingly opened my mind that the pilot's cognitive function wasn't right'.

The whole premise of aviation safety is acknowledging that human beings make errors. Undoubtedly Andrew Hill's were serious. But if every error led to a criminal prosecution, what effect would that have on aviation itself? I conclude the jury did the right thing in acquitting him. The defence raised reasonable doubt. The prosecution raised overwhelming doubt.

By far the worst aspect was the decision to gamble that an injustice would be perpetrated. The CPS rolled the dice, which they thought loaded in their favour, and failed spectacularly. Is the public allowed to ask why the decision makers remain in office, when they have committed misconduct in that office by, for example, condoning conspiracy to pervert justice?

To end this section, I will simply repeat the words of one of the defence team, which I agree with entirely:

> 'A number of people have remarked that the best/most expensive lawyers won. Whilst extremely flattering, the prosecution lawyers are both highly respected, capable barristers who could only act with the hand they were dealt. They dealt with the case doggedly and professionally and I retain nothing but the highest respect for them. They suffered from an inherent lack of aviation knowledge, and more importantly a lack of such amongst some of the people who were advising them. As a result the prosecution proceeded on a number of false assumptions, including a number of criticisms of Andy Hill's previous flying that they subsequently had to abandon. There were further criticisms that they had to withdraw before ever getting to the jury, as a result of representations we made to the prosecution and the trial judge.
>
> The burden on the prosecution was to prove that Andy Hill was guilty of Gross Negligence Manslaughter. Once there was credible evidence that he may have been suffering from Cognitive Impairment, then it was for the prosecution to disprove it. There was sufficient evidence to raise a credible case, and not only did the evidence exist but the jury accepted it as credible and possible. The jury could have rejected the evidence if they so wished.
>
> Regarding Andy Hill saying he was not made aware of anti-g straining during training, that was misreported. What he actually said was that when he went through training, g-training was not dealt with as formally and to the extent that it is now. That was an agreed position with the prosecution experts. The newspapers misreported it as him saying he didn't know anything about anti-g straining. I am afraid there was a lot of misreporting in the press. As an example, when I cross-examined one of the prosecution expert witnesses it was reported in the papers that my colleague had cross-examined that witness. On that particular day my colleague was not even in the country, he was in New York. I use that as a non-contentious example. There were a number of criticisms levelled by the prosecution, nearly all of which ended up being binned. In a way it was a shame, as our evidence would have made for some uncomfortable moments in the witness box'. [52]

---

[52] https://www.pprune.org/military-aviation/619209-shoreham-airshow-crash-trial-25.html (8 August 2019).

'I am truly sorry…'

On the steps of the Old Bailey, an hour after his acquittal, Hill read out the names of the deceased, also referring to the injured, and said:

'I am truly sorry for the part I have played in their deaths'.

He was criticised for *'the part I have played…'*, which implied others shared blame. Yet that was a simple fact, and was set out in the AAIB report. But he was not allowed to refer to it, having to choose his words carefully. In fact, it is likely he went further than he should have, because his words begged the question: *Who are you referring to?* Had he replied, he would have been committing contempt and might have been whisked back into court, because he could only be referring to the AAIB report.

Have these others been asked to apologise?

It is entirely normal for accused to be advised not to speak publicly until after the trial. History shows us their words, and events in general, will be distorted by the media. Military pilots, in particular, are tight-lipped after an incident or accident, for the very good reason they are deemed guilty until they prove themselves innocent. In the most bizarre extension of this, it remains the government and MoD's formal position that it is for deceased aircrew to prove themselves innocent - a position has never been retracted.[53]

That same day Sky News broadcast a 12-minute piece on the case, their opening shot being *'There was nothing wrong with the plane'.*[54] Well, there was plenty wrong with the plane, and the AAIB had spelt it out in excruciating detail. Later, they broadcast another piece with an 'aviation safety expert' claiming Hill was 300 feet lower than his authorisation when he commenced his loop manoeuvre. Yet that had already been refuted in court, without challenge. One must question the motives of those who would willingly overlook the established facts and mislead the public.

---

53 Lord Alexander Philip, Mull of Kintyre Review, paragraph 4.4.5.
54 https://www.youtube.com/watch?v=TC1Oezipcu8

Request to reopen AAIB investigation

I sense disagreement within the AAIB. The Senior Inspector thought the possibility of Cognitive Impairment should be included in the AAIB report. He was overruled; and I have discussed why senior AAIB (and MoD) management would not wish this raised. In 2017 Hill requested the AAIB reopen its inquiries, primarily because the known facts left its report unsupportable. In May 2019, after the trial, the Chief Inspector invited 'new' evidence; plainly a reaction to his report being revealed in court as flawed and deficient (for the same reasons cited in 2017). Commencing the following month, Hill had a number of meetings with the AAIB, submitting a lengthy list of reasons and evidence.

It would seem the outcome was unsatisfactory, as he then wrote to a Director General in the Department for Transport (DfT), nominally in charge of the AAIB and CAA. She replied, offering a meeting, with Hill urged to send any safety concerns to the CAA; who attended the subsequent meeting along with the AAIB's Chief Inspector.

On 2 August 2019 the Chief Inspector issued this statement:

> 'Following a detailed review of the g-forces, the AAIB has decided not to re-open its investigation into the accident near Shoreham Airport on 22 August 2015. The results confirm that the findings of the AAIB safety investigation published in 2017 remain valid and we will not be reopening the investigation. However, we will publish a Supplement to our Final Report with full details of the review conducted which we hope all parties will find informative'.

The scope (g-forces) was limited, yet even so the review deficient, in that:

- It considered only isolated events, rather than the whole.
- The RAFCAM analysis only addressed two aspects, the pull-up into the climb, and apex.
- The AAIB continued to base its analysis on RAFCAM's significantly incorrect Gz calculations and methodology, providing no rationale for ignoring that its Appendix M (RAFCAM report) had been proven inaccurate in court, and that this had been accepted by the prosecution and their own Human Factors expert witness, Wing Commander Green.

And, plainly, the Supplement, issued on 19 December 2019, was in breach of the High Court order of 2016 by virtue of discussing the cockpit video. In fact it went further, publishing more video extracts. It did not advance knowledge of cause, but was priceless to the CAA and MoD.

With no mechanism by which the decision could be appealed, the official record shows the AAIB declared itself and RAFCAM right, and the CAA and senior DfT staff concurred, to the exclusion of all evidence to the contrary. And all the while delaying the Inquest.

What rules did the AAIB work to? The Civil Aviation (Investigation of Air Accidents and Incidents) Regulations 2018 state:

> *'Following publication of a final safety investigation report relating to an accident or serious incident, evidence has become available which, in the Chief Inspector's opinion, is new and significant, the Chief Inspector <u>must</u> cause the safety investigation to be reopened'.*

In this context, the following definitions may be used:

<u>Evidence</u>: This must be factual.

<u>New</u>: Unknown to, or previously unused by, the AAIB.

<u>Significant</u>: Sufficient to alter analysis, conclusions or recommendations.

The evidence from the trial (and of equal import, lack of evidence) was clearly 'new and significant'. The real reason the AAIB didn't want to reopen was because to do so would be to admit its report was deeply flawed, and it did not want this examined at the Inquest (or in a civil case).

For the most part I have avoided quoting anonymous internet posts, but thought I'd offer one that sums up my own feelings on the Supplement:

> *'It is difficult to read the AAIB supplementary report without gaining the impression that they were somewhat peeved to have been required to write it. It does not evidence their customary open mindedness, instead reeking of a desire to bury Cognitive Impairment by whatever means they can. It seems to start from the premise that it doesn't exist, and seeks out all the material they can find to support that premise'.* [55]

---

55 https://www.pprune.org/military-aviation/619209-shoreham-airshow-crash-trial-27.html, 21 December 2019.

Other voices (2019 - 2022)

A question of contempt

The following is a personal observation arising from a post made on the Professional Pilots Rumour Network (PPRuNe) internet forum by a serving RAF officer. I should say *'claims to be...'* because PPRuNe is a largely anonymous forum, but if he is not an RAF officer then the following is even worse...

On 8 August 2019 he revealed he had access to data protected by the 2016 High Court ruling:

> *'Those currently serving may also have seen a RAFCAM note to duty holders on the issues raised...'.*[56]

He was referring to a RAFCAM letter (it is more formal than a 'note') to the Air Officers Commanding (AOC) 1, 2 and 22 Groups, copied to AOC 38 Group and the Head of the Air Safety Centre, and headed 'Shoreham Airshow Crash Trial Verdict - Initial Impressions'. At the time, 1 Group was essentially frontline aircraft fleets such as Typhoon; 2 Group was air transport, refuelling, Airborne Early Warning and Air Battle Management; and 22 Group was training, including the Red Arrows (now within 2 Group). 38 Group was Engineering, Logistics, Communications and Medical Operations.

The Air Vice Marshals who hold these AOC posts are termed 'Operating Duty Holders'. In the Duty Holder construct they sit between Delivery Duty Holders (usually Group Captains) and the Senior Duty Holder (the Chief of the Air Staff). The addressees owned and were accountable for the Air System Safety Cases for their platforms, and were required to record and justify an argument in the Safety Statement that risks were As Low As Reasonably Practicable (ALARP) and tolerable. They are the only officers required to answer in court for ALARP and tolerable statements. At time of writing, none have.

It was therefore incumbent upon them to have their Safety Cases updated and re-issued to include an assessment of the data being provided by RAFCAM. That is, RAFCAM (whether intentionally or not) were notifying a possible hazard, and even if it was later deemed or thought not to exist, or to have zero

---

[56] https://www.pprune.org/military-aviation/619209-shoreham-airshow-crash-trial-25.html (8 August 2019).

impact, it had to be recorded and the reasoning set out, in case a future event proved the assessment wrong. Moreover, this audit trail must be retained in perpetuity, because even after an aircraft has left service one may have to justify decisions in court. A good test of any Safety Management System, and of the AOCs satisfying their duty of care, would be to confirm this was all done.

Given the continuing uncertainty over Cognitive Impairment, the risk mitigation would be to continue to fund RAFCAM research, along with allies such as the US. And a positive statement would be required to say the current fleets could continue flying. If the Chief of the Air Staff did not feel able to make this decision, it had to be referred to the Secretary of State.

The author (or least signatory) was Deputy Assistant Chief of Staff Aviation Medicine, a Group Captain. He refers to analysis of the cockpit GoPro footage, which Sussex Police could only release to experts instructed by themselves, and to the CPS for use by prosecuting counsel or experts they engaged. It comments on the video and analysis in a way Hill was not allowed to. The letter aligns with the prosecution's case, which had been challenged and found severely wanting, to the point the Judge directed jurors not to heed it.

To recap, the 2016 *Sussex* High Court ruling said:

'The material that is disclosed to the Chief Constable of Sussex <u>shall not be further disclosed by him</u> save that he may disclose the material to:

(i) Any experts instructed by the Police in the furtherance of their investigation.

(ii) The Crown Prosecution Service for the purposes of advising him and pursuing a prosecution if that is the decision of the CPS and any Solicitor or Counsel engaged by them to act as their agents or representatives or any expert instructed by them.

The results of any <u>analysis and any subsequent opinion</u> as a result of the expert consideration referred to in 3(i) above shall be treated on the same confidential as the rest of the material'.

MoD itself was not 'instructed' by Sussex Police; but Wing Commander Green, the prosecution's *g*-force expert, was. He also acted for the AAIB, and assisted the CAA. The issue here is that protected data was relayed back to RAFCAM, in doing so breaching the High Court order; and then presented as authoritative. The author of the letter also breached the order by publishing this opinion. Both the PPRuNe post and passage of data were in contempt of the High Court ruling.

Asked by another party for the RAFCAM letter in September 2019, the RAF refused on the grounds it was part of *'ongoing research'*, and releasing it may *'prejudice the outcome of the research'*.[57] Yet its existence and general content had already been discussed in public.

If he saw the letter, Hill would not be able to challenge its technical and factual accuracy, as that would be a breach of the High Court ruling. He would be restricted to making it clear that, at most, it had been read to him. How to deal with this? Any formal complaint referring to the letter might be construed as contempt. Better to notify one's concerns to the parties involved, allowing them a way out by accepting their actions may have been unintentional or inadvertent; and if they took steps when made aware, the Judge (if it got that far) might take that into account. If such a 'warning shot' were ignored, and disclosure or discussion continued, then that would certainly be contempt. He did this, and no action was taken.

More recently, the RAF officer said on PPRuNe:

'Hill argued in court that he had suffered from a <u>hitherto undocumented</u> medical condition known as "cognitive impairment"...' [58]

This inflammatory claim went further than MoD's previous position of immature understanding. And, as I said, it had cited Cognitive Impairment in, for example, the Sean Cunningham case (2011). This step change in its disinformation campaign was clearly intended to influence public and media opinion, diverting attention from the principals' failings. (The media monitors and quotes PPRuNe, and in many ways it is MoD's primary source of corporate memory).

For any officer to post in such a manner is indicative of the top cover this ethos enjoys. He had clearly sighted the letter, placing him close to one of the addressees; if not one himself. Notably, it was addressed to the AOCs themselves, not their Personal Staff Officers or Group HQs.

It is easy to see why MoD got involved with, for example, the post-accident test flights. But with RAFCAM providing, free of charge, its own 'Subject Matter Expert' on the effects of g, a major step was taken towards it being the *de facto* co-prosecution. RAFCAM's initial aims were, I believe, laudable. But

---

57 MoD letter FOI 2019/09679, 6 September 2019.
58 https://www.pprune.org/military-aviation/619209-shoreham-airshow-crash-trial-58.html (2 October 2024).

they (or their proxy) now went too far, one clear aim being to try to salvage reputations.

If the principals want to continue arguing their lost case, then justice demands the High Court rulings be lifted. RAFCAM drew conclusions from a brief review of some uncorroborated opinions arising from incomplete research. As such, the letter is little more than a (poor) business case for funding to commence serious research by an independent body; one which should feel able to express an opinion without fear of self-incrimination.

On 12 December 2017 the Head of RAFCAM had stated at a Royal Aeronautical Society medical symposium:

> 'Cognitive decline can be spotted at medicals and simulator checks'.[59]

The keynote speaker was Mr Keith Conradi, Chief Investigator of the Healthcare Safety Investigation Branch. He had recently left his role as AAIB Chief Inspector, replaced by Colonel Crispin Orr, formerly of the Military Aviation Authority.

I mention this because it illustrates the close links that exist between MoD, CAA and AAIB. Indeed, the current Chief of the Air Staff (CAS) sat on the CAA Board when an Air Vice Marshal, and the current chair is a former CAS. All quite natural, in fact essential to everyday business and mutual aims. But was a boundary crossed when acting (yet again) for the prosecution at a criminal trial? This is an unseemly trait, and a common factor is MoD 'expert' witnesses being exposed as no such thing. I need only cite the Sean Cunningham case where, prior to the trial of Martin-Baker, MoD gave public presentations of the 'evidence' that was later proven untrue. Had Martin-Baker even attempted such a thing, they would have been held in contempt. Indeed, the trial Judge warned them of this, while ignoring MoD's actions.

MAA Duty Holders Air Safety Course / Flight Safety Officers Course

In May 2019, an MAA safety course was revealed to have a module on 'Shoreham - How was it allowed to happen?', expressing the MAA's opinion. It was highly critical of the CAA in aspects that, if made public, would have been useful to Hill at the forthcoming Inquest:

1. The CAA had not recognised the societal change relating to loss of life.

---

59 https://www.aerosociety.com/media/7674/20171219-raes-presentation-timperley-pdf-0.pdf

2. The CAA had not considered the parties involved in planning, conduct and regulatory oversight.
3. The CAA had no requirement for a Safety Management System.
4. Lack of clarity in ownership of risk and safety.
5. No organisation or individual had considered <u>all</u> hazards associated with display flying, including:
   - What could go wrong?
   - Who might be affected?
   - What could be done to mitigate risks to As Low As Reasonably Practicable and Tolerable. An example given was: *Who supervises the Display Authorisation Evaluators?*

I try not to be cynical, but it's difficult. This could have been paraphrased from any number of rejected recommendations from MoD's own staff, with it being guilty of the same failures across many fatal accidents. There had been a recurrence just the previous year, with the death of Red Arrows engineer Jon Bayliss. So, while I applaud those involved in the MAA, might I suggest MoD gets its own house in order before criticising others. Were those who attended the course asked *How was Jon's death allowed to happen?* Or do you still advocate lying in court?

CAA review of low-*g* impairment (2020)

In December 2020 the CAA published a 242-page review. Citing the AAIB and MoD as sources, it said Hill experienced no more than $4g$ (the AAIB said $2.7g$), claiming no other estimate exceeded this. This completely ignored the evidence of the prosecution's Jonathon Whaley, and others, who had agreed ~$4.8g$. Biased and self-serving it brought no added value, and there is little to gain from discussing it.

The torturous route to the Inquest (2015 - 2022)

General

A Coroner has a choice. Either open and immediately adjourn the Inquest pending publication of the AAIB report; or proceed promptly on the assumption that the reasons for the accident will be determined by that report, and so the issues treated as outside the scope of the Inquest. In the cases I have looked at - primarily military accidents - both routes have been taken. Here, Ms Schofield opened and adjourned on 22 March 2016, seven months after the accident. The Inquest (properly, 11 Inquests) was eventually held in November/December 2022.

The conclusions available to the Coroner are: Accident, Industrial Disease, Natural Causes, Open Verdict, Suicide, and Unlawful Killing. These are termed 'short form' conclusions, but a Coroner may choose to record a narrative conclusion, which seeks to explain the circumstances in a descriptive way. Here, a recent change in law meant the standard of proof for Unlawful Killing and Suicide was now the criminal standard *Beyond Reasonable Doubt* and no longer the civil *Balance of Probabilities*; following the Maughan Supreme Court judgment of 13 November 2020, overturning the existing Coroners (Inquests) Rules of 2013.[60] That is, these two possible conclusions were now aligned with the other short form conclusions.

However, there has been much debate and even dissent in legal circles; particularly over the need to mitigate the prejudice arising from a conclusion of Unlawful Killing. This is because an Inquest is not adversarial, so the 'accused' (properly, an 'Interested Person') is not permitted to cross-examine witnesses, challenge their evidence, or present his own. Many believe Inquests must now be adversarial in cases where Unlawful Killing and Suicide are possible conclusions. A related issue is that the Inquest is now a quasi-trial, yet there are no parties (defence, prosecution), and there is no indictment. The *Maughan* ruling avoids the issues, leaving the Coroners Service to deal with the fallout.

So, if the Coroner's conclusion seems to contradict the outcome of a criminal trial - as happened here - one cannot read too much into it. Different evidence may have been led, and key witnesses may not have been called. Here, the

---

[60] R (on the application of Maughan) (Appellant) v Her Majesty's Senior Coroner for Oxfordshire (Respondent) [2020] UKSC 46. On appeal from [2019] EWCA Civ 809.

criminal trial was not allowed to consider the AAIB report, despite it being the basis of the prosecution case; yet the Coroner was required to regard it as wholly accurate, knowing that it was not. Regardless of one's feelings for or against the pilot, most fair-minded people would see the potential for a miscarriage of justice.

The Coroner's Court is a court of inquiry, not litigation. The Inquest is a fact-finding exercise, the Coroner's role to find facts based on the evidence led. As the Coroner principally determines what evidence is led, and more to the point what is <u>not</u> led, there is a large degree of pre-determination. Put another way, there exists judicial truth and actual truth. The proceedings are similar to a civil case (but see *Maughan*), however the Coroner may sit alone or call a jury. Here, she initially stated she *would* sit with a jury, but later changed her mind.[61] The Coroners Service says:

> 'A Coroner will hold an Inquest with a jury in certain circumstances, such as when someone dies in prison or police custody or other state detention such as an immigration detention centre'.

This differs radically from Coroners' websites, which add *'or in circumstances which may affect public health or safety'*. The former might explain Ms Schofield's decision; but the latter would make Shoreham a shoe-in for a jury. Very confusing, the bereaved relying on the integrity of individual Coroners.

If the Coroner decides to hold a jury Inquest, he/she can advise that certain verdicts are not appropriate in law, for the case before them, so cannot be used. Sometimes that means only one verdict can reasonably be reached, in which case it is effectively a direction. However, if more than one verdict is possible, then the jury should not be steered as to which to return. This is different from a criminal case, where the Judge can decide that the evidence on a particular charge is so weak that no reasonable jury could consider convicting; and can direct the jury to acquit. (Which is so close to what happened at Hill's trial, as to make no difference).

Importantly, the bereaved should bear in mind the Coroner is not there to act in their interests. Some are sympathetic and bend over backwards to help (e.g. Nimrod XV230, Hercules XV179); others are rabidly anti-family (e.g. Sea King ASaC Mk7 mid-air, Jon Bayliss). And like Judges, they can declare 'facts' even though provided with evidence that they are not facts.

---

61 Hansard, 9 January 2018.

Disclosure to the Coroner

Disclosure of evidence is at the discretion of the Coroner. If one does not wish to disclose, one must challenge or influence the scope of the Inquest. Under the Coroners and Justice Act, Interested Parties are not under a legal duty to disclose material which is or may be relevant to the Inquest, unless asked to do so by the Coroner; so may withhold material that may be helpful to the Coroner. This contrasts sharply with civil or criminal proceedings, where there is a well-defined burden to disclose that which may assist the defence or undermine the prosecution, pursuant to the *Criminal Procedure and Investigations Act 1996*. Again, justification for these very different regimes is that an Inquest is not adversarial. (But see the effect of *Maughan*).

In theory, if material is relevant the Coroner is entitled to see it. But this case highlighted basic flaws - how does the Coroner know what is relevant if evidence is allowed to be concealed, Departments of State and their agents are allowed to determine relevance, and the 'accused' is not permitted to mention it? Ministry of Justice protocols call for *'openness and honesty, including supporting the disclosure of all relevant and disclosable information to the Coroner'*. This, they suggest, should be a *'model of behaviour'* for all interested parties. But it is unenforceable.

Here, the AAIB and CAA were allowed to decide what they should and should not disclose. Once more, the law was biased towards allowing concealment and perjury, denying a fair hearing. Under these circumstances, it is difficult to see how a Coroner can meet his/her obligation to ensure the *'relevant facts are fully, fairly and fearlessly investigated'*.

Route

I shall set this out in diary form. It has been gleaned mainly from press releases by the West Sussex Senior Coroner, and I have added explanatory comments where necessary.

Of particular note, many of the court papers (including trial transcripts) were made available via ShareFile, a secure document and file sharing application whereby authorised persons are given a login code. The problem was, hundreds of people were given access to Shoreham files, and inevitably many 'leaked' into the public domain - most benign, but some I believe 'protected'. One reason for this was that interested parties were at liberty to challenge the use or admissibility of any document, so gave access to their experts and advisors to gather their arguments together. As a result, the Coroner agreed to many changes; and at each change everyone had to be notified and... This secure system was not private or confidential; and it is likely many recipients did not realise some of what they held was protected (it is not marked as such).

It is important to acknowledge that the law governing Coroners Inquests is impressively complex, and changes with bewildering regularity. It is not difficult to see why Coroners must take time out to consider what to do in the face of any given circumstance, and seek guidance as to the law.

17 March 2017

Date scheduled for Pre-Inquest Review. Postponed due to the close timing of the release of the AAIB final report (issued 3 March), and the ongoing police investigation which was awaiting that report.

20 June 2017

Pre-Inquest Review. Sussex Police provided an update; their investigation was 95% complete, and a file being submitted to the CPS. The Coroner set the date for a second Pre-Inquest Review for 24 January 2018 at Crawley Coroner's Court, indicating she would like the full Inquest to be set for September 2018. However, she added that it may have to be suspended if the CPS decided to bring criminal charges.

29 September 2017

Sussex Police reported progress has been made, and a further update would be provided by 30 November. No further information was revealed, the full Inquest still scheduled for September 2018.

30 November 2017

Sussex Police's reported their file was with the CPS, and a charging decision awaited. The Pre-Inquest Review scheduled for 24 January 2018 was postponed, as the CPS had notified the Coroner no charging decision *against the pilot* would be reached before that date. This was the first indication that the offences committed by others were to be overlooked.

26 March 2018

Scheduled second Pre-Inquest Review; again postponed, the CPS having decided to bring charges. Due to their nature, the full Inquest would have to await the conclusion of the criminal case. A new date of 22 February 2019 was set, the Coroner saying she did not anticipate the full Inquest taking place until mid-late 2019. With this announcement, she released her ruling on the scope of the Inquest.

8 April 2019

Following Hill's acquittal, a Pre-Inquest Review, Lawyers' Meeting, and Case Management Meeting was held on 8 April in Crawley Town Hall. The Review heard that disclosure could now be made to the families of the documentation held by Sussex Police. A further Pre-Inquest Review was scheduled for July, at which time the Coroner hoped she could set a date for the Inquest proper. She reiterated that the trial had concentrated on the actions of the pilot, but an Inquest can consider wider issues that are linked to the deaths. She would have to decide, having heard the evidence, whether or not she needed to make any Regulation 28 Report (Prevention of Future Deaths Reports) relating to the organisation and planning of future air shows.

16 June 2019

The AAIB made a submission to the Coroner on 'The effects of the *Norfolk* judgment'. The thrust was familiar and to be expected - the AAIB report should not be referred to. However, this was almost four years after the accident, and could have been made soon after the 2016 High Court ruling. *Inter alia*, the AAIB claimed the Hunter was safe; completely ignoring its own report that had detailed why it was not. The AAIB also argued that its (i.e. MoD's) incorrect g-calculations and invalidated work on Cognitive Impairment should be heeded over the pivotal evidence produced by the defence at trial.

15 July 2019

Pre-Inquest Review. The Coroner advised the families that it was not possible to fix the Inquest dates, stating she was:

> 'Not persuaded that the circumstances of the deaths (rather than the general facts of the crash) have been sufficiently established. Moreover, there are potential issues arising under Article 2 (European Convention on Human Rights)'.[62]

Article 2 Inquests are enhanced Inquests held in cases where *'the State or its*

---

[62] Coroner's ruling, 7 August 2019. (Resumption of Inquest).

agents have failed to protect the deceased against a human threat or other risk'. The crucial difference is that, under Article 2, not only does the cause of death have to be established, but also the broader circumstances surrounding the death. Article 2 <u>must</u> be invoked if it *appears* to be arguable on the evidence that substantive duties have been breached. But arguable on what evidence, if the only report is prohibited? The Coroner clearly realised that it pointed the finger fairly and squarely at CAA failures.

Subsequently, it was decided this would <u>not</u> be an Article 2 Inquest. The reasoning has not been published.

She explained there had been recent correspondence from the Government Legal Service indicating that the AAIB was now considering whether to reopen its investigation, and that it would advise this position on 2 August 2019. If there was to be further investigation, she anticipated the Inquest would be delayed until late-2020.

<u>2 August 2019</u>

The AAIB decided not to reopen its investigation. The Coroner set a date for the next Pre-Inquest Review, to be held in Crawley on 29 January 2020, at which she anticipated setting a date for the Inquest.

<u>22 August 2019</u>

Hill made a Subject Access Request to MoD seeking details of the December 2015 test flight, and correspondence between RAFCAM and AAIB; perhaps indicating the direction he would take at the Inquest.

<u>7 October 2019</u>

In an interesting development, the Chief Coroner issued Guidance #33, 'Suspension, adjournment and resumption of Investigations and Inquests'.

<u>29 January 2020</u>

The Coroner set a date of 14 September 2020, setting aside six weeks. Before that, a further Pre-Inquest Review was scheduled for 24 June 2020, to agree the list of required witnesses and finalise any other administrative matters. She ruled she would not be sitting with a jury:

> *'I have taken into account all the views of the interested persons, but it is my view that there is not sufficient reason for departing from the*

> *presumption in Schedule 1 Para 11(3) Coroners in Justice Act 2009 in favour of me sitting alone without a jury. I do accept that this case raises questions on matter of great public importance. However, as a Coroner I will be able to make very detailed and reasoned factual findings, which will be announced publicly. It is my position that public interest can be better served by sitting alone'.*

What lay behind this ruling needs explaining. A jury may ask questions that the Coroner may not have the remit to pose; for example, arising from the AAIB report. Once aired, they would become part of the Inquest narrative, and unavoidably expose systemic failures by the CAA, and serious offences by the AAIB and MoD. Her decision was, in effect, a control measure to contain the adverse.

May 2020

Due to the impact of the COVID-19 pandemic, the Inquest could not take place safely in open court on the scheduled date. A future date, likely to be in June or September 2021, was pencilled in; the aim being to allow the families to attend in person:

> *'My present view is that these Inquests are not ones that are appropriate to be held remotely given the importance to the families of being fully involved in the hearings, the benefits of hearing the first-hand evidence in person and the overall public interest'.*

24 June 2020

Pre-Inquest Review, via remote hearing. Counsel for the Inquest stated the Coroner was awaiting a report from the CAA, due in September 2020; and coupled with the pandemic, the Inquest would be delayed a year. Cockpit video footage was raised, and whether it would be available to the Inquest; the 2016 High Court ruling applying only to the criminal trial.

4 July 2020

The Coroner issued draft findings of the Pre-Inquest Review. These centred on the impact of the *'Norfolk'* legal ruling that there was *'no public interest in having unnecessary duplication of investigations or enquiries'*, unless it can be demonstrated that the official investigation *is* incomplete, flawed or deficient. Only then may an investigation or Inquest be re-opened.

This is why I have emphasised this phrase. If the AAIB investigation could be shown as incomplete, flawed or deficient, then *Norfolk* would not apply. But here, the AAIB was permitted to judge its own case, and of course denied that its investigation was incomplete… Ms Schofield now shifted her thinking regarding scope. Hitherto she had intended to dig deep, but now talked of a '*narrow purpose*' . This change was brought about by AAIB pressure, effectively throwing up a smokescreen.

Discussion

By this time, Hill had made a number of detailed submissions regarding the AAIB's report, the failings it noted, and the failings of the AAIB itself. The Coroner, as required, sent them to interested parties. Many advised her to stop using the AAIB to adjudicate on these submissions, for two reasons. First, the information was protected; second, allowing it to judge its own case defeated the purpose and aim of the legal process.

At this time it became evident that the police had seriously considered corporate manslaughter against the CAA. From events at the trial, it is clear Hill did not wish to drop anyone else in it, but it is likely his attitude changed when the collusion and conspiracy over the test flights emerged, legal authorities condoning it. Now, despite him having been acquitted, the CAA was still pushing the *only the pilot is guilty* line. This was blatant self-protectionism. The Coroner knew this, but did not reject the AAIB and CAA's obvious bias. (A quite different approach to that of the trial Judge).

Poor administrative control meant the process was going round in circles. I'm afraid this is what happens when entities with much to lose if the truth comes out are allowed to dictate matters; and is common at Inquests into military deaths. There is also an element of the 'prosecution' (AAIB, CAA and MoD) trying to wear down the 'defence' (Hill and the families) with delaying tactics. They have an almost unlimited budget, whereas time is money to families. It is not uncommon for the bereaved to say they feel as if *they* are on trial.

In September 2020 Hill presented to the Coroner Dr Mitchell's report, 'Cognitive Impairment in a fast jet', discussed earlier. She noted that Dr Mitchell professed no expertise in aviation medicine or neurology, clearly swayed by the fact he knew Hill. Yet plenty of the prosecution witnesses knew each other, and so too staff in the AAIB, MoD and CAA. Mitchell's credentials were impeccable, in his field. Just because he specialised in genetics and therapy of childhood illnesses, and was 'only' the Director of Children's Services at a major university hospital in England, does not mean he could not offer medical opinion on the facts of the case. And if Hill were so inclined, he could have pointed to the Coroner declaring herself sufficiently expert to rule on all technical and airmanship aspects of aircraft operations.

Yet...she did read Dr Mitchell's work, concluding it presented a *'credible suggestion that the AAIB's investigation of the Cognitive Impairment issue was incomplete'*. Her QC, Bridget Dolan, claimed Ms Schofield did not actually have *'credible evidence that the investigation was incomplete'*. But she did - because she knew by 11 October 2019, at the very latest, the precise reasons why the aircraft was not permitted to fly. Also, she knew the AAIB had barely touched on the events of December 2015; where it was not only *incomplete*, but seriously *flawed* and *deficient* by virtue of crucial evidence being concealed.

3 January 2021

Hill asked for Ms Schofield's recusal, saying the West Sussex Coroners Service (not Ms Schofield) may have contributed to the deaths through the six recommendations from a previous fatal accident at Shoreham not being implemented, and there was potential for bias. (Hurricane G-HURR, 15 September 2007). The concerns behind each recommendation had arisen again after 2015. In particular, recommendation 2009-057 related to CAA oversight, the AAIB's Shoreham report noting this had actually regressed.[63]

While acknowledging Hill was not represented, she correctly pointed out a misunderstanding existed regarding what powers the Coroner had. It would perhaps have been better to submit to the Coroner (and police) that the CAA had not implemented the recommendations, and that this should be taken into account. Nevertheless, the concerns expressed by the families and Hill were entirely valid, it being clear that if the CAA had taken action after G-HURR, Shoreham 2015 would have been avoided.

On 26 February 2021 the Coroner advised she would not stand down; adding she had sought the views of interested parties, and the CAA had not responded. This illustrated perfectly the limited extent of her powers.

26 April 2021

At a further Pre-Inquest Review Ms Schofield explained why she would be applying to the High Court for access to material from the criminal trial. Bearing in mind the 2016 High Court judgment prohibiting use of the AAIB

---

63 AAIB Accident Report No.6/2009, issued September 2009.

data, she was compelled to make a similar application, seeking:

> 'An order pursuant to Regulation 25 of the Civil Aviation (Investigation of Air Accidents and Incidents) Regulations 2018/321 that specified records which may be protected under Art 14 of the EU Regulations on the investigation and prevention of Air Accidents No.996/2010 be made available to her for the purpose of the Inquests. The main record sought by the Coroner is the cockpit video recording from the aircraft'.

Hill supported the application despite being listed as a defendant. As no High Court could sit until the Autumn, the Inquest was further delayed.

December 2021

The Coroner stated a further Pre-Inquest Review, to be heard remotely, would take place on 6 January 2021; but subject to the High Court making its ruling by then. The Inquest was now scheduled to commence on 28 February 2022.

20 December 2021

The Coroner's application was heard by a Divisional Court (part of the High Court and one sitting with at least two Judges, in this case Lady Justice Sharp and Mr Justice Saini) at the Royal Courts of Justice in London. The court reserved its judgment, saying it would be handed down in the New Year. The planned Pre-Inquest Review was postponed until 11 February 2022, the Coroner announcing the Inquest would also be postponed again.

4 February 2022

The High Court issued its ruling against the Coroner and Hill.[64] He and others had been allowed to present some evidence, the court confirming this *'included substantial exhibits'*. However, it did not examine the merits of this evidence, dismissing it on legal technicalities. Henceforth, Ms Schofield had to regard the AAIB report as 100% accurate, knowing with absolute certainty it was not.

---

64 High Court of Justice Queen's Bench Division Divisional Court - Approved Judgment Case No: QB-2021-002090 (Her Majesty's Senior Coroner for West Sussex v (a) Chief Constable of Sussex Police, (b) Secretary of State for Transport (AAIB), and (c) Mr Andrew Hill; and Sue & Philip Grimstone, Jonathan Smith & Julie Smith, Robert Henry, Jack Schilt & Caroline Louise Schilt, 4 February 2022).

22 June 2022

The Coroner issued a private ruling on administrative matters to interested parties. Also, a ruling regarding Hill's attendance at the Inquest:

> 'It seems to me that any matter that Hill, the pilot, might address in his evidence is already covered by the AAIB investigation and I do not propose that he should be called to give evidence'.

This was prejudicial, and complete and utter nonsense. As shown by his request of August 2019 for test flight data and RAFCAM/AAIB correspondence, he was eager to learn what the AAIB report <u>omitted</u>, and the evidence it and MoD had concealed, which was <u>not covered</u> by the High Court ruling. Who benefitted from her decision? The CAA and AAIB, who would both be spared the embarrassment of their errors. Also, MoD's flawed g-calculations would not be discussed. This ruling was made public on 1 September 2022. On that date it was announced the Inquest would commence on 30 November 2022, in Horsham.

***

I felt it necessary to set out this convoluted and frustrating path. One can understand the legal necessities, but why did the AAIB take over two years following Hill's acquittal to make its move, and challenge the use of its report at the Inquest? Quite apart from the unforgiveable heartache it caused the families, one effect was that any proposed civil action became time-expired.

Was this deliberate? The High Court rulings did not apply to a civil case; where the AAIB report and its content, and more importantly what it omitted, would be exposed to detailed examination, and violations revealed. The principals, and legal authorities, would not want this.

My own submissions

Having read the AAIB report, I felt the same concerns any engineer would. When it was announced the Inquest process would recommence, on 11 October 2019 I made a submission to the Coroner offering brief observations on airworthiness, non-disclosure of evidence, and recurrence. I finished:

> 'Might I suggest it is important the court understands why the pilot was provided with an unairworthy aircraft. He was misled. The families of the deceased deserve to know why, and how recurrence can be prevented'.

The Coroner's Office acknowledged receipt on 5 November. In the interim I had received confirmation from MoD that neither it nor the RAF had ever been Design Authority for the Hunter, and I submitted this on the 6th. I was told my submission had been sent to the AAIB for comment.

Almost a year later, I was informed of its reply:

'The design authority for G-BXFI prior to transfer to the civil register was the Royal Air Force, as detailed in Airworthiness Approval Note (AAN) No: 26172. After being approved by the CAA to operate on the civil register, G-BXFI had been maintained by several organisations which held CAA design and maintenance approvals. Therefore, at the time of the accident the design approval for the aircraft rested with its approved maintenance organisation and the CAA, not the RAF'.

As noted before, the Approval Note was wrong, and the AAIB knew it. The remainder conflates Maintaining and Continuing airworthiness, and Design Organisation and Design Authority. If the maintenance organisation and CAA had assumed responsibility for the design (a big 'if'), then the Approval Note should have been up-issued to reflect this change to the single most important part of it (as everything else is predicated on that part being correct). If correct, the AAIB report did not say the CAA and Weald had assumed responsibility from the RAF, or when, instead presenting the Approval Note as the authoritative document. Crucially, it didn't mention to the Coroner that, regardless of who now did what, the work wasn't done properly, if at all.

Of most relevance to the current process, the AAIB now confirmed the Approval Note (and hence its report, which reproduced it without comment) was flawed in a safety critical area; and the terms of the Permit to Fly were not (and could not be) complied with. And, having now changed its mind about the accuracy of its report, it did not issue a Bulletin or Supplement to this effect, so any reader remains unaware.

The reply is meaningless without satisfactorily addressing these issues. Of huge concern must be an organisation, headed by a former Military Aviation Authority officer, simply accepting and repeating that the RAF were the Design Authority (until, apparently, some undefined date between 2008 and 2015) - especially after MoD had expressly denied it. Yet, it clearly understood the issues, saying in its (excellent) section 1.18.13:

'When the aircraft type retired from military service the support provided by the Original Equipment Manufacturers ceased. The CAA should establish a process for the effective dissemination of ex-military jet aircraft experience and type-specific knowledge to individual maintenance organisations'.

Of equal concern is the Coroner accepting the AAIB's reply, which is carefully worded to avoid an outright lie of commission. But it plainly contains lies of omission. At best, this proved she was incapable of reaching informed decisions on engineering matters and was now duty bound to include this in her application to the High Court. She did not.

The Coroner was grossly misled. But she brought it upon herself by asking the AAIB, when it was the CAA documentation that was in question. What else was the AAIB going to say? *Yes, our report is incomplete, flawed and deficient through blindly accepting CAA documentation at face value, but according to the High Court it isn't?* Bearing in mind the AAIB and CAA are part of the same Department of State, with the same line manager, the truth would incriminate both the AAIB and its partner MoD; and compromise, at Ministerial level, the Department for Transport.

One must therefore consider if a higher authority dictated the AAIB's position; in turn related to a wider question over the dynamics of the prosecution. Having trashed the CAA in its report (an understatement), at what point did the AAIB decide to change tack to the point it was arguing against its own report, join forces with the CAA and MoD, and act for the prosecution by misleading legal authorities and families? Why? What influence was being brought to bear? Who benefitted? I answers, I suggest, are crystal clear.

I summarised this to the Coroner on 13 December 2020, and the following day Counsel for the Inquest invited me to attend the Pre-Inquest Review remote hearing by audio link. But her decision was made, and she would not change it.

All this implies there are a number of different Aircraft Design Authorities for Hunters in private hands, defying the whole point of the Design Authority construct. That is, to have a single, focal point for all engineering/safety matters pertaining to the type. The aim is standardisation. Who now holds and maintains the Master Drawing Set? Or do they all hold a set of Secondary Masters? Who maintains them? The process is now extraordinarily convoluted, confusing and expensive, and can only lead to severe safety problems that the CAA, on its own admission, is poorly equipped to control. I have no doubt it knows what is needed, but without the resources…

I of course agree that if the CAA were to suddenly be given the resources to enforce its regulations, many private owners would have to consider giving up display flying on cost grounds. Much as Team Viper did in 2012 when it could no longer afford to operate G-BXFI. But would that be a bad thing? The natural effect would be to concentrate ownership, and move closer towards the intent of the regulations. Elsewhere, the case touched on a related factor.

Individuals are at liberty to place <u>themselves</u> at risk, the reward being the thrill. There are many such examples. The difference here is that when something went wrong entirely innocent passers-by were killed.

In what way was the AAIB report incomplete, flawed or deficient?

First, common definitions, and then a few examples:

<u>Incomplete</u>: lacking some parts, not finished.

<u>Flawed</u>: having, or characterised by, a fundamental weakness or imperfection.

<u>Deficient</u>: lacking or not good enough.

- The report was *incomplete* in that it did not include analysis of the *flawed* Airworthiness Approval Note, or the failure to maintain airworthiness. It was made *deficient* by not explaining why the aircraft should not have been flying, and how this affected other Hunters and legacy fast jets in general.
- It was *flawed* by including, without checking, the errors in the g-calculations made by RAFCAM; and then made *incomplete* by not updating the report when these errors were advised.
- It was *flawed* in that a fundamental imperfection was that it was constructed, in part, following improper collusion between the AAIB and MoD over the 2015 test flights. Concealing this rendered it *incomplete* and *deficient*.
- It was made *incomplete* by concealing other wrongdoing by parties who were at least partly culpable, and was *deficient* in that it did not fully investigate these failings.
- Failure to adhere to the AAIB's own investigative protocols and requirement for independence rendered it *deficient*.
- It was *incomplete, flawed* and *deficient* by its classification of recommendations to the CAA as *'closed'*, knowing the risks had not been mitigated.

Not only are these examples undisputed fact, they are fundamental to the entire criminal case and conduct of the Inquest. The basic flaw in the *Norfolk* ruling is that it assumes the investigating authority is truly independent and can substantiate the claims in its report. For the reasons I have set out, this can never be said of the Shoreham investigation.

The Inquest finally opens: 30 November 2022

An Inquest must not determine, or appear to determine, any question of criminal or civil liability on the part of a named person. It is limited to ascertaining who the deceased was, and how [65], when and where he or she came by their death, and *'neither the Senior Coroner…nor the jury (if there is one) are entitled to express an opinion on any other matters'*.[66]

It is important to restate Ms Schofield's position. In her 'Findings of fact and conclusions including the ruling on law', she stated:

> *'I am bound by law to accept the findings of the AAIB. As a consequence of the Divisional Court judgment these Inquests have proceeded on the basis that there is no credible evidence that the AAIB investigation was <u>incomplete, flawed or deficient</u> and I may not reinvestigate any matters the AAIB investigation has already covered'.*[67]

Yet, the AAIB had confirmed to her it <u>was</u> incomplete…

However, she went further, refusing to consider evidence that was <u>not</u> in the AAIB report; because that would emphasise it was incomplete… Had Hill so much as mentioned this, he would be in contempt. This probably goes some way to explaining why he did not argue with the Coroner's decision to agree with the AAIB that he should be excluded; and he could do nothing about her allowing the AAIB to give evidence over two days. While naturally cautious about going beyond the scope of its report, the AAIB proceeded in the safe knowledge that the Coroner was bound by it, and Hill was not permitted to challenge its errors and inconsistencies.

For their part, the CAA pushed for an Unlawful Killing verdict, their position being they had nothing to do with it all. This of course contradicted the severe criticism and recommendations in the AAIB report, which the Coroner was bound by.

It can be seen she was faced with an insurmountable dilemma. In effect, two branches of the same government department were in opposition, and the evidence proving both wrong was not allowed in court. That being so, I could

---

65 And, in an Article 2 Inquest, *'in what circumstances'*. (s.5(2) Coroners and Justice Act 2009).
66 S.10(2), s.5 and s.5(3), Coroners and Justice Act 2009.
67 https://www.westsussex.gov.uk/media/18404/shoreham_facts_conclusions.pdf

stop there, because the rest of the one-sided proceedings were rendered meaningless, largely because she did not attempt to resolve this conflict. But for completeness sake I'll carry on, although skip to her 'findings of fact' and conclusions.

Ms Schofield took the reader through events in roughly chronological order, briefly summarising the airshow, the deceased, pen portraits offered by family, and emphasising:

> 'It should be acknowledged that these 11 men played absolutely no part in their own deaths. They were all going about their lawful business, but at a time which placed them into the path of this aircrash'.

The first major contradiction came when she declared:

> 'I therefore accept the AAIB investigation's findings in their entirety in respect of the mechanical safety of the aircraft...'

If she accepted the AAIB's findings in respect of safety, by definition she <u>had</u> to accept that the aircraft was <u>unsafe</u>. As she did not, she was seen to reject and disobey the High Court order.

She was critical of the event planning and organisation, which the AAIB reported had failed catastrophically through poor application of safety protocols by the organisers, committee, and the CAA; confirming the Flying Display Director had now accepted the AAIB's:

> 'There were a number of deficiencies compared to what would be expected for a risk assessment to control risks to the public. [It] was not fit for the purpose of identifying and mitigating the risks and hazards to the public from the air display activities of the airshow'.

At this point one would reasonably anticipate her recommending the CPS consider action against the airshow organisers and CAA.

Moving on to ground safety and emergency planning, a witness who had not been called at trial had given evidence of his Event Plan and an Emergency Response Plan. He confirmed he had not seen the flawed Flying Display risk assessment (so what was the Response Plan in response to?). His Event Plan had identified risks that later materialised - again, the implication being these were not linked to the Flying Display Risk Register - but the 'agreed' mitigation could not be followed-through because it was outwith the control of the Committee.

In short, he had been told that the A27 would <u>not</u> be closed, and so did not ask for it to be. I discussed this earlier. A mitigation plan that cannot be implemented is no plan at all. But if there was a viable risk to life, then there <u>had</u> to be viable mitigation; including re-routing of displays (but perhaps further away and rendering them unappealing to paying spectators). Logically, then, one had to question the very existence of the airshow so close to a busy trunk road and huge built-up area. Bringing us back to the regulator...

Linked to this was the poor signage, and the impracticality of imposing temporary 'rules'; which were not rules, but unenforceable aspirations. The Coroner agreed the signs were ambiguous and wrongly positioned. This related to the deaths of two cyclists, Dylan Archer and Richard Smith, who may not have been where they were had the signage been correctly positioned and they adhered to it. At which point one might anticipate, at the very least, a finding against the organisers and/or CAA for *these* deaths.

Ms Schofield repeated the AAIB's (correct) assessment of the confusion that reigned over risk ownership, severely criticising the CAA's:

> '*...shortcomings in the conduct and oversight of flying displays in the UK in the areas of operation, risk management and maintenance. In total 14 Safety Recommendations were published to inform the air display community ahead of the 2016 air display season. A further 11 Safety Recommendations are made in the full AAIB report. Whilst some of these were looked at in detail during the evidence I do not recite them here given that all have now been addressed to the satisfaction of the AAIB*'.

But it was not for the AAIB to adjudicate, merely comment and recommend. The recommendations had <u>not</u> been addressed satisfactorily, and so a deep chasm existed in the process. She omitted that the AAIB had 'closed' its recommendations simply because the CAA had stated an <u>intent</u> to implement them. Also, that many of these recommendations were already mandated, and the CAA (primarily) had <u>already declared</u> they had been implemented (by virtue of approving the airshow). Moreover, many had been made before, meaning Shoreham was a recurrence. This last is perhaps the most obvious deficiency arising from the Inquest. If the aim is to prevent recurrence, surely it was incumbent upon the Coroner to record that the accident in question was a recurrence?

She then moved on to Hill, the flight conduct, his training, and expertise. Suffice to say, she repeated the prosecution's false and disproven claims as if they were fact. For example, the alleged breach of height minima. She claimed he had <u>deliberately</u> changed the ground track to align with the A27. Also, she stated one of the reasons the crash occurred was because *'the <u>thrust applied by the pilot</u> in the upward half of the manoeuvre was insufficient'*; which was incompatible with the AAIB's *'an <u>uncommanded reduction in thrust</u> during the accident manoeuvre could not be ruled out'*, and the evidence at trial from expert pilots that these two reductions in power (be they commanded or uncommanded) were the real problem. She did not mention the faulty and unairworthy fuel pump.

When addressing *'poor flying'*, she ignored that the prosecution's 'evidence' on Cognitive Impairment had been shredded in court; simply saying that the AAIB found no evidence of any impairment during the manoeuvre. But absence of evidence is not evidence of absence - a 'deliberate' error routinely made by government and MoD. She continued:

'I accept those AAIB conclusions. On the balance of probabilities this poor flying is not explained by Hill suffering a cognitive impairment'.

She did not say what she had 'balanced' the decision against. Not surprising, as there *could* be no balance, as she had allowed no relevant evidence and the AAIB had come to no firm conclusions. Yet, in her application to the High Court she had said:

'Dr Mitchell's paper presents a <u>credible suggestion</u> that the AAIB's investigation of the Cognitive Impairment issue was incomplete'.

'Credible' means believable. That, I suggest, falls below the 51% bar for 'balance of probabilities'. And bearing in mind the AAIB's 'investigation' was actually the discredited RAFCAM report, revealed as incomplete, flawed and deficient in court, who or what persuaded her (and the High Court) that Dr Mitchell's <u>additional</u> evidence to this effect was no longer believable?

After repeating the legal considerations at length, Ms Schofield concluded that the 11 victims had been Unlawfully Killed. Technically she did not name Hill, referring to *'the pilot'*. However, the majority of her adverse comments had not applied to him, but to the CAA and organisers. She did not issue a 'Matters of Concern' letter or a 'Prevention of Future Deaths Report', the implication being that the gross errors made by these others could never be repeated, and she was unconcerned about the AAIB and MoD conspiring to conceal evidence. Above all else, she omitted the lead anomaly - the aircraft was neither airworthy nor serviceable, and should not have been flying. This had been confirmed by the AAIB report she was bound by; and disregarding it was like writing a book about popular music and omitting The Beatles or Elvis.

Assessment

Despite confirming she was *'bound by law'*, Ms Schofield ignored the law; to the benefit of the AAIB and CAA, but detriment of the families. One can readily see the effect of excluding Hill, as there was no-one else to challenge her, the allegedly independent and neutral principals all remaining silent in order to conceal their own culpability. She ignored every investigative protocol by only looking at the proximate act, and she failed to address *all the circumstances* that led to the deaths. She said *'lessons had been learnt'*. Well, if they'd been learnt and acted upon after previous fatalities (and the Nimrod Review), Shoreham would have been avoided.

Once again, the CAA was off the hook. What persuaded her to place absolute trust in an organisation that had manifestly failed so often? What persuaded her it had improved to such a degree she felt no need to formally express concern? This, more than anything, revealed the protection provided to the principals.

Regardless of the High Court ruling, she had the authority to suspend the hearing and refer any concerns to the police. All I can say is, it is possible she submitted a confidential briefing to the Chief Coroner - who, if consistent, would reject it. (Having recently shown no concern over the same violations in the Jon Bayliss case).

I accept there needs to be a judgment call on 'proximity' and how far back one goes to examine factors. But the aircraft having no proper authority to fly doesn't require much regression. If there is a single fact/event which could have prevented the accident, and therefore deaths, then Ms Schofield was bound to note it. She didn't. The report she was ordered to accept confirmed that other organisations played major parts in the accident sequence. Was it fair, then, to place all the blame on one person and say only he could have prevented the deaths?

I can only conclude her conclusion of Unlawful Killing was unjust. Notably, when she handed it down Ms Schofield already knew a civil case was time-expired. Had such a case still been possible, one wonders if she would have exposed herself to ridicule in the civil court by issuing the same finding.

In hindsight, Hill's application for recusal was prescient. It may have been wiser and safer for Ms Schofield to say something like: *'In light of the evidence prohibited by the High Court, I can only issue an Open Verdict'*. This is the proper finding when there is not enough evidence to reach any other conclusion, and appropriate here if applied to the evidence she was restricted to considering. The effect was to deny the families the truth. They left court having been ruthlessly misled.

The pilot challenges the Coroner's findings

It was probably inevitable Hill would challenge Unlawful Killing; not least because Ms Schofield had aimed most of her criticism at the CAA and organisers - until right at the end she laid sole blame on him.

There are two routes. A judicial review, which must be started within three months; and a *fiat,* a legal, authoritative decision that has absolute sanction to the Attorney General, which has no time limit.[68] To achieve this requires a High Court ruling. The reason is that once Ms Schofield closed the Inquest, as a judicial officer she was seen to be *functus officio,* meaning she had discharged her function and had no authority to revisit or remake her decision; even in the certain (prior) knowledge its basis was flawed. If granted, a review would be limited to dismissing the finding of Unlawful Killing as irrational or unsafe, forcing her to reconsider; which would amount to the High Court calling itself irrational...

One aim of her Inquest was to uncover *'Why was the plane flown that way'.* That would require her to refer to trial evidence showing many of the prosecution's allegations had been disproved - in turn confirming the AAIB report was flawed. She had asked the High Court to allow her access to the information necessary to be able to explore the question. In this, she was supported by Hill, but opposed by the AAIB and CAA. She lost, and at that point should have seriously considered calling off the Inquest, as her aims could <u>never</u> be met. Thereafter, whatever her conclusion, it would be tainted by the known facts. The fundamental issues were (a) the AAIB had admitted to her its report was incomplete..., and (b) the AAIB and MoD had acted together, for the prosecution. Either made her position impossible. But she did not mention any of this, serving to facilitate her ruling.

On 6 February 2023 it was widely reported that Hill had sought a judicial review. He had not. He had submitted a 'judicial review pre-action letter', as

---

[68] https://www.inquestrepresentationservice.com/appealing-an-inquest-conclusion-or-coroners-decision/

part of the process necessary to avoid time expiry. The primary basis of the request was that the AAIB report was based on wrong g-calculations, and that this had been accepted at his trial. Put another way, there had been no reason for the jury to consider if there was *reasonable doubt* on this matter, and so on what basis was the Coroner considering *balance of probabilities*? And if she was to hear new evidence, or regurgitate discredited prosecution evidence, should he not be present?

Those who had read her findings and the High Court ruling of 2022 could glean another reason - he believed she had acted *ultra vires*, beyond her powers. This was simply a logical conclusion. His dilemma was that, if he chose to challenge the finding, he would have to do so without actually mentioning her breach, or why it was a breach.

Ms Schofield advised the AAIB and CAA, inviting them to judge their own case. It would seem their replies gave him no reason to back off, and he formally requested permission to seek a review. On 23 May 2023 the High Court refused the application, giving him seven days to appeal. On 1 June he informed all parties he had decided against further action. Why would he back down now, after pursuing his case so vigorously? One reason might be that the High Court's decision meant it had placed itself in conflict with itself. To argue this, he would have to breach the High Court order. He had nowhere to go. This would be so obvious to the court, it must have been a deliberate attempt to shut him down.

In summary, the Inquest was itself incomplete, flawed and deficient. Ms Schofield was required to treat the AAIB report as 100% accurate. Where she did (repeating its errors), it was to Hill's detriment. Where she didn't (attributing certainty when the AAIB was uncertain), it was also to his detriment. She went further, revisiting the trial and accepting the prosecution's disproven claims; while expressly rejecting the evidence of expert witnesses for the prosecution who had destroyed its case; again causing detriment. It hardly mattered then that she also rejected the defence experts - and the Judge's decisions.

Logically, the AAIB investigation should now be reopened. The AAIB dare not do that, as it would expose itself, the Coroner and the High Court to derision and mockery. No action has been taken.

ACTUAL TRUTH

'The AAIB report raised serious questions about the protection of [the right to life under Article 2 of the European Convention on Human Rights] by certain public agencies - the systemic failure by the State and its agents in the safe regulation of public flying displays'.

Hansard, 9 January 2018

Collective responsibility

Andrew Hill

He buggered it up. The prosecution cast him as cavalier, over-confident, and negligent to a gross degree. It made a number of accusations as to his airmanship - all proven false with the partial exception of Southport in 2014, where he stopped his display after an error. That merely demonstrated no-one is perfect all the time. But not being perfect does not equate to manslaughter; the jury agreed, and he was acquitted.

Perhaps they also thought the litany of misconduct by others was unacceptable. I do not agree with the law permitting government departments and agencies to do this with impunity, and it is difficult not to have a sneaking admiration for his fortitude in the face of it. He was dealt a poor hand by the court rulings. Had he been imprisoned, he would have been a free man long ago and deemed to have 'done his time'. In many ways his acquittal condemned him to a worse fate. This will be unsatisfactory to the bereaved, but I ask them to accept they have been grossly misled.

Airshow organisers

At the time of the accident the CAA did not require risk assessments (never mind agreed control measures) to be submitted when applying for approval for an airshow. When considering applications for flying displays, and when attending displays to conduct inspections, it did not inspect or request copies of Hazard Logs or risk plans.

Correctly, the AAIB commissioned the Health and Safety Laboratory (HSL) to conduct a review of these 'assessments'. It was blistering:

'The Shoreham Airshow Air Display risk assessment contained a number of deficiencies compared to what would be expected to control risks to the public. There is little, or no, evidence that:

- *All relevant parties were consulted.*
- *A comprehensive list of foreseeable hazards was identified.*
- *Sufficient and achievable mitigation measures were considered and <u>implemented</u>.*
- *Lessons were learned from near misses or incidents at previous airshows (either previous Shoreham airshows or other airshows).*

- *The hazards and risks identified have been managed sufficiently.*
- *The risk assessment complies fully with the CAA guidance for air displays.*

The conclusion of the review is that the 2015 Shoreham Airshow Air Display Risk Assessment is not fit for the purpose of identifying and mitigating the risks and hazards to the public from the air display activities of the airshow'.[69]

The HSL made appropriate recommendations as to qualifications and experience required of these risk assessors, and that they should explicitly state the rationale behind risk mitigation plans. In other words, adopt basic safety management protocols. It was also noted that the Display Director acted in the same capacity at two other displays shortly afterwards. In each, he had offered the CAA essentially the same document when seeking authorisation, which was granted without comment. He took this as confirmation his work was fit for purpose. It was not; although it must be said its quality far exceeded that required by the CAA.

Lancing College

The college is 1,000m from the end of the display line, and no overflight was permitted. Yet it would seem that here was no obligation to consider a large fuel storage facility located 500m closer, and estimated to contain up to 600,000 litres of road vehicle fuels.

Traffic lights

The organisers had correctly identified:

'Fast moving trunk road. 70 mph dual carriageway. Traffic lights and queuing traffic'.

And proposed the mitigation as:

'Traffic management plan in place. No right turns. Traffic Lights off and 40 mph limit in place'.

The decision to go ahead with the show was predicated on there being no stationary traffic at the junction. The mitigation was to set the lights at green, so there wouldn't be the usual line of cars waiting for them to change. But they were not set to green, and nor was the 40 limit requested of the local Council. The plan was 'in place', but not implemented - again, the thrust of the Nimrod

---

69 AAIB report, 1.17.6.

Review. Much was made of this, it being mooted there would have been fewer casualties had the traffic been moving. This doesn't follow. All that can be said is there may have been different casualties. There may have been circumstances were the road happened to be clear at impact; but equally the aircraft may have landed on a packed bus, or fast moving traffic may have veered and caused secondary accidents. The issue is not the colour of the lights, or whether or not the traffic was moving. It is the inadequate risk management, with no accountability.

It is prudent and fair to point out that Duxford Airshow, an airfield and aviation museum immediately adjacent to the busy M11/A505 motorway junction in Cambridgeshire, and despite having had fatal accidents immediately either side of the motorway in the past, continues to have a number of large airshows each year with the motorway remaining open.

This is where life's realities kick in. Airshows are required to have experienced aviation people on their committees - and Shoreham did. Organisers seek out former CAA employees. Fine, they know the regulations; but they also know the way around them, and the Old Boy Network waives risks through without proper assessment and mitigation. That is not to imply anything untoward. But the CAA acknowledged it didn't have sufficient staff to carry out its regulatory and oversight role. It would be tempting to look at the Display Committee, say *Good old Percy is there, he'll know what to do*, and ignore what's going on. I can't say that's exactly what happened, but I'm pretty close. The background to this deserves scrutiny.

Canfield Hunter and Weald Aviation Services

The AAIB report did not explore these operations in any detail, so I will confine myself to pointing out the aircraft carried a number of faults and defects, and it must have been obvious there was no airworthiness audit trail. In mitigation, Weald were a maintenance and design organisation, not a Design Authority, so would only be expected to be competent in a small part of the process. Nevertheless, they had a duty to report concerns to the CAA. Irrefutably, they contributed by stating the aircraft met its Approval Note requirements. The AAIB confirmed this was not the case.

Air Accidents Investigation Branch (AAIB)

I should say first of all it pains me to be critical in any way of the AAIB. Theirs is a difficult job. My experience is limited to study of a few MoD accidents where, as I said, the Branch was constrained by only being required to report on physical evidence from the scene; which is routinely removed or otherwise concealed by, primarily, MoD and the police. The law doesn't permit this, but legal authorities do. It is also clear, and has been admitted by MoD, that the AAIB's conclusions are ignored if they don't fit the predetermined official narrative. Chinooks ZD576 (1994) and ZA721 (1987) are prime examples. The Inspectors must be very frustrated. In fact, I know they are, as one wrote the foreword to my second book, Breaking the Military Covenant.

Any anomaly uncovered in an investigation must be fully investigated and resolved, regardless of suspected impact on the investigation in hand; and must be reported in the official investigation report. Otherwise, the report is incomplete; with recurrence likely, which is a factor to be considered when considering negligence. While the AAIB uncovered multiple errors and violations, they were not all expressed as such, and so no associated recommendations were made.

The perception of AAIB Inspectors naturally adjusts over time; which is why they must give equal weight to Legal, Technical, Airmanship, etc. until the lead anomaly is agreed. But the report lacks much critical analysis. The CAA made an absolute howler affecting the airworthiness, and hence serviceability, of all Hunters, meaning there could be no valid safety argument. The AAIB was duty bound to ask if this had occurred before, if it was still happening, and what the CAA was doing about it. Only then could it properly form an opinion on causal, contributory, aggravating and other factors, and make recommendations. On Shoreham that work remains incomplete.

Nevertheless, the report is utterly scathing of the CAA's failed regulatory oversight. Reading it, one can see the Inspectors working towards a logical conclusion. And then…nothing. Not a word. That needs explaining.

But, overall, what seems to be a comprehensive and independent report has been exposed as a façade. In mitigation, I believe the mass exodus of Inspectors - those who carry out the core task - in the mid/late 2010's left the AAIB open to outside pressure, when its entire being is predicated on total independence. Unlike MoD, where the same state of affairs has been allowed to fester for over 30 years, the situation is not irretrievable. The Branch simply needs to step back and decide that it is going to do what it is meant to do. It is not a business. It is not a pseudo-military organisation. It is there to make safety recommendations that will prevent recurrence.

If you wish to learn more of the AAIB's illustrious history, I suggest 'Safety Is No Accident' by the late Bill Tench. Read it and ask if the procedures and rules he describes so well were followed in this case, would the outcome have been different.

Crown Prosecution Service

With the AAIB report amounting to *We don't know about Hill's culpability, but we're certain about the CAA's*, the CPS decided to go all-in against Hill with deliberate act. The Judge instructed the jury that the Crown had to prove this, or Hill was not guilty. There was no in-between. Ultimately the decision backfired. They would have been better advised to gather evidence for the purpose of coming to an informed decision, rather than a preconceived one.

Sussex Police

There is evidence suggesting the police rejected the adverse; for example, the work of an expert they engaged, Dr Mudassir Lone from Cranfield University, whose g-calculations were above those of their advisor, the MoD/AAIB/CAA/prosecution's Wing Commander Green, and inconvenient to the CPS. It was a serious miscalculation to allow this conflict to develop and stand. It would indeed be interesting to see their report, and the correspondence with the CPS. Given the standard of proof, it should cite Professor Lone's report and explain why it was entirely wrong. It there was the slightest doubt, or unresolvable disagreement between he and Green, then the outcome of a criminal prosecution could be anticipated.

Nevertheless, when the concealed test flight evidence was revealed in November 2018, Sussex Police acted impeccably.

Health and Safety Executive

The HSE's violations had a greater effect on a concurrent case they were prosecuting - the killing of Sean Cunningham. On 10 September 2019, six months after Hill was cleared, they were asked under Freedom of Information if they had voiced concern over any part of the Shoreham report, given it contradicted their sworn statements to the Judge and categorically cleared Martin-Baker. At first they refused to reply, but eventually said the information was *'not held'*. After further pressure, they clarified this as meaning no action had been taken.

At this point they were required, by law, to review the exculpatory evidence and report to the Judge. They did not; as to reveal the timeline would be to admit both they and MoD deliberately lied to the court, perverting the course of justice. I explore these links a little more in the Annex; and in detail in my book Red 5.

I exclude the Health and Safety Laboratory from the above. Their work on Shoreham was exemplary.

Ministry of Defence

If MoD participants are honest, they will bitterly regret becoming involved.

I can understand why none spotted the error in the Approval Note. Its staff are no longer trained in the subject. But when the error was identified by the public as soon as the AAIB report was released, it was incumbent upon them to notify the CAA and police. They didn't.

MoD and the AAIB provided mutual protection. They couldn't both be right. But they could both be wrong, and were. Their joint aim was to transfer sole blame on to the pilot, and their conduct regarding the test flights was truly malevolent.

Senior Coroner for West Sussex

Ms Schofield was required to take account of *all the circumstances*, but was prevented by High Court order. The court took the easy way out, off-loading the problem back onto her.

She did not permit Hill to give evidence; instead seeking 'experts' who, in the main, sought to hide their own deficiencies. She was unconcerned about the active concealment of evidence, and that the accident was a recurrence. But, had she spoken out, the truth would reveal as incompetent the High Court's ruling that the AAIB report was 100% accurate; meaning the aims of her Inquest could never be met, contaminating the entire process.

Civil Aviation Authority (CAA)

The CAA is charged with regulating civil aviation. It is the licensing authority for *(inter alia)* aircraft types, individual aircraft, pilots, maintainers, Air Traffic Control and the controllers, and airports. It also licences air navigation aids such as radar, radio beacons and landing aids; and their operators, and those who regulate and oversee this activity. This is a huge and complex undertaking, the foundations of which are:

1. A set of rules and regulations
2. Implementation, audit and inspection

3. Enforcement

The regulations are in places deficient; for example, the crowd line rule assumes that the display is on a remote airfield, not adjacent to a conurbation. (Or in the case of Farnborough, very close to the town centre; meaning part of the population might be considered part of the crowd). Implementation is rendered optional by the lack of enforcement. The AAIB reflected on an ongoing internal CAA audit, which said there were *'significant weaknesses'* in the CAA's Safety Division, concluding that the CAA's *'capability does not match the true demands'*. What needs to be made public is the CAA's submission(s) to the Department for Transport seeking *the capability to match the true demands*, and what the reply was.

Once again there is a parallel with the Sean Cunningham case. Nine months before his death, in February 2011 the Red Arrows Senior Engineering Officer made a submission direct to the Chief of the Air Staff seeking the resources to ensure continuing airworthiness. It was rejected. After the accident he was given a modest uplift. Too little, too late.

Even if the CAA wished to implement the AAIB's recommendations, which (like the Nimrod Review) amounted to *reverse policy decisions and return to implementing mandated regulations*, where are the resources? The intent may be there, but without the wherewithal implementation remains a distant aspiration. The problem is, the beancounter who insists on a 20% cut in a given year is never around when the effect bites, and an accident occurs that can be directly traced to this decision. Pilots have no say in these policies. Hill was the only person accused, the implication to the layman being he was responsible for all the failures noted by the AAIB.

When Hill began to fly Hunters, he was required to attain an Aircraft Type Rating Exemption, first issued in June 2011 and valid for one year. Annual renewals were based on him retaining a current licence, not on any specific flight training or checking requirement. It was current at the time of the accident. So, too, his Display Authorisation. However, the AAIB noted:

> 'Under the regime that existed at the time, the pilot was able to renew his Display Approval for all of the categories by renewing his Approval in one of them. Consequently the evaluation he conducted in the RV-8 also renewed his Approval for the Hunter and Jet Provost'.

In my view, the differences between a self-build propeller driven RV-8 and jet aircraft are too great, and this 'read across' is unsafe. (The Hunter can be flown at over 3x the speed). The CAA disagrees, and the AAIB's report is a comment on *that* aspect, not Hill's ability.

The suspicion must be that the CAA recognised its exposed legal position, and thought a little self-flagellation would go down well. Such moves are typical of government departments. *Look, we've set up an internal audit and sent a questionnaire to staff, nothing can go wrong again.* But there's no point flogging a dead horse.

In the past, the UK had a Director of Flight Safety to oversee all this. But the post was abolished as a savings measure. Likewise the RAF, and throughout the 1990's a series of excellent postholders issued numerous airworthiness review reports on individual aircraft types, detailing the decline in safety standards. They were completely ignored. Why? Because their views did not align with the recent policy of *savings at the expense of safety*. This background formed the central evidence to the Nimrod Review, which Mr Haddon-Cave accepted. It applies equally to civil aviation. The government fully accepted the Review's report, and directed that its recommendations be implemented. But neither acknowledged that most were mandated anyway, and Nimrod XV230 was a recurrence. But crucially, and correctly, the Review regressed sufficiently to identify the lead anomaly - flat refusal to implement mandated safety regulations. On Shoreham, the authorities baulked at this. No lessons had been learned, despite the Review being regularly cited as having led to a reset of aviation safety.

There have always been close links between MoD and the CAA. For example, when searching for a viable error reporting system the CAA adopted that of the RAF Institute of Aviation Medicine at Farnborough. The essential issues are whether to make error reporting mandatory or voluntary, and confidential or completely open. The problem, of course, is that the person committing the error has to report himself, submitting to the mercy of an organisation whose default position is to blame the final act, when it is frequently judging its own case. Plainly, a separate, independent, overseer is required. (This applies equally to MoD).

The result of these conscious attacks on safety are set out in painful detail in the AAIB report, and nothing I say can be any worse. My aim has been to join the dots, and explain the subtleties and effects, in the hope you realise there is far more to this than Andrew Hill failing to get out of his loop. Indeed, the solicitors representing the families (*pro bono*), Stewarts Law, said this:

'There is a valid, proper and serious legal argument that the CAA failed as a regulator in properly implementing a safety recommendation made over

six years ago by the AAIB from a previous fatal Hawker [Hurricane] crash at Shoreham in 2007'.[70]

All very familiar. Little wonder the pilot wanted the AAIB report read out in court, but the principals did not.

The CAA took the view that once it approved/licenced someone to do something, it had no further responsibility. Former Chief Inspector Bill Tench got it right:

'The CAA has a lamentable record when it comes to implementing recommendations made by the AIB'.[71]

The subsequent clamp-down on vintage jet displaying was inevitable, a tacit admission of administrative and regulatory failures. This can clearly be seen as another self-protection measure. *Look, we've acted quickly.* But you didn't do your job properly in the first place, so how can anyone be sure your current actions will help?

Those who attend an airshow rather assume (if they even think about it) that the aircraft they're watching are fit for purpose. It could be said they enter into a contract with the organisers to this effect, who in turn rely upon the CAA, the operator, maintainers and, finally, the pilot. But the approach here was to equate 'finally' with only the pilot being at fault. That chain of responsibility was broken by the organisers and the CAA long before he entered the aircraft.

Should these legacy fast jets be flying? Is it really possible, technically and economically, to keep them airworthy? How can a new owner conduct due diligence? Do they even understand the issues I have set out? And how does a pilot acquire enough hours to safely perform high energy manoeuvres at a public display? The CAA's solution is to hand out licences to display fast jets after examining the pilot in a dissimilar aircraft. Nor are they asked to demonstrate an ability to carry out their intended display manoeuvres. And yet the same Department for Transport, quite sensibly, doesn't allow a driver with a standard car licence drive a 40-wheel articulated lorry. Similarly, are the medicals for flying a civilian airliner sufficient for flying aerobatics in a fast jet?

Shoreham was the CAA's Nimrod XV230. Did it not read the Nimrod Review?

---

70 Hansard, 9 January 2018.
71 'Safety Is No Accident' (W H Tench, 1985) (AIB - Accidents Investigation Branch, before being renamed Air...).

Folland Gnat T.1 G-TIMM (XP504), 1 August 2015

Having mentioned recurrence, I should offer a relevant example. On 1 August 2015, two weeks before Shoreham, Kevin Whyman died when the Folland Gnat he was displaying crashed during a synchro exercise at the CarFest North event at Oulton Park in Cheshire, organised by TV celebrity Chris Evans. (The Red Arrows flew Gnats, which are of similar vintage to Hunters, before acquiring Hawks in 1979). Kevin was an RAF trainee pilot between 1998 and 2001, and later became a member of the Gnat Display Team. The Chief Pilot of the Gnat team was later a witness for the prosecution at Hill's trial.

Kevin was one of two pilots executing a 360-degree manoeuvre known as an aileron roll. His aircraft was into its second roll when it reached a 107° angle of bank to the left, and the nose of the jet dropped unexpectedly. The AAIB reported he had attempted to reverse the direction of the roll and that the situation was *'probably recoverable'* at that point. He then applied *'a large pitch input'* which was *'inappropriately timed'*, the rate of descent increased, and he lost control. It was believed inexperience probably contributed to the outcome.

A medical condition diagnosed in 2000 that caused his heart to beat abnormally fast had curtailed his RAF career, and there had been no subsequent medical intervention. He had not declared this condition when seeking his medical certificate from the CAA.

On 12 May 2016, the AAIB reported:

> *'Typical symptoms of the pilot's medical condition include chest pain, rapid heartbeats (palpitations), dizziness, light-headedness, fainting, and shortness of breath. Some people do not experience any symptoms but, in others, episodes can last for seconds to hours and, in rare cases, days with the frequency varying from person to person. When the heart beats with an irregular or abnormal rhythm, there can be a drop in blood pressure which can <u>compromise the supply of blood to the brain</u>. The CAA stated that, if this is <u>combined with circumstances where high acceleration (g) forces are experienced, such as in aircraft during high-performance manoeuvres, g-induced loss of consciousness (G-LOC) is more likely to occur. In addition, high-g manoeuvres can in themselves precipitate the arrhythmias which trigger the symptoms</u>. The CAA also stated that the requirements for the*

issue of a Class 2 medical certificate, valid for use in display flying, do not include routine ECGs (before age 40) which might have highlighted this pilot's condition'.[72]

A feature of the case was that the Flying Display Director had briefed one display line to the pilots; they had briefed a different, parallel one; and noted a third, parallel one in their notes, which they had flown. None of these display lines were in accord with the CAA authorisation, which was set at a quite different angle. There was no associated recommendation.[73]

Of further interest, the AAIB noted that the engineer who serviced the ejection seats in G-TIMM, and who *'eventually'* travelled to the accident site to assist:

'Was thought to be the only person in the UK with the appropriate expertise to respond to an accident involving the type of ejection seat fitted to the Gnat'.

(The Gnat seats were designed and built by the aircraft manufacturer, Folland).

These vintage Gnats flew with the front ejection seat armed, and the unoccupied rear seat disarmed but with live explosive cartridges in place. Interestingly, some images posted in the media showed both seats occupied. That being so, one might reasonably expect the AAIB to have recommended the CAA issue an amendment to Gnat Airworthiness Approval Notes and Permits to Fly. Unlike Shoreham, the AAIB report did not reproduce these documents. And it would seem the continued ability to fly Gnats is predicated on one elderly engineer remaining fit enough to carry out this work. That can never be satisfactory; yet it is common with vintage aircraft. I recall in 1983 the RAF were struggling to find the necessary skills to repair Spitfire instrumentation - they were relying on a single, long-retired fitter. And a few years earlier the RN had scrapped their only remaining Lancaster auto-pilot test rig, which had been used by MoD engineers to carry out 'repayment' work for private owners. In such circumstances the work becomes very expensive, and short-cuts are tempting.

However, the AAIB did, correctly, note that its Safety Bulletins were *'relevant in the context of the accident to G-TIMM'*; and the second Bulletin correctly referenced the Gnat accident and linkages.

Notably, the Inquest was held before a jury. But because 'only' Kevin was killed, the aeroplane crashing in woodland, there was relatively little publicity.

---

72 AAIB Bulletin 5/2016, G-TIMM Pages 69-70, Medical Information.
73 AAIB Bulletin 5/2016, G-TIMM, Figure 6.

Yet many of the same issues arose on Shoreham, but to a lesser degree, the AAIB making three familiar recommendations.[74] These related to (a) managing risk to the ALARP principle, (b) authorised height minima should be appropriate to a pilot's experience, and (c) examinations to improve the likelihood of medical conditions being identified.

Unreported was that at Abingdon airshow the previous year a Gnat from the same team had been involved in an incident, possibly due to pilot disorientation in heavy rain. The pair did a low fast circuit of the airfield, one appearing to lose orientation in a turn, flew towards the ground, but fortunately pulled up. His height was around 100 feet.[75]

I think this context crucial. It is directly relevant to Shoreham as the medical symptoms described can be summarised as resulting in Cognitive Impairment. I also note that in a case where the investigation ran in parallel with Shoreham, the AAIB sought medical advice from the CAA, not MoD. But the CAA did not give evidence on medical matters on Shoreham. Why was it deemed sufficiently expert on one, and not the other? Also, on G-TIMM the AAIB issued a Field Investigation Report, not a Formal Report.

The difference in approach to similar accidents is quite startling. By comparison, Oulton Park was perfunctory; although it is probably better to say that resources were thrown at Shoreham and the subsequent report bloated. Why? The number of deaths should not be the main determining factor. What is important is the number, and repetitive nature, of safety violations requiring recommendations. Many (in both accidents) were immediately obvious, as they were recurrences. Had Oulton Park been afforded these resources, it is entirely possible the preliminary findings would have been sufficient to affect Shoreham - by, say, curtailing aerobatics in vintage jets. Why the different approach? Who benefitted? However, this should not detract from the fact the AAIB had made the same recommendations many years before.

---

74 AAIB G-TIMM Safety Recommendation Document (Undated, but no earlier than 20 August 2016, and updated on 9 June 2022 to reflect CAA responses).
75 https://www.youtube.com/watch?v=7mt7i9zCs-c

Where do matters stand?

The possibility of civil proceedings

Action Limitation periods impose time limits within which a party may bring a claim or give notice of a claim to another party. Here, the limit is six years from the date of the cause of action (i.e. 22 August 2021). Had action been brought, the High Court rulings would not apply, the AAIB report permitted in evidence.

A civil case is decided on the balance of probabilities. But, just because an accident happened and people died (two separate issues) doesn't mean somebody must be liable. And just because the Coroner said 'Unlawful Killing' doesn't mean a civil case would succeed. Far from it, as the AAIB report would immediately be seen to undermine her conclusion. And, unlike the Coroner, the court would not be able to ignore the disproved prosecution evidence led at the criminal trial. And, strange as it may seem, Hill would probably have welcomed this, as the evidence he wished to present in court would finally be out in the open. (The question of cost is another matter).

A related question is whether he can be prosecuted again. The double jeopardy protection in criminal prosecutions bars only an identical prosecution for the same offence; however, a different offence may be charged on identical evidence. Acquitted of manslaughter unanimously by the jury, that is the end of *that* matter. The CPS could bring an alternative charge based on the same fundamentally flawed evidence. But what charge, and in any case why risk further ridicule? There will be no appetite for further self-destruction.

Application for licence renewal

Post-AAIB report publication, on 23 March 2017 Hill's licences were provisionally suspended by the CAA *'pending the complete investigation and consideration of the case'*. It was unclear what part of the investigation it considered *incomplete*. The CAA did not request a medical examination, and no explanation of the decision was offered. He has not flown since.

On 10 July 2023 CAA's Safety and Airspace Regulation Group (SARG) proposed that his licences be revoked. On 21 July 2023 he requested an Internal CAA Review, which must be carried out by an independent person within the CAA. Can this be possible given the violations set out by the AAIB?

The Review considered whether the correct procedure had been followed, concluding that the CAA took proper account the evidence available, and followed the correct process in reaching its decision. It may have followed its own process, but any suggestion it took proper account of the evidence is risible. On 18 January 2024 SARG decided to revisit its use of the AAIB's reports. It concluded, unsurprisingly, that its use of the evidence was appropriate. Hill was informed of this on 28 May 2024. The following day he requested a review. In a ruling of 17 October 2024, the CAA refused his application. The full decision is available on the CAA's website.[76]

As it is essentially a self-protection measure, a large bucket of salt is needed. The CAA's regulatory role meant it had a significant conflict of interests. To protect itself, it <u>had</u> to place all blame on Hill. Instead of focussing on the evidence gathered by the AAIB, it focussed on his demeanour; ignoring that he was required by law to remain silent on the evidence. To accept collective responsibility would be to admit its own gross failings, and raise questions as to why it had not properly and proactively discharged its duties. From there, it would be one small step to confirming the AAIB was correct - the accident would have been avoided had the CAA done its job. The CAA could not make the report disappear, but it could divert attention from it.

I cannot second guess Hill's motives. It has been suggested to me that he has a living to make, which is true. But both he and his Counsel agreed there could be no expectation of him being employed as a pilot again, due to the bad publicity, so I can only assume he wishes to fly his small private aeroplane for recreational purposes.

(Update)

On 6 March 2025 the CAA confirmed it had *'received a judicial review claim on behalf of Mr Andrew Hill following the CAA's decision to formally revoke his pilot and flight radio telephony licences'.*

---

76 https://www.caa.co.uk/publication/download/23182

An alternative explanation?

Hill was vastly experienced on Jet Provosts, far less so on Hunters. A theory emerged that Cognitive Impairment led him to subconsciously revert to using Jet Provost parameters. I can find no mention of it being formally considered in the case; although close study of the AAIB report suggests at least one of the Inspectors pondered it, but the theory was not developed:

'The majority of the pilot's jet display flying was in the Jet Provost, which has significantly different performance and lower apex gate heights in looping manoeuvres than the Hunter. His greater experience and recency on the Jet Provost meant that he was more likely to be familiar with the speeds and handling characteristics of this type, and to recall them more easily than those for the Hunter'.[77]

The phenomenon is well-known, and called 'reversion to type' (i.e. the type of aircraft one is most familiar with), whereby the subconscious demands familiar cues, but muscle memory decides the actions, every other higher level cue being ignored. Two commonly cited fatal accidents involved a Red Arrows Hawk T.1A and a Tornado F.3, both occurring when at the vital moment the pilots flew their manoeuvres using Lightning parameters.

It is held that there are three primary circumstances:

1. High Stress (e.g. the Hawk case)
2. Very low stress (e.g. the Tornado case)
3. High fatigue

The basic evidence supporting this theory is:

- Hunter apex - 4,000 feet, 150 knots
- Jet Provost apex - 2,800 feet, 110 knots
- Actually flown - 2,700 feet (±200) , 105 (±2.5) knots

Reversion to type is considered a human error, and so is not negligence.

---

77 AAIB report, 2.4.4.2.

Final conclusions

I sincerely hope I have achieved my aim of conveying to you why Andrew Hill was acquitted; and that this was a classic case of the holes in the Swiss Cheese lining up on 22 August 2015.

In doing so, I have highlighted recurring contributory and aggravating factors, and two themes that have become familiar across many accidents:

1. The consistent refusal of authorities and regulators to implement their own rules, or the recommendations of investigations, Inquiries and Reviews. Had the existing regulations been applied at each stage, these accidents would not have happened.
2. Investigating authorities, airworthiness authorities, and the regulator, must be wholly independent of each other. The government defines this as having separate line management chains. The AAIB and CAA's are the same, in the Department for Transport.

It was said the CAA's Safety Management System did not reflect the environment. But there *was* no system, because it didn't require itself to have one; which to an engineer is perhaps the most astonishing aspect of this entire case. When you allow that, in such an obviously hazardous domain, you reap what you sow. Stand back, and you can see there are a number of elephants in the principals' room. In fact, it's a circus. What happened at Shoreham was a long time in the making, all the warning signs were there, just waiting for the holes to line up. Where was the oversight?

The political solution is simple. Give these authorities the wherewithal to do their jobs properly. And if they don't, appoint someone who will.

My final words must be about Andrew Hill and the errors he admitted.

The prosecution expected the jury to believe that a pilot with impeccable credentials, including a history as an RAF fast jet instructor and a job as a British Airways Captain, deliberately disregarded all he had been taught, ignored all his natural instincts of self-preservation, and flew a routine that should have killed him. It was right to question whether his actions amounted to negligence (inadvertent); but wrong to consider them gross negligence (deliberate). The case was sheathed in veneer. When stripped away, there was nothing of substance beneath.

Ultimately, it was not he who was found to have wilfully deceived the court. He will be satisfied at being found not guilty; but also, I suspect, dissatisfied at not being permitted to place the whole truth before the jury or Inquest. As a consequence, many believe he 'got away with it'. The outcome has been unsatisfactory for the families and the public. It has been wholly satisfactory for the principals. The inevitable not guilty verdict effectively closed the book on the bigger picture, guaranteeing recurrence. That's the biggest elephant in the room. A public inquiry is needed.

The brain is a magnificently complex computer which science cannot begin to fully understand. One can survive dreadful head injuries, but a seemingly innocuous bump or fall can kill you instantly, leave you in a coma, or floating impaired in the middle. Asked for a prognosis, doctors shrug: *We don't know, wait and see.* When they can only offer the same in court, what expectation can there be of securing a conviction to the required standard? The only person who can tell the whole story is Mr Hill, by lapsing and revealing details of the accident. He hasn't come close.

Finally, rest in peace those who perished. I hope their families find their own peace. Please do not harbour ill-feeling, but in quiet moments think of the good times. Do not forget.

ANNEX - Links to the death of Sean Cunningham

In any investigation it is important to understand what is going on elsewhere. Sean Cunningham had been killed at RAF Scampton on 8 November 2011, when he inadvertently ejected from his Hawk T.1 and his main parachute failed to deploy. His seat had been incorrectly serviced by RAF tradesmen, who had been instructed by superiors <u>not</u> to implement the mandated regulations governing this safety critical escape system. As a result, a nut in the parachute release mechanism was over-tightened, and the shackles which were meant to separate were jammed together.

As with Shoreham, the MoD investigation only looked at the final act, despite it being clear that prior negligence had taken place elsewhere in MoD and the RAF. (The AAIB was not involved). The Inquest was held in 2014, and the CPS then had to consider whether to prosecute, and who. Correctly, they decided not to prosecute the seat manufacturer, Martin-Baker. No action was taken against MoD or the RAF.

The Health and Safety Executive (HSE) then decided to prosecute Martin-Baker, accusing them of <u>never</u> providing the information necessary to allow safe servicing of the seat. They, too, ignored the MoD/RAF offences, and joined with them to conduct a joint prosecution. In doing so, they ignored voluminous written and verbal evidence to the contrary. Images in company manuals actually showed RAF armourers being taught - on the release mechanism - at the company's school. Far worse, 12 RAF training films were uncovered in the Imperial War Museum, showing how to check shackle disengagement. They were based on information provided by Martin-Baker. The HSE told the trial Judge all this was *'irrelevant'*, as it did not refer to the parachute release mechanism; despite an RAF Instructor staring into the lens and declaring: *'Check <u>again</u> the release of the Scissor Shackle'*. These films were exculpatory.

In February 2018 the company were fined £1.1M for failing to provide information, despite the Judge naming the (correct) MoD recipient of the written information.

The AAIB's Shoreham report provided further proof of the HSE's corruption, and that both they and MoD lied to the Judge and Coroner. Published 10 months before the Martin-Baker trial, it reproduced the G-BXFI

Airworthiness Approval Note of 3 July 2008, which required (mandated) the seats to be serviced in accordance with AP 109B-0131-series. (The Topic 5F contains Bay Servicing Schedules). The Approval Note completely destroyed the HSE's case against Martin-Baker - but only if led in evidence. Instructed by the Judge to disclose relevant evidence, the HSE told the her that the Hawk seat, a Mk10B, was the <u>only</u> variant with a mechanical drogue shackle parachute release system. The AAIB report, and the AP109B-0131-series, confirm the Hunter Mk4HA seat had the same design. In fact, and as explained, Andrew Hill survived because the shackles disengaged correctly.

Asked to reconsider its position in light of the Shoreham Report, the HSE refused; confirming they had not mentioned these discrepancies to legal authorities or the AAIB, and did not intend to. For their part, the authorities (the CPS and Lincolnshire Police) expressed themselves content with the courts having been lied to, and also refused to take action.

A complaint of prosecutorial misconduct was made, but the Lincolnshire Chief Constable ruled that the HSE could judge their own case. I do not have the HSE's reply - they refuse to release it - but the extracts quoted by the Chief Constable make it clear he was lied to. Informed of this, and given irrefutable written and video evidence, both he and his Police and Crime Commissioner expressed themselves content to let matters rest.

After the Shoreham trial, the head of the HSE was notified again of the exculpatory evidence in the Martin-Baker case, and asked if she would now review it and advise the Judge and police (the latter also being under an obligation to review it). She declined to comment.

The Cunningham and Shoreham cases produced different outcomes, but both served to protect those who allowed and even encouraged the legal and technical failings. Justice? No. And once again the bereaved families were left in limbo.

Terms and abbreviations

AAIB	Air Accidents Investigation Branch
ALARP	As Low As Reasonably Practicable
AMOC	Alternative Means of Compliance
ASIMS	Air Safety Information Management System (MoD)
A-LOC	Almost Loss of Consciousness
CAA	Civil Aviation Authority
CAP	Civil Aviation Publication
CAS	Chief of the Air Staff
CPS	Crown Prosecution Service
DASOR	Defence Air Safety Occurrence Report
DfT	Department for Transport
FCC	Flying Control Committee
FDD	Flying Display Director
FRC	Flight Reference Cards
g	Gravito-inertial forces
G-LOC	g-induced Loss of Consciousness
HSE	Health and Safety Executive
HHA	Hawker Hunter Aviation
IAS	Indicated Airspeed
MAA	Military Aviation Authority
MPD	Mandatory Permit Directive
P-LOC	Partial Loss of Consciousness
RAFA	Royal Air Forces Association
RAFCAM	RAF Centre of Aviation Medicine
SI	Servicing Instruction
STI	Special Technical Instruction
SQEP	Suitably Qualified and Experienced Person

The Author

The author is a retired aircraft engineer, spending much of his career as an avionics and aircraft project/programme manager in the Ministry of Defence. After retiring in 2004 he assisted families and Coroners in a number of cases, including Hercules XV179 where he uncovered the crucial evidence that MoD had denied the existence of. His evidence in the aftermath of the Nimrod XV230 accident identified that the aircraft was not airworthy, leading directly to the Nimrod Review (2007-09) and the reset of aviation safety management. He then delivered the main technical submission to the Mull of Kintyre Review (2010-11) proving the same.

Between 2016 and 2024 he published a trilogy about the 1994 Mull of Kintyre crash, covering the campaign to clear the pilots, cause and culpability, and the evidence concealed from investigators, families and the Fatal Accident Inquiry.

Having been invited to submit a report to the Defence Committee on the 2003 Sea King ASaC Mk7 mid-air collision, in 2018 he published this as the main case study in 'Breaking the Military Covenant', linking the failures to over 110 other avoidable deaths sharing the same root causes.

Continuing this theme, his two Red Arrows books 'Red 5' and 'A Noble Anger' describe the manslaughter of pilot Sean Cunningham in 2011, and engineer Jon Bayliss in 2018. These reveal that the same systemic failures rejected by MoD in 1992, and confirmed by the Nimrod Review in 2009, caused both deaths; and repeated the root causes of previous Red Arrows fatalities.

Printed in Great Britain
by Amazon